A HISTORY OF JEWISH LITERATURE
VOLUME IV

Israel Zinberg's *History of Jewish Literature*

An Analytic Index to the *History of Jewish Literature* will appear in Volume XII.

Israel Zinberg

A HISTORY OF
JEWISH
LITERATURE

TRANSLATED AND EDITED BY BERNARD MARTIN

Italian Jewry in the Renaissance Era

HEBREW UNION COLLEGE PRESS
CINCINNATI, OHIO
KTAV PUBLISHING HOUSE, INC.
NEW YORK, NEW YORK
1974

Library of Congress Cataloging in Publication Data   (Revised)

Zinberg, Israel, 1873–1938.
  A history of Jewish literature.

  Translation of Di geshikhte fun der literatur bay Yidn.
  Vols. 4– published by Ktav Pub. House, New York.
  Includes bibliographical references.
  CONTENTS: v. 1. The Arabic-Spanish period.—v. 2. French and
German Jewry in the early Middle Ages. The Jewish community of
medieval Italy.—v. 3. The struggle of mysticism and tradition against
philosophical rationalism.—v. 4. Italian Jewry in the Renaissance era.—
v. 5. The Jewish center of culture in the Ottoman empire.

  1. Jewish literature—History and criticism.
I. Title.
PJ5008.Z5313   809′.889′24   72–183310
ISBN 0–87068–240–7 (v. 4)

Printed in the United States of America.

Contents

PART V: ITALIAN JEWRY IN THE RENAISSANCE ERA

Chapter One: **ITALIAN JEWRY IN THE RENAISSANCE ERA; JEHUDAH ABRAVANEL   /   3**

The Renaissance era and the Jews—Italian Jewry and its unique way of life—Mystical currents—Menaḥem Recanati and his world view—The influence of humanism on the Jewish community in Italy—Moses Rieti and his *Mikdash Meat*—Rieti's inclination toward the Kabbalah—Platonic influence on the philosophy of the Renaissance era—Jehudah Abravanel and his tragic life —Abravanel's *Dialoghi di amore*—Love as the foundation of the world—Beauty as the mother of love—The human personality as the connecting link between the world and its Creator.

Chapter Two: **JEWISH MYSTICISM AND THE ITALIAN HUMANISTS; GRAMMARIANS AND SCHOLARS   /   25**

Jewish mysticism and the humanists of Italy—Pico della Mirandola—Elijah Delmedigo and his *Beḥinat Ha-Dat*—Yoḥanan Alemanno and his doctrine of the "divine madness"—Reuchlin, Widmanstadt, Baruch of Benevento, and Jacob Mantino—The Hebrew language and the ancient world—Moses Ibn Ḥabib and his *Darchei Noam*—Messer Leon and his *Nofet Tzufim*—The Latin classics and Bible exegesis—Abraham de Balmes and his *Mikneh Avraham*—Elijah Levita as philologist—His Christian

friends and pupils—The first Hebrew printing establishments—
Levita as proofreader—Missionary tendencies; Sebastian Muenster
and Paulus Fagius and their conversionist works—Bonet de Lattes
—Joseph Ibn Yahya and his *Torah Or.*

The intensified interest in cosmography and the descriptions of
the newly discovered lands—Abraham Farrisol and his *Iggeret
Orehot Olam*—Joseph Ha-Kohen and his description of "Spanish
India"—The flowering of historiography as a result of the expulsion from Spain—Abraham Zacuto as astronomer and historian—
The family Ibn Verga and their *Shevet Yehudah*—Samuel Usque
and his poem—Joseph Ha-Kohen as community leader and historian; his *Divrei Ha-Yamim* and *Emek Ha-Bacha*—Elijah Capsali
and his *Dvei Eliahu;* Capsali as stylist and scholar—Gedaliah Ibn
Yahya and his *Shalshelet Ha-Kabbalah*—The importance of Ibn
Yahya's work as a source of Jewish folklore—Interest in archaeology; Abraham Portaleone and his *Shiltei Ha-Gibborim.*

The belated battle against Aristotle's philosophy—Yehiel of Pisa
and his *Minhat Kenaot*—David Messer Leon's *Tehillah Le-David*—
Obadiah Sforno and his *Or Ammim*—The Bible as the source of
all the sciences—The decline of philosophical thought—Mantua as
cultural center—Jewish artists at the court of the Gonzagas—
"Friends of women" and "enemies of women"—Jehudah Sommo
and David Messer Leon—The Provençal (Provinciali) family and
the proposal for a Jewish academy—Jehudah Moscato as humanist
and orator—His *Nefutzot Yehudah* and *Kol Yehudah*—Azariah
dei Rossi as founder of critical historical science—The battle against
his *Meor Enayim.*

The decline of the Renaissance era—Spanish power and the
Catholic reaction in Italy—Ignatius of Loyola and Gian Pietro

Carafa; the Jesuits and the Theatines—The Inquisitorial censors and persecutions of Hebrew books—The burning of the Talmud and of Marranos—The decree of Pope Paul IV and the role of the Jewish doctors—Further censorship of Hebrew books—The reaction in the Jewish environment—The strengthening of mystical currents—The first printed editions of the *Zohar* and other Kabbalist works—Israel Saruk (Sarug) and Menaḥem da Fano—The role of the German rabbis in Italy—Jehudah Minz and Joseph Colon—Jacob Landau and Meir Katzenellenbogen—German rabbinic piety and the legacy of the Renaissance—The life of the Venetian ghetto and Leo de Modena's letter and autobiography—Samuel Archevolti and his *Arugat Ha-Bosem*—Leo de Modena's childhood, character, and literary talent; de Modena as a person—"Common sense" as the highest authority—De Modena's view of the final goal of the world—A rabbi as fierce opponent of rabbinism—De Modena and Jean Meslier—The significance of *Kol Sachal*—The "destroyer" and the "builder"—De Modena's battle against the Kabbalah—His *Ben David* and *Ari Nohem*.

Joseph Solomon Delmedigo; his wandering life; his correspondence with the Karaites—Delmedigo as disseminator of Copernicus' doctrine—Delmedigo's world outlook; the tragedy of his soul; his true face and the strange mask—Delmedigo's attitude toward mysticism; his allusory and disguised style in *Matzref Le-Ḥochmah* and other works—The orthodox movement and its representatives: Azariah Figo and Samuel Aboab—The decline of the Renaissance current in Italian Jewry—Moses Zacuto as poet and mystic.

A Note on
Israel Zinberg

D R. ISRAEL ZINBERG is widely regarded as one of the foremost historians of Jewish literature. Born in Russia in 1873 and
educated at various universities in Germany and Switzerland, he
devoted more than twenty years to the writing, in Yiddish, of his
monumental *Die Geshichte fun der Literatur bei Yidn* (History of
Jewish Literature). This work, published in eight volumes in Vilna,
1929–1937, is a comprehensive and authoritative study of Jewish
literary creativity in Europe from its beginnings in tenth-century
Spain to the end of the Haskalah period in nineteenth-century
Russia. Based on a meticulous study of all the relevant primary
source material and provided with full documentation, Zinberg's
History is a notable exemplar of the tradition of modern Jewish
scholarship known as *die Wissenschaft des Judentums* (the Science
of Judaism).

In addition to his *magnum opus*, Zinberg, who earned his living
as a chemical engineer, wrote numerous other valuable monographs
and articles on Jewish history and literature in Russian, Hebrew,
and Yiddish. In 1938, during the Stalinist purges, he was arrested
by the Soviet police and sentenced to exile in Siberia. He died in a
concentration camp hospital in Vladivostok in that same year.

The reader who wishes a fuller introduction is invited to consult
the Translator's Introduction to Volume I of Zinberg's *History of
Jewish Literature*.

Foreword

In 1972 the Case Western Reserve University Press began publishing an English translation of Israel Zinberg's *History of Jewish Literature*. Zinberg, an engineer by profession, was a scholar by choice and inclination. In thirty years of intensive study in the great Jewish libraries of St. Petersburg (later Leningrad), he produced eight volumes in Yiddish portraying the course of literary creativity among the Jews beginning with the Golden Age of Spanish Jewry and continuing to the end of the last century. It was not until many years after Zinberg's death that a Hebrew translation was prepared and published in the State of Israel.

There has been no work of similar scope and magnitude in the English language, despite the fact that the Jewish reading public in Britain, South Africa, Canada, and the United States constitutes about half of the Jews in the world. Now, however, the Zinberg volumes have been beautifully translated into English by Dr. Bernard Martin, Abba Hillel Silver Professor of Jewish Studies and Chairman of the Department of Religion at Case Western Reserve University in Cleveland, Ohio. All the English-speaking lands are indebted to Professor Martin for his endeavor to make accessible a literary history such as Zinberg's, a history which depicts the intellectual strivings of the Jews, their aspirations, yearnings, and spiritual search in the medieval and modern worlds, in both of which they have played a not undistinguished role.

Special gratitude is due to the Press of Case Western Reserve University which inaugurated the challenging task of publishing this handsome and very important series of books. Each volume is an aesthetic as well as intellectual delight. The Case Western Reserve Press was aided in publication by a generous grant from the Memorial Foundation for Jewish Culture. The grant is, indeed, a memorial to the martyred Zinberg, who was arrested by the Soviet police in 1938 and deported to Siberia, where he died. We, for our part, are pleased with this opportunity to express our gratitude to the Memorial Foundation for the support which made possible the publication of the first three volumes.

Unfortunately, the economic difficulties from which many universities are now suffering has led to the dissolution of the Case Western Reserve Press and made it impossible for it to continue with the remaining nine volumes. That is why the Hebrew Union College—Jewish Institute of Religion, realizing the importance and cultural implications of this work, is cooperating with the Ktav Publishing House, Incorporated, in the publication of the remaining volumes.

The completion of this series will make available to the English-speaking world a magnificent account of the literary and cultural treasures created by the Jewish people during their millennial history.

Hebrew Union College— Alfred Gottschalk
Jewish Institute of Religion President
Cincinnati, Ohio
January 1974

TRANSLITERATION OF HEBREW TERMS

א is not transliterated

ב = b

כ = v

ג, ג = g

ד, ד = d

ה = h

ו = v (where not a vowel)

ז = z

ח = ḥ

ט = t

י = y

כ = k

כ = ch

ל = l

מ = m

נ = n

ס = s

ע is not transliterated

פ = p

פ = f

צ = tz

ק = k

ר = r

שׁ = sh

שׂ = s

ת, ת = t

◌ָ = a

◌ַ = a

◌ֹ, וֹ = o

◌ֻ, וּ = u

short ◌ָ = o

י◌ֵ = ei

◌ֶ = e

◌ִ = i

◌ֵ = ei

◌ְ = e

◌ֳ = o

◌ֲ = a

vocal *sheva* = e

silent *sheva* is not transliterated

Abbreviations

JQR	*Jewish Quarterly Review*
JQR, n.s.	*Jewish Quarterly Review*, new series
MGWJ	*Monatsschrift für die Geschichte und Wissenschaft des Judentums*
PAAJR	*Proceedings of the American Academy for Jewish Research*
REJ	*Revue des Études Juives*
ZHB	*Zeitschrift für hebräische Bibliographie*

This volume is dedicated
to
Jack A. Goldfarb
One of nature's noblemen
with his heart in his hand

ITALIAN JEWRY IN THE RENAISSANCE ERA

CHAPTER ONE

Italian Jewry in the Renaissance Era; JEHUDAH ABRAVANEL

 RULY remarkable is the fate of the Jewish people. In the very year when brave sailors, equipped with the most ingenious instruments produced by Arabic-Jewish inventiveness, ventured out on uncharted seas to discover a new world, the major center of Jewish civilization, the Jewish community of Spain, was destroyed. For western Europe this was the dawn of a bright new age; for Jewry, it was the harbinger of twilight and cultural decline. The Renaissance era in Europe is known in Jewish history as a period of spiritual sunset, when the last rays of secular culture still flickered, soon to be snuffed out, and the night of darkness and cultural retardation was about to begin. At the very time that in Christian Europe thought began to free itself from its medieval chains, Jewish thought, as a result of the bitter hostility and oppression directed against the Jewish people, was locked up in the narrow, dark streets of the ghetto and became ever more entangled in the thick fog of mysticism and in the confusion of arid scholasticism and fruitless hairsplitting.

Only beneath the blue sky of Italy, under the rays of the Renaissance era, did the relatively small Italian Jewish community preserve for a time the cultural heritage of earlier generations. Until the middle of the seventeenth century it faithfully guarded the sparks of secular Jewish culture. At times these sparks even flared up brightly and for a short period chased away the shadows of night.

The obdurate ideological struggle which lasted for generations in Spain and Provence had virtually no echo in the Jewish community of Italy. The rigorously consistent rationalism of Jacob Anatoli and his disciples did not find favorable soil there. The spiritual influence of Palestine and Babylonia, with their mystical tradition and legendary world, was very powerful in Italian Jewry. We have observed[1] that the most significant representative of philosophic thought among the Italian Jews of that age, Hillel of Verona, resolutely declined to accept the view that the only criterion for evaluating human bliss is man's perfection in matters of speculation and his proficiency in dealing with philosophical ideas and theories. One-sided rationalism could not satisfy Hillel's soul. The popular tradition, with its religious-mystical emotion and ecstasy, was too precious to him. To be sure, his ideological opponent, the Spaniard Zeraḥyah Ḥen, achieved considerable success in Rome, and his radical views attracted numerous followers. But this success was quite superficial, without any firm foundation. Zeraḥyah's teaching aroused interest only by virtue of its novelty; it made no profound impression. We have noted how Zeraḥyah sarcastically advised Hillel of Verona: "Leave philosophy alone; turn rather to the ancient tradition. Read the *Sefer Yetzirah*, immerse yourself in the *Shiur Komah* and the *Sefer Ha-Razim*."[2]

That these works were, indeed, extremely popular among the Italian Jews is attested by Kalonymos ben Kalonymos, who lived in Rome some thirty years after Zeraḥyah Ḥen. We read in his *Even Boḥan* that men were prepared to pawn their last possessions, so long as others believed them expert in knowledge of *maaseh bereshit* (the work of creation) and proficient in such books as the *Shiur Komah* and *Sefer Yetzirah*.[3] It is quite characteristic that even such an ardent disciple of Maimonides as Kalonymos' friend, Immanuel of Rome, devoted himself greatly to Kabbalist books, studied the *Sefer Yetzirah* and *Sefer Ha-Bahir* with diligence, and even composed in his youth a work on the mystical-symbolic significance of the Hebrew alphabet.[4] The *Zohar* itself, which first

1. In Part Three, Chapter Four, of our work.
2. See Volume II, p. 200 of our work.
3. *Even Boḥan*, 41 (the 1865 edition).
4. This work was eventually lost. Only the poem which served as an introduction to it is introduced by Immanuel in his *Maḥberot* (Makama XI).

appeared in Spain, was disseminated in Italy earlier than in all other lands and, indeed, it was there that it found its first enthusiastic disciple and exponent, Menahem Recanati (c. 1300), a contemporary of Immanuel.

A fervent mystic, Recanati spent all his life poring over such works of the Kabbalah as the *Sefer Yetzirah, Sefer Ha-Bahir, Hechalot,* and the like. One of his favorite authors was the Kabbalist Azriel,[5] but transcending all other works in value for him was "the wondrous book of the *Zohar.*" In his mystical commentary on the Torah, *Perush Al Ha-Torah Al Derech Ha-Emet,*[6] Recanati faithfully reports the fundamental ideas of the *Zohar.* The spirit of the *Zohar* also dominates his well-known work *Taamei Ha-Mitzvot.* "All things in the world below," he teaches,

are dependent on the upper worlds . . . and, indeed, from the lower world we understand the mystery of what occurs in the upper world. . . . Everything we see in the creatures here on earth is a copy of the ten *sefirot.* The form of earthly man is a reflection of the heavenly form. . . . Man here below is the mirror image of the ten *sefirot* in the distant heights. . . . We must represent all phenomena to ourselves as rungs of a ladder that is all good, that rises higher and higher to the most exalted level of complete perfection—to God Himself.

The well-known dictum of the *Zohar* that "the Holy One blessed be He, the Torah, and Israel are one" receives in Recanati an extremely original form. God, the Torah, and the universe are merely various revelations of one and the same primordial source—the Creator. Every man is to be loved, for each bears the image of the heavenly form. Every man is an organic part of the great tri-unity, and every commandment, every good deed accomplished by man, is strictly connected with the universal harmony, with the heavenly "chariot." In every commandment, Recanati assures us, a special mystery is concealed. But it is not only man's

5. Recanati declares quite frequently in his works: "and Rabbi Azriel, may his memory be for blessing, said," and "thus said the sage, Rabbi Azriel."
6. This work was not completed. The commentary to the last *parashah* (weekly reading) of the Pentateuch is missing, and the first editor makes the following remark at the end: "To this point have we found this book, and we have heard that the master, may his memory be for blessing, was summoned to the academy on high before he finished the book and did not complete the commentary to the *parashah, Ve-Zot Ha-Berachah.*" Incidentally, this is the first Kabbalist work that was printed.

deeds that are foundation stones in the great structure of the universe, but also his thought and feeling, which are incorporated in the word of prayer. Like all other Kabbalists, Recanati frequently underscores the vast importance of sincere prayer. He also quotes the well-known passage of *Sefer Ha-Merkavah*[7] to show how beloved, as it were, by God is the prayer that rises out of the heart.[8]

These mystical tendencies among the Jews of Italy became an important cultural factor in the heyday of the Renaissance. They also found resonance in the external world, and in the Christian humanist environment of that age assumed altogether unique forms. Recanati was a contemporary of Dante and Immanuel of Rome, living at the time when the earliest rays of the Renaissance manifested themselves in Italy. The first shoots of humanism, which set itself the task of liberating the human personality from the heavy yoke of church supervision, had just appeared. To overcome the ascetic and scholastic world outlook of the Middle Ages, the humanist movement, with all its youthful ardor and sacrificial fervor, embarked on the exploration of the ancient world of the Greeks and Romans. In the old pre-Christian culture the new movement saw the most effective weapon against the congealed theological formulas of the medieval way of life. The men of the ancient pre-Christian centuries and their manner of life came to be regarded as the ideal pattern of perfection. This contributed greatly to the decline of interest in purely religious questions and in scholasticism.

The truly powerful and exalted, the ideals of grandeur and beauty, displaced the medieval Christian ideals of holiness and sinlessness. The Christian European for the first time experienced his own "ego" and realized that he was a free and independent personality. This was a revelation of immense importance. Until the Renaissance era self-consciousness, respect for one's own personality, was generally known only among the Arabs and the Jews who lived in their midst, not in Christian Europe. In the first volume of our work we had frequent occasion to call attention to the exaggerated terms in which the Hebrew poets of Andalusia and Provence praised the beauty of their songs and their own fame. This was not common boasting, the banal clamor of petty arrogance. Here the proud consciousness of the ego, the triumphant cry of spiritual richness springing out of the talented and powerful personality, was heard.

This phenomenon was repeated in Christian Italy, but only in

7. See Volume II, pp. 62–63 of our work.
8. *Taamei Ha-Mitzvot*, pp. 36–37.

the era of the Renaissance, for in the Middle Ages the Christian
European generally did not know of an independent moral personality which acts and creates on its own account. Deifying man
in the person of Christ, the Christian of the Middle Ages lost his
own ego, his clearly defined individuality. To be saved, to attain
eternal beatitude, to approach his God—this, man could not do
on his own, but only through the Church and its representative,
the priest. Man by himself was nothing; the Church and its *pontifex maximus*, the pope, were everything. Only the pope could
"bind and loose"; all others were his servants, not merely bodily
but, above all, spiritually. Only in the age of the Renaissance did
the Christian European again obtain his human face. Only now
was self-consciousness, regard for his own personality, aroused in
him. And this flowering of self-awareness, this awakened ego feeling, found its strongest expression in a brief but intoxicating word:
fame. The brilliant Dante yearns with all the ardor of his soul
to obtain the laurel wreath of the acknowledged poet. He is not
content with his own awareness that he is singular and chosen;
he desires that all know this, that the whole land publicly recognize
that he has no peer.

In the celebrated poet Petrarch the thirst for fame and glory
assumes literally pathological forms. He himself in his old age admits this in his letters, and regrets it as a grievous sin. But he repeats
his *mea culpa* in vain. For it was not his self-love or pride that
was responsible for his diseased yearning for glory. It was rather
the characteristic feature of the entire age in which the poet lived,
the age that had as its motto: The person is more important than
all else. The sounds of the fruitful earth came to be heard ever
more loudly, the awareness that the earthly is not the sinful grew
ever more prominent. Together with the heavenly and everything
having to do with the world to come, the demands of the earthly,
the human, and the this-worldly came to the foreground. In the
social life of Italy highly gifted persons with a cosmopolitan world
view appeared.[9] An altogether new and, for the Europe of that
day, still strange attitude arose, which the humanist Galeoto
Marizius clearly expressed in the following words: "Whoever leads
a decent life and whose actions harmonize with the moral sentiment
residing in his heart has a place prepared for him in heaven, no
matter to what people he belongs."

It is quite understandable that the new humanist tendencies
found a powerful resonance in the Jewish milieu. We noted, in
the third part of our work, the relatively favorable economic and

9. See Jacob Burckhardt, *Die Kultur der Renaissance in Italien.*

civic conditions under which the Jews lived in Italy. There caste distinctions and the dominance of the nobility were significantly less noticeable than in other lands. The intensive political life of the cities and republics, the constant party strife, and the frequent revolutions in the social-political order destroyed the barriers which so frequently separated the various classes and created conditions under which any energetic and talented individual could display his venturesome spirit without hindrance. The officials and rulers of Italy in the fourteenth and fifteenth centuries were mainly persons who had risen from rather lowly lineage. They obtained their power and honor not through inheritance but through their own energy and capability. Hence, in social life men considered family distinction of slight importance but looked rather to personal distinction. One took account not so much of the class to which an individual belonged as of the individual himself, with his own capacities and merits. Under such conditions, it is not surprising that even the Jews in Italy enjoyed far greater freedom than in other Christian lands in the Middle Ages. In the Italian universities, Jewish youths studied natural sciences, astronomy, and medicine along with Christians. Christian scholars would frequently engage in friendly correspondence with their Jewish colleagues.[10] Even the severe edicts and restrictions which the popes in the Middle Ages issued against the Jews remained largely on paper in Italy and were not enforced. Moreover, during the Renaissance era, freethinkers with a cordial attitude toward Jews not infrequently sat on the papal throne itself. When the pious Catholic Ferdinand expelled the Jews from Spain, many of the exiles found refuge in Rome, where Alexander VI was then pope. Shortly afterwards, when the highly cultured Leo X (Giovanni de Medici) ruled as pope, the Jews of Rome lived in such freedom and tranquillity that several pious leaders of the community inquired of the Jews in Jerusalem whether the signs announcing the speedy advent of the redeemer had already appeared in the Holy Land and the "times of the Messiah" were beginning.

Hence, it is quite natural that the cultured Jews of Italy warmly welcomed the new spiritual and intellectual movement and were

10. In Vogelstein and Rieger, *Geschichte der Juden in Rom* (II, 65), it is noted: "Die erworbene Bildung zeigen sie (die italienischen Juden) in zahlreichen Schöpfungen auf allen literarischen Gebieten. In der italienischer Muttersprache dichten und denken, in der hebräischer fühlen und beten sie. Hochsinnige Fürsten und Edle fördern ihre Studien und gewähren ihnen Schutz. Christliche Gelehrte stehen im Wechselverkehr mit jüdischen Meistern. Christliche Humanität unterstützt das jüdische Streben. Das ist das Bild des jüdischen literarischen Rom bis in der Mitte des XVI Jahrhunderts."

devoted to it heart and soul. But a very significant point must be emphasized here. We have noted how, because of the neighboring Arabic civilization, Hebrew literature was revived in Spain. Under the influence of the Spanish Jewish poets there arose, at the dawn of the Renaissance era in Italy, a poet of such major stature as Immanuel of Rome, a contemporary of Dante. But while Dante was the harbinger of a new and brilliant period in Italian national poetry, the Jews of Italy did not produce a single significant poet after Immanuel. The golden age of the Italian Renaissance had virtually no influence on Jewish poetry. The reason for this is easily understandable. The ancient pagan world of the Greeks and Romans, which so enchanted the humanists of the Renaissance era, was utterly foreign to Judaism. The power and beauty of the antique world of the gods found no echo in the Jewish milieu and could evoke scant enthusiasm there. The Renaissance forged the ancient pagan world together with the Christian world of the Middle Ages. The gods and demi-gods of Greece and Rome fraternized with the saints of Catholicism. But both the pagan and the medieval Christian worlds remained alien to Judaism and its creative spirit; it could not create from them its own artistic concepts or forge them into rich symbols and images.

The efflorescence of painting and art in Italy did, indeed, call forth an enthusiastic response in the wealthy and intellectual circles of the Jewish populace. The art historian Giorgio Vasari (1511–74), in his *Vite de' più eccellenti architetti, pittori, e scultori italiani*, describes the great excitement elicited among the Jews by Michelangelo's famous marble statue of Moses. "Every Sabbath day," Vasari relates, "Jewish men and women would pilgrimage in hosts to the sculpture and marvel in rapture and reverence at Michelangelo's masterpiece." But to raise themselves to artistic creation, to become themselves masters of stone and color—this the Jews of Italy were unable to do. In the entire course of the Renaissance era there was not a single significant Jewish sculptor or painter in Italy.[11]

Only in that field of art which from ancient times on was loved by Jews, music, did Italian Jewry play a prominent role. It is worth mentioning the musician and fluteplayer so celebrated in his day,

---

11. To be sure, the painter and Bible illustrator Moses Castellazzo, who lived in Venice in the fifteenth and sixteenth centuries, did acquire some fame in his day, but his talent is hardly original and not of a significant magnitude. (On him, see Burckhardt, *op. cit.*, I, 371 [1908], and D. Kaufmann, *Die Haggadah von Sarajevo*, pp. 302–3.) Only in the art of miniature painting did Italian Jewry produce a few talented artists (see D. Kaufmann, *op. cit.*, p. 290).

Giovanni Maria, the favorite of Pope Leo X, who bestowed on the Jewish artist a palazzo and the title of count. No less renowned was another Jewish musician, Giacono Sansecondo, who served as the model for Raphael's painting of Apollo on Parnassus. These musicians were not the only ones. The scholar Giovanni Paolo lists in his register of the famous artists in Italy of his century, *Trattato del arte della pittura* (1584), numerous Jews among the celebrated musicians.

We obtain an altogether different picture when we move from the realm of music to the realm of the creative word. Aside from some awkward, cumbersome imitations[12] and some more or less successful rhetorical efforts, Italian Jewry produced nothing noteworthy in the course of the whole Renaissance era (from the middle of the fourteenth to the middle of the sixteenth century). Characteristic in this respect is the most prominent poetic work of the period, *Mikdash Meat* by Moses ben Isaac (Maestro Gaio) da Rieti.[13]

Moses Rieti was a person of distinction, a well-rounded man, a *uomo universale*, as such a figure was then called in Italy. An excellent Talmudist,[14] he was also proficient in all areas of contemporary science. He studied natural science, philosophy, and especially medicine, whereby he earned his living. Until 1422 he was engaged in medical practice in his native city, Rieti. Later he moved to Rome, where he became rabbi and at the same time occupied the post of court physician to Pope Pius II. In his youth Rieti also devoted himself greatly to poetry. Dante's *Divine Comedy* made such a profound impression on him that he decided to produce a Hebrew poem patterned after this great model. Rieti began his work in 1416 and worked on it for many years without completing it.[15]

This unfinished work consists of two parts. The first part, *Ha-Ulam* (the Forecourt), is divided into five cantos, which contain a mixture of all kinds of things. There is a listing and discussion of the meaning of the thirteen dogmas or principles of the Jewish faith. Shortly thereafter comes a description of all the fields of

12. E.g., that of Zeraḥ Barfat, who, in 1364, rewrote the Book of Job in poetry. Fragments of Barfat's stilted and cumbersome verses were published in *Literaturblatt des Orients*, 1841, pp. 313–14.
13. Born in Rieti in 1388, died sometime after 1460.
14. He studied Talmudic literature with his father, Maestro Gaio (Isaac).
15. Originally Rieti set as his goal the composition of a poem in three parts (following the pattern of Dante's work), but he did not manage to write the third part, *Devir*, and the second part also remained incomplete. Rieti's poem was first published in 1851 by Jacob Goldenthal.

science, including alchemy.[16] Then the content of Aristotle's *Categories* is given—this with Averroes' commentaries and Gersonides' notes, etc. The second part, *Ha-Hechal* (the Palace), consists of eight cantos. Through the "holy palace," in which the souls of the patriarchs, prophets, Tannaim, and martyrs[17] who died for the sanctification of God's name rest, the poet reaches the *meon ha-shoalim*, the room of those who are praying, and here he pours out his own petition before God.[18] Thence the poet proceeds into the "divine city" (*ir ha-elohim*) which is the symbol of Holy Scripture. From the divine city he passes over to the upper deck of the *oniyot ha-nefesh* (ships of souls), an allusion to the Mishnah and Gemara. In the last cantos, in which the men of the Talmud, the Geonim, and the codifiers and decisors of later generations are listed, there are numerous details which have a certain interest for the historian of literature.[19]

It is astonishing that a man with such limited talent as Moses Rieti should have been crowned with the honorific title "the Jewish Dante." In the sixteenth century Elijah Gennazano manifested so little taste as to declare Rieti "the head of the Jewish people" who is "like the divine Dante."[20] Taking their cue from him, many others also spoke with great enthusiasm of the "Hebrew Dante."[21] To be sure, Rieti set himself a difficult task: to create a monumental work which would reflect the culture of Judaism with its entire world of ideas in the same measure as Dante's immortal *Divine Comedy* does in regard to the Christian Middle Ages. Such a tremendous task, however, was beyond his weak capacities. The mirror which Rieti created is obscure and blurred, unilluminated by the rays of true poetry, unexalted by the breath of life, of creative sentiment and inspiration. Rieti was doubtless a very competent versifier: he has the merit of having liberated himself from the cumbersome and complicated Arabic metrical forms and of ingeniously utilizing, and naturalizing in Hebrew poetry, the unique

16. *Mikdash Meat*, 20a.
17. *Ibid.*, 40b, where Rieti speaks of those who were burned, slaughtered, and hanged.
18. This petition was especially loved by the Jews of Italy, who introduced it into their Festival Prayer Book. It was also translated into Italian a number of times (see Vogelstein and Rieger, *op. cit.*, p. 71, and Steinschneider, *MGWJ*, XLIII, 92–93).
19. Especially important are the explanations that Rieti gives of several verses.
20. See *Letterbode*, X, 104.
21. See Reggio, in *Bikkurei Ha-Ittim*, IX, 14–15; Franz Delitzsch, *Zur Geschichte der jüdischen Poesie*, p. 54; Goldenthal, in his introduction to *Mikdash Meat; Literaturblatt des Orients*, 1843, p. 36.

terza rima which Dante employed in his *Divine Comedy*. But he lacked the most significant and essential things—genuine inspiration, rich imagination, and poetic intuition.

As far as the first part of *Mikdash Meat* is concerned, there is no more true poetry in it than in all the handbooks and manuals of instruction on rhyme that were so fashionable in the Middle Ages. In the second part there are, indeed, some tercets in which the fervor of a profoundly believing, pious heart is felt, but here also the flame of true poetry is missing.[22]

Rieti's work, which testifies how weakly the poetic art was represented among the Italian Jews in the Renaissance era, shows quite clearly, on the other hand, what an honored place Italian Jewry occupied in the realm of the sciences. Rieti was a rather poor poet, but his poem reminds us quite frequently how familiar he was with all branches of contemporary science. He was, first of all, a highly skilled physician. We observed in Part Three of our work the prominent role of Jewish physicians in Italy in the thirteenth century. Their importance became even greater in the Renaissance era. Jewish doctors were renowned throughout Italy, and most of the court physicians of the popes and princes were Jews.[23] These Jewish doctors were mainly men of multifaceted, philosophical culture. Moses Rieti himself wrote commentaries on important works of Arabic thinkers. He used to engage very successfully in theological debates, and also composed in Italian a polemical work in which he carries on a philosophic-religious disputation with a priest who had created a sensation in Rome with his anti-Jewish sermons.[24]

In this work Rieti appears as an ardent adherent and admirer of Aristotelian philosophy. "I follow the ways of Aristotle's system," he admits in his *Mikdash Meat*. But higher than all other sciences or wisdoms for Rieti was the wisdom of the Kabbalah. "And to the sages of the generation," he emphasizes in his poem, "the highest, fourth world, the world of the Kabbalah, which is

22. Even slighter is the literary value of Rieti's other poem, *Iggeret Yaar Levanon*, in which the author describes in rhymed lines the vessels of the Temple in Jerusalem (see Vogelstein and Rieger, *op. cit.*, p. 70). Leo de Modena mentions in his *Hayyei Yehudah* (p. 44) a piece for the theater entitled *Esther* that Rieti wrote, but this work has been lost.

23. See Vogelstein and Rieger, *op. cit.*, pp. 111–12; L. Fürst, *Beiträge zur Geschichte der jüdischen Ärtze in Italien* (*Jahrbuch für die Geschichte der Juden*, II, 325–70).

24. Rieger conjectures (Vogelstein and Rieger, *op. cit.*, p. 73) that this priest was Giannozzo Manetti, secretary of Pope Nicholas V and Callixtus III (Alfonso Borgia).

called *olam ha-sefirot* [world of the *sefirot*], revealed itself." He speaks with great emotion of the Kabbalist Recanati, "who concealed many profound mysteries under his cloak." On the other hand, Rieti indignantly barred the gates of heaven before the learned Moston de Herrera merely because the latter had permitted himself to mock the sages of the Kabbalah.[25] In his old age the pious Rieti even regretted that he had once "wasted time" on natural science and poetry.[26]

Rieti, however, was by no means the only fervent Kabbalist. Intense interest in mysticism was a unique feature of the entire era. One must take account of the mystical currents noticeable at that period in certain Jewish circles as a cultural factor of broad compass, for they found an echo in the external world as well and had a definite influence on some of the major spirits of the Renaissance era. The powerful drive to be liberated from the medieval theological chains, to tear through the web of arid scholasticism and dogmatics, brought many humanists to look coldly, often even inimically, on the foremost authority of the learned scholastic world, Aristotle. Precisely that which pleased the theologians and scholars of the Middle Ages so, the calm self-containedness and strict dogmatism of Aristotle's system, could least satisfy the restless, seeking spirits of the Renaissance who dreamed of a new way of life and struggled with all their powers to burst out of the choking atmosphere of frozen, obsolete dogmas. They saw in Aristotle's system[27] a conservative force barring their way to a new world of ideas. It was precisely this feeling that motivated the scholar Peter Ramus when he wrote on the gates of a French church in large letters: "Everything that Aristotle teaches is vanity and falsehood."

The causes that called forth the Reformation in central Europe and the humanist currents in Italy are extremely complex and various. Social-political and intellectual-spiritual factors were here interwoven. The human personality, which had just awakened to independent and conscious life, struggled to display all its spiritual powers and could no longer be content with the ingenious, entangled, hairsplitting syllogisms of medieval scholasticism, which were based ostensibly on Aristotle's assumptions and theories. More

25. *Mikdash Meat*, 106a.
26. The author of *Iggeret Ḥamudot* testifies: "For after he had tested all the sciences, he regretted that he had occupied himself with the secular ones and had written of them in his poem entitled *Mikdash Meat*, and he called it a waste of time."
27. That is, in the form that it assumed among the Christian scholastics in the Middle Ages.

congenial to it were the fervent, dreaming teachings of Plato and the neo-Platonists, which glistened with the most vivid colors of poetic enthusiasm. Precisely for this reason the transition from Christian scholasticism to the philosophy of the Renaissance was associated, first of all, with a revolt against the exclusive dominion of Aristotle's authority and with the increasing influence of neo-Platonic and mystical conceptions.

This transition from Aristotelianism to Platonism manifested itself quite clearly in the first half of the fifteenth century, especially in the work of the most significant thinker of that era, Nicholas of Cusa. The process was even more noticeable in the second half of the century. The famous patron Cosimo de' Medici discovered and published Plato's most important works, which had been completely forgotten in the Middle Ages. At Cosimo de' Medici's court lived the eighty-year-old Greek scholar Gemistus Pletho, who in inspired lectures and addresses, delivered with youthful enthusiasm in a prophetic, mystical style, would disclose the "profound mysteries" and "eternal truths" concealed in the writings of the "divine" Plato. Later, during the reign of Cosimo's grandson, Lorenzo, a Platonic academy was established in Florence in which many prominent humanists participated, chief among them the famous Platonic scholar Marsilio Ficino, who translated Plato's works into Latin. The members of this academy would frequently come together in sessions at which philosophical discussions were conducted and the most varied problems illuminated from the neo-Platonic point of view. Among these humanists it was a firmly accepted principle that whoever is not thoroughly familiar with Plato's world outlook cannot be a right-thinking Christian and citizen. Medieval man regarded this world as a sorrowful vale of tears, a place of sin and filth. But the members of the Platonic academy, who saw in the universe an emanation of God's infinite light, were imbued with the idea that the earthly world was created by God out of *love*. Hence, for them it was not a world of "sin" but a reflection of the highest prototype, the Creator and dynamic power.

These philosophical trends of the Italian humanists found a response also in Jewish intellectual circles and intensified in them mystical tendencies and interest in the Kabbalah, in which the fundamental ideas of neo-Platonism were employed in a very unique way. But this was not self-depreciation, a merely passive acceptance of alien ideas, but what Ahad Ha-Am called "competitive imitation" (*hikkui shel hitharut*), a mutual cultural influence of two groups living in closest proximity.

One must also take into consideration the powerful influence which the Jews who had been driven out of Spain exercised on the Jewish community of Italy. The Italian seaports were the first places of refuge where many of the miserable exiles found protection and rest after all the hardships they had to suffer on their difficult way. It was these highly educated immigrants who contributed not a little to the fact that Italian Jewry was all at once raised to greatness. While in the Middle Ages, as a numerically small community, this Jewry played merely a secondary role, in the sixteenth century it appears in the foreground and occupies the most important place in Jewish cultural history of that era.

The horrible afflictions which the expelled wanderers had to endure in their roamings contributed greatly to the strengthening of mystical currents among them. We noted in the third volume that mystical-messianic hopes constitute the fundamental motif of Isaac Abravanel's work. All believed that they were living through the "pangs of the Messiah" and were certain that soon the "times of the Messiah" would begin.[28] Jehudah ben Jacob Hayyat, who went into exile together with Isaac Abravanel and left for later generations a heart-rending description of the sufferings and troubles which the exiles had to endure,[29] was quite certain that only because of the support of the sacred books of the Kabbalah, in which he was engrossed day and night, was he saved from all the afflictions he encountered on the way. In Mantua, where he spent the remainder of his years, he delivered sermons on the *ḥochmat ha-nistar* (hidden wisdom) and composed an extensive commentary to the well-known Kabbalist work of the fourteenth century, *Maarechet Ha-Elohut*.

It is therefore not surprising that one of the most original flowers of the Renaissance era, glistening in neo-Platonic colors, grew on the Jewish soil so richly fertilized by mysticism. This was Jehudah ben Isaac Abravanel's[30] "conversations on love," *Dialoghi di amore*.[31]

28. A visionary Kabbalist named Asher Lemlein appeared, wandered from city to city, and proclaimed that he was the Messiah the son of Ephraim, and that soon after him the Messiah the son of David would appear in all his glory. Many, indeed, believed that they already heard the ram's horn of the Messiah. The historian David Gans relates how his grandfather, who was a rabbi in Asher Lemlein's time, ordered the Passover oven in which they used to bake *matzot* destroyed, for he was certain that the following year he would celebrate Passover in Palestine (*Tzemaḥ David*, Part I).

29. In the introduction to *Maarechet Ha-Elohut*.

30. In the Christian world he is known as Leo Hebreo, Leo Hebraeus, or Leon Medigo.

31. Some scholars believe that Jehudah Abravanel wrote this work first in Hebrew and only toward the end of his life, under the influence

The life of this highly gifted man was tragic, for his fate was intimately associated with the catastrophe which befell his brethren in Spain. Richly endowed, philosophically schooled, distinguished as a physician and astronomer, he was compelled in his youth[32] to flee from Lisbon, together with his father, Isaac Abravanel, before the wrath of the despotic king João II, who confiscated their entire fortune. Jehudah settled with his father in Castile. When the decree of expulsion was issued in 1492, he decided to go into exile with all the other Spanish Jews who had been driven out. The government, however, had no desire to let such a competent physician out of the country and, in order to compel him to adopt the Catholic faith, decided to kidnap his little son and forcibly convert the child. But Jehudah Abravanel was informed of the plan in time and sent his child by stealth over the Portuguese border. He himself was afraid to return to the land where his enemy João II still reigned and went with his father to Italy. But there he learned that the Portuguese king had kept his child a hostage as Isaac Abravanel's grandson, and João's successor, the pietist Manuel, in 1495 ordered the little Abravanel forcibly converted, together with thousands of other Jewish children, to save their still-guiltless souls from hell.[33]

The wound was so deep that even time could not heal it. Seven years later Jehudah Abravanel expressed his pain in his moving poem "Telunah Al Ha-Zeman."[34] "Twelve years have passed," he declares, "since I have seen my child. I can find no rest, no comfort. Not for me shines the light of the sun; my eyes are veiled in dark night. Not for me blooms the lily in the garden; my flowers are withered. The memory of him has robbed me of sleep. I have hung my harp on the weeping willow, transformed my song into lamentation." In tender verses he begs the child not to forget his sorrowing father, not to remain deaf to his mother's weeping, and to return to his parents' roof.

In the same year (1502)[35] that Abravanel lamented his bitter

---

of his Italian friends, reworked the *Dialoghi* into Italian (see *MGWJ*, 1928, p. 436). Some basis for this conjecture is to be found in the statement of a contemporary of Abravanel's which we shall introduce at the end of this chapter.

32. Abravanel was born around 1460 and died around 1521.
33. All these details are related by Abravanel himself in his poem "Telunah Al Ha-Zeman."
34. This poem was composed in 1502. It was published for the first time in *Otzar Neḥmad*, II, 70–75, and later reprinted in the introduction to *Vikkuaḥ Al Ha-Ahavah* (the Hebrew version of *Dialoghi di amore*).
35. The author himself indicates the year in which he began his work in the third dialogue.

fate in his poem, he also began his masterwork, *Dialoghi di amore*, the inspired song of songs of ardent love. This half-Portuguese, half-Spanish Jew, in the course of the ten years that he spent in the cities of Italy, penetrated so profoundly into the spirit of the Italian Renaissance that he became one of its major standard-bearers. He, the alien Iberian Jew, became the first to deal with purely philosophical problems in the Italian vernacular. Only much later, in the seventeenth century, did an anonymous but extremely competent translator render *Dialoghi di amore* into Hebrew and thereby firmly establish Jehudah Abravanel's name in Hebrew literature.[36]

Isaac Abravanel insists in one of his letters that his elder son, Jehudah, is "doubtless the major thinker in Italy of the present generation,"[37] and Jehudah himself declares proudly in his previously mentioned poem: "My keen thought surpasses that of all the scholars of Edom, who were like grasshoppers in my sight; I went to their schools, and none of them could compare with me." It must be admitted that Abravanel did not greatly exaggerate his importance. The author of the *Dialoghi* was, indeed, a man of comprehensive knowledge. He was proficient in Greek-Arabic philosophy and very familiar with Aristotle's medieval commentators. His native poetic sentiment and the orthodox religious traditions which he carried with him from his father's house, however, contributed significantly to the fact that he could not be content with the rationalism of the Aristotelian-Maimonidean system. He was more attracted to the mystical world of ideas of the medieval Kabbalah, with its strong inclination toward neo-Platonism.[38] These sympathies were considerably strengthened in Abravanel after he settled in Italy and absorbed the humanistic atmosphere in which the influence of Plato and the neo-Platonists was so powerfully felt. He calls the author of the *Phaedo* and the *Sym-*

36. Graetz believes that Abravanel's work was translated by Leo de Modena. This conjecture, however, has not the slightest foundation, for Leo de Modena lists in his autobiography all of his literary works but the *Dialoghi di amore* (*Vikkuaḥ Al Ha-Ahavah*, in Hebrew) is not mentioned there. Also unfounded is the conjecture of S. Sachs (*Ha-Maggid*, XV, 335) that the translator was Joseph Baruch of Urbino, who lived in the seventeenth century. We believe that the *Dialoghi di amore* was translated by Joseph Solomon Delmedigo, who explicitly claims this in his letter to the Karaite, Zeraḥ ben Nathan (see *Melo Chofnajim*, 21). The Hebrew translation was first published by the Mekitzei Nirdamim Society in Lyck in 1871.
37. *Otzar Neḥmad*, II, 58.
38. Abravanel himself notes the influence that the Jewish neo-Platonist Solomon Ibn Gabirol and his *Mekor Ḥayyim* (*Fons Vitae*) exercised on him (*Vikkuaḥ Al Ha-Ahavah*, 58a).

posium the "divine" Plato,[39] and when he discusses important problems of philosophy, e.g., the question whether wisdom is the essence of divinity or merely its emanation, he emphatically adopts Plato's view and rejects Aristotle's basic principle.[40] Abravanel, incidentally, accepts the ancient legend that when Plato lived in Egypt, the sages of Israel dwelling there acquainted him with the Torah of Moses and the Jewish world of ideas in general, and for this reason his system is more correct than the Aristotelian.[41]

"Hatred, war, and human evil have destroyed far more persons than all the diseases and afflictions of nature together," writes Abravanel, who himself had to suffer so much from hatred and fanaticism. Yet he is firmly convinced, and sets forth as the major item of his credo, that love is the foundation of the world and that nothing besides it exists. From the cold, inanimate stones to the highest celestial spheres, love everywhere reigns. Everything strives toward harmonious union. The entire universe is pregnant with love, and the higher the stage, the higher the degree of love. Even the primordial chaos before the work of creation is permeated with sexual love, the love that creates and unites, that is in constant, impetuous motion in its insatiable yearning for union. Everything is imbued with the drive for constant creation; everything breathes an unquenchable desire for constant exchange of forms, for new birth. And everything strives toward a single goal: attainment of the supreme degree of harmony, union with the primal source of wholeness and absolute unity—the Creator.[42] All creatures are imbued with love for one another, the higher for the lower and the lower for the higher, for they are all parts of one organic whole.[43]

Abravanel employs in lovely poetic form the dictum of Pythagoras on the "harmony of the heavenly spheres." Just as in music a unitary melody is created through the most varied individual chords and tones, so also out of the tremendous movements of the planets and the unceasing exchange of forms and structures is born the incomparable, harmoniously complete, universal song of praise. And everything is so closely intertwined, one thing is so powerfully dependent on another, that where even the slightest

39. *Vikkuaḥ Al Ha-Ahavah*, 22a.
40. *Ibid.*, 86a.
41. *Ibid.*, 85a; cf. 71a.
42. *Ibid.*, 67a; cf. 55a and 43a.
43. *Ibid.*, 20b. Abravanel incidentally dwells at length (17–20) on the analogy, so popular in antiquity and the Middle Ages, between the structure of the human body and the arrangement of the planets. He endeavors to show that the human body is a microcosm, a miniature image of the world, and that every part of this microcosm has its reflection in the macrocosm, the structure of the universe.

link falls out of the infinite chain, this suffices for the entire harmonious wholeness to be destroyed.[44] This love permeating the entire universe does not intend merely the pleasure and satisfaction of each part by itself; it strives to universal, harmonious unity, for without this harmony all the individual parts are at once destroyed. Of such universal compass, Abravanel insists, is the conscious love of the elect persons who have obtained the supreme level of perfection.[45] Not only do the lower levels strive toward the higher in order to obtain the desired harmonious perfection, but the higher also strive toward the lower and less perfected, "because," Abravanel points out, "no true perfection can be conceived where the lower and defective is near it."[46]

Proceeding from this profound idea, Abravanel arrives at the conclusion that there are two kinds of love. One is of a purely passive character; its source is the feeling of dissatisfaction, the consciousness of unattained perfection. This is the love that yearns for bestowal on itself and fructification. But there is another of a completely different kind: the active, creative love which bestows and gives. It strives to rejoice and satisfy everything around it with its immense opulence, which streams forth from it as out of a mighty spring.[47] The highest revelation of such wondrous love, with its desire to give without any indemnity or compensation, and with an immense drive to raise everything around itself to the supreme level of perfection, is the love of God for the world.[48] No true perfection can be conceived that would not strive to work on everything around itself and not bestow upon others of its perfection. "The fruit-bearing tree is more beautiful and perfect than that without fruit, and the living spring which fructifies and is in constant motion is incomparably lovelier than standing, though crystal-clear, water."[49] Because God is the acme of perfection, He must, by His very nature, influence everything around Him, irradiate and illuminate it with His perfect splendor. Hence, everything is created and ruled by Him; hence, His love for everything He has created is so vast and His desire that all creatures attain His level of perfection so powerful.[50]

Because the existing world is the product of the divine love, the perfection of divinity is strictly correlated with the perfection

44. *Vikkuaḥ Al Ha-Ahavah*, 21a.
45. *Ibid.*, 21b.
46. *Ibid.*, 36b.
47. *Ibid.*, 36a.
48. *Ibid.*, 50a; 90b.
49. *Ibid.*, 94b.
50. *Ibid.*, 53a.

of its creatures, whose highest goal is to return to the Creator and unite with Him. God is the first cause as well as the final goal. Just as one ray of the sun is reflected in all the wealth of the rainbow's colors, so the first and only cause reveals itself in the diversity of its creatures, all of which strive to return to the unity which gave birth to them.[51] Abravanel portrays in magnificent imagery the enchanted "circle of love"—how the whole cosmos is, as it were, split into two halves that strive ceaselessly to become reunited. The lower levels strive upward toward the symbol of perfection, and the exalted and perfect strives to raise to itself the low and gross, to irradiate it and endow it with its own beauty and perfection.[52] And at the very center of this mighty cosmic circle is man, whose soul is "a small part of the infinite divine light." The soul, with its marvelous capacity for knowing God, is the connecting link binding the supernal world of spiritual perfection with the lower, material world.

Here Abravanel deems it necessary to dwell on a point which occupies an important place in the Aristotelian-Maimonidean ethic. Certain thinkers, he notes, assert that the supreme happiness of man consists in inquiring or speculating about God; others, again, believe that it consists in love for Him. There is no doubt, Abravanel concludes, that reason is the guide of man's emotions; the understanding leads man's spiritual capacities to the goal of comprehending God's greatness. Without this, no genuine love is conceivable. But reason is not the only "king in the chamber." The stronger love grows, the closer man comes to the highest spiritual level, at which the sober understanding remains behind and the former guide is overcome and led by another, stronger power. Man attains the degree of such indescribably blissful joy as neither reason nor even love can provide. Through the feeling of transcending corporeality, through the utmost exertion of the will, suddenly arises the unexpected revelation, the crystal-clear vision, and man's soul feels its cleaving (*devekut*) to, its union with, divinity, its oneness with God.[53]

Reason, Abravanel further declares, certainly contributes greatly

51. It is interesting that the theoretician of the German Romantic movement and scholar of neo-Platonism Friedrich Schlegel repeats almost verbatim this idea of Abravanel's. "Divinity," says Schlegel, "is eternally the Infinite Unity. But it must also be the Absolute Perfection. Herein lies the secret of the creation of the world: out of the depths of the Absolute Unity is born the longing for content and abundance, for this alone can provide the revelation of the Infinite, the history, as it were, of divinity, the highest degree of perfection."
52. *Vikkuaḥ Al Ha-Ahavah*, 92–93.
53. *Ibid.*, 10a.

to arousing love for God. However, once this love is awakened, it no longer remains under the dominion of the sober understanding; on the contrary, it governs the understanding. It is not the practical, calculating, and coldly analytic mind that leads a man when he sacrifices himself with great ardor for his deeply loved God. What can be nobler than this burning love, and what lovelier than this sacrifice? The sober, practical mind, which thinks above all of purpose and utility, is utterly incapable of grasping the immense sweetness and the beatifying feeling of joy deriving from the sufferings and pain that are accepted out of great and ardent love.[54]

Here we approach the core of Abravanel's philosophical world view. Love, declares this faithful son of the Renaissance era, is the foundation of the world, the mother of all good. And yet love is not the truly most important thing. There is something even higher, and this highest is *beauty*, the active beauty that reveals itself in the process of becoming and creating. But true beauty is inconceivable where spirit and spirituality are lacking. The corporeal or material can be useful, it can attain the level of good, but it is not the category of beauty. The true grace of beauty glistens only in the kingdom of the spirit.[55]

When Abravanel expounds the foundation and nature of beauty, which occupies the focal point in his *Dialoghi di amore*, he employs the idea, so favored among the neo-Platonists as well as the Kabbalists, of the tri-unity of the divine nature. We have observed that the *Sefer Yetzirah*, the *Zohar*, and many other medieval Jewish sources insist that, in God's knowledge, consciousness and being are merged into one whole, since God is, as it were, simultaneously knowledge, the knower, and what is known. This idea obtains a new dress in Abravanel. He places the emphasis not on knowledge but on love. God, says Abravanel, is not only the One who loves but also the One who is loved. He loves, with His eternal love, His own divine beauty. "In God beauty precedes love. . . . The progenitor of love is beauty." "The first point, the origin of everything, is the divine beauty."[56] Beauty transcends everything else, it is the primordial source of all, the author of the *Dialoghi* several times insists. And the beloved divine beauty, the loving divinity, and love itself are one.[57] With our intellect, Jehudah Abravanel adds, we cannot grasp this, for limited as it is by the concepts

54. *Ibid.*, 11b.
55. *Ibid.*, 53a.
56. *Ibid.*, 60a. Here no doubt the influence of Plato's famous dialogue, the *Symposium*, is discernible.
57. *Ibid.*, 60.

of time and place, the intellect must separate the thought, the thinker, and that which is thought. From the splendor of the beloved divine beauty is radiated the *sechel ha-kolel*, the universal reason, the father of all structures, the source of all forms and phenomena. From the divine creative intellect is radiated primordial matter, the mother of the world; and from the love union of these two fundamental elements everything that exists is born.[58] As is the case with most mystics, Abravanel's world outlook has a definite erotic coloration. In sexuality itself he perceives something divine and holy, a revelation of mystical experiences. Sexual love, the union of man and woman, is the earthly reflection of the heavenly mystery—the sacred, divine union of the supreme beauty and the supreme wisdom.[59]

Only God, the source of beauty, can grasp, as it were, the degree of His own beauty. Our language, with its material images and symbols, is too weak and awkward to be capable of giving us a clear concept of this divine beauty. We can speak of it only in parables and allusions, and the loveliest and deepest in this realm, the most marvelous parables of divine love and divine beauty, Abravanel insists, were revealed by King Solomon in his Song of Songs, in which the profoundest divine mystery, the secret of secrets, is rendered in symbols of human passions and desires.[60]

Since the divine beauty is the highest criterion by which every degree of beauty is measured and evaluated, the true perfection of beauty is without the least trace of corporeality. The beauty that hovers over material bodies and earthly creatures is merely a pale shadow, a weak reflection, of the true, spiritual beauty. Only he who is endowed with a deeply sensitive, spiritually rich soul can grasp the extraordinary beauty of the world soul. As a blind man cannot properly appreciate the glory of colors, so, Abravanel insists, a man with a gross, unpurified soul cannot grasp the splendor of true spiritual beauty which illuminates, like the rays of the sun, the whole extent of the world.[61] The more exalted and inspired a person is, the more his soul is permeated with divine beauty. Man's purified soul is the focus which gathers in itself all

58. *Ibid.*
59. *Ibid.*, 87a; cf. 61a.
60. Abravanel sees in the Song of Songs an allegory on the holy bond between the divine beauty and the divine wisdom (*ibid.*, 86–87, 95). It is, incidentally, worth emphasizing the following point, which is very characteristic of that era: just as the Maimunists endeavored to allegorize numerous passages in the Bible, so Abravanel saw only parables and allegories in the whole of Graeco-Roman mythology as well (*ibid.*, 21–33, 68, 74, etc.).
61. *Ibid.*, 77.

the sparks of beauty scattered over the vast distances of the world, with all its wealth of creatures and phenomena. Man, with his love and longing for beauty, is the link uniting the world with its Creator.[62] And in this role, in his consciousness that he is the essential link, the supreme happiness and pleasure of man are hidden.

While in the Christian Middle Ages terrified and despondent man regarded the world as a vale of sorrow and affliction, Abravanel, who was educated on the ideas of the medieval Judeo-Arabic philosophers and of the humanists of his generation, speaks with pride and self-consciousness, in rich, figurative language, of the immense significance of the human personality and of the universal role it plays in the limitless cosmos. He is firmly convinced that on every human soul the rays of the infinite divine beauty rest, and every man, if only he lovingly strives toward God, bears in his limited being divinity with all its beauty; for God, the superlative degree of justice, righteousness, and lovingkindness, is not only our creator but also our true counselor and guide.[63] Jehudah Halevi's mastery lines

> I have sought Thy nearness
> With all my heart have I called Thee,
> And going out to meet Thee,
> I found Thee coming toward me

find in Abravanel their further, philosophical-mystical interpretation. Great, infinitely great, does man's soul become when it strives on the wings of love toward its God. For the more exalted the love, the more marvelous and splendid is the divine beauty which shines toward it; and in beatific enchantment the trembling, loving human soul merges with God, unites itself with His beauty.[64]

The Italian *Dialoghi* of the Jewish philosopher made a colossal impression. In the course of fifteen years (1535–50) his work went through five editions. "If the Jew Leo's *Dialoghi*," notes an important Italian writer of that time,[65] "had been written in as beautiful Italian style as he composed it in his language [*in lingua sua*],[66] then we would have no reason to be envious either of the Romans or the Greeks." Two French writers, Denis Sylvester and Du Parc, translated the *Dialoghi* into French and dedicated the translation

62. *Ibid.*, 63a.
63. *Ibid.*, 6b.
64. *Ibid.*, 95.
65. The Italian Tolomeo Claudio in a letter in 1547.
66. By the expression *in lingua sua*, one ought perhaps to understand the Hebrew language. See Note 31, above.

to the French queen, Catherine de Médici (1551). Soon thereafter Abravanel's work was translated into Latin, and the Jewish historian Gedaliah Ibn Yaḥya translated it into Spanish[67] and dedicated it to the king of Spain, the cruel Philip II. The romantic book on love was thus presented as a gift to one of the most venomous haters of men.

The reputation Abravanel's *Dialoghi di amore* obtained in Spain is attested by the brilliant creator of *Don Quixote*, Miguel de Cervantes. "If you would speak of love," the author advises his friend in the prologue, "turn to Leo Hebraeus; he will instruct you in full measure."

67. In 1905 a new Spanish edition of Abravanel's *Dialoghi* appeared.

CHAPTER TWO

Jewish Mysticism and the Italian Humanists;
GRAMMARIANS AND SCHOLARS

E have noted the sensation produced by Jehudah Abravanel's *Dialoghi di amore*. Its philosophical views were so congenial to the humanists of that era that the work became one of the most popular of the time. The author's philosophical mystical ideas about the active and passive elements, as well as about the tri-unity of the creating "father," the receptive "mother," and the fruit of their love, were in such close affinity to Christian religious conceptions that a legend was created to the effect that Abravanel converted to Christianity at the end of his life. Very little was known at that time about the historical development of neo-Platonic ideas. There was no understanding of the fact that both Jewish mysticism and the religious-philosophical vesture of the Christian faith drew, to a certain extent, from a single source, that both were under the influence of the same world of ideas, whose origin was neo-Platonism. The humanists, who were acquainted with many Jewish scholars, soon realized that certain neo-Platonic ideas of which they were extremely fond had been erected by the Jewish mystics, especially the authors of the *Zohar*, into a complete system. Hence, they began to concern themselves with Jewish mysticism and developed an intense desire to become familiar with the books of the Kabbalah. Jewish scholars were in general very well received in Italy, and it is therefore no surprise that among the humanist neo-Platonists the view that treasures of profound wisdom are hidden in old Hebrew manuscripts was widespread. As a result, in Christian humanist circles at the end of the fifteenth century interest in Jewish studies, especially in the Kabbalah, became quite considerable. Many humanists requested the Jewish scholars whom they knew to acquaint them orally or through translation with the fundamental ideas discussed in the Hebrew books.

Here we must dwell first on the influence exercised by Jewish savants on the famous count Pico della Mirandola (1463–94), whose youthful powers were devoured by his unquenchable thirst for truth and knowledge and who came to his premature grave at the age of thirty-one. This remarkable man, though not a significantly original thinker, was one of the elect few, one of those who know of no rest or contentment but, with longing hearts, search indefatigably in their drive to uncover the mysteries that veil human life and cosmic being.

Pico della Mirandola could in no way agree with those who were interested only in the ancient Graeco-Roman world and refused to recognize any other civilizations. He was deeply persuaded of the great value of the cultures of various peoples and eras, and constantly insisted that even in the half-forgotten manuscripts of the Middle Ages solutions may be discovered to highly significant problems which were not even posed by the ancient world. Out of these yellowed and forgotten pages, Pico della Mirandola maintained, the following words are clearly and distinctly heard: Forever shall we live—not, however, in the minds of dry philologists but in the hearts of true sages who do not split hairs about every petty detail of mythological legends but devote themselves to the profound problems of God and man. He who has open eyes can see and understand that even the peoples stamped with the contemptuous name "barbarians" were rich in spirit, not only on their lips but within their hearts.[1]

Pico della Mirandola was especially interested in medieval Jewish literature, which is written in such difficult and inaccessible language. With great energy he sought, with the aid of his learned Jewish friends, to penetrate into the treasures assembled in the numerous Hebrew books of speculation and Kabbalah. Jehudah

1. See Jacob Burckhardt, *Die Kultur der Renaissance in Italien* (tenth edition), I, 217.

Abravanel composed especially for the great Italian humanist his work in Latin on the harmony of the celestial spheres, *De coeli harmonia*,[2] and Elijah Delmedigo taught him Judeo-Arabic philosophy.

Characteristic of that era is the significant role played by Delmedigo, who was a prominent physician and scholar, in the Christian circles of Italy. Born in 1460 in Crete, which at that time belonged to Venice, Delmedigo died in 1497. As a youth he was already renowned as a prodigy and expert in the "sea of the Talmud."[3] At the age of twenty he was invited to occupy the post of head of a *yeshivah* or Talmudic academy in Padua. Soon he also became known in the local Christian learned circles as one thoroughly proficient in the realm of philosophy. His reputation as a philosophical scholar was so great that the University of Padua invited him to be the arbitrator and conciliator in the heated philosophical controversy which at that time divided its professors and students into two hostile camps.[4] At the age of twenty-three Elijah Delmedigo occupied the chair of philosophy at the University of Padua. He also lectured in Florence, Venice, Perugia, and other Italian cities, familiarizing his Christian auditors with the philosophical systems of Aristotle, Averroes, and Maimonides.[5]

At that time Delmedigo became acquainted with Pico della Mirandola, and the two quickly became close friends. At the wish of his Italian friend, Delmedigo translated numerous philosophic works (mainly Averroes' commentaries) from Hebrew into Latin, and also composed in Latin[6] two independent works in which he attempts to define the boundaries distinguishing faith from philosophy. The same theme is discussed by Delmedigo in his well-known

2. See A. Geiger in *Otzar Neḥmad*, II, 224–25. Steinschneider denies the historicity of this piece of information (*Hebräische Bibliographie*, XXI, 111). Some scholars even wish to show that Pico's friend Leo Hebraeus is in no way related to the author of the *Dialoghi*. Against this view, however, see H. Pflaum's article in *MGWJ*, 1928, pp. 344–50.
3. The greatest Talmudist of that age, Joseph Colon, mentions Elijah Delmedigo in terms of high praise. See his *Responsa*, No. 54.
4. See *Matzref Le-Ḥochmah*, Chapter 2.
5. See the well-known letter of Delmedigo's disciple Saul Cohen to Isaac Abravanel, 10a: "Our teacher, our master, Elijah Delmedigo, may his memory be for blessing, was a wise and understanding man, perfect in theoretical speculation. . . . He taught multitudes in the academies of the gentiles in Padua and Florence. . . . His name was famous among their scholars . . . and most of his disciples were from the nobility of the land." See also Conforte, *Kore Ha-Dorot*.
6. See Perles, *Beiträge*, pp. 197–98. For a discussion of Delmedigo's Latin works, see Steinschneider, *Hebräische Bibliographie*, XXI, 60–71.

Hebrew work *Beḥinat Ha-Dat*,[7] which he wrote at the request of his Jewish pupil, Saul Cohen Ashkenazi. This work provides the best evidence that its author was, indeed, a talented popularizer, a man of broad philosophical knowledge, but not an original thinker.

In *Beḥinat Ha-Dat* the old questions that had already been debated so many times in medieval Jewish literature are raised once again. May a pious Jew study philosophy without apprehension that he may thereby arrive at heresy? Is philosophic knowledge in general necessary to understand the commandments of the Torah accurately? To the latter question Delmedigo replies with a decisive No. The Jewish religion, he maintains, is not a philosophical system which must first be grounded through logical argumentation; it teaches and demands fulfillment of the commandments and observance of such precepts as lead to a pure moral life. Hence he speaks with great disgust of the *mitpalsefim* (philosophizers) who argue that the chief thing is knowledge and understanding rather than deeds, thought rather than action, and who have a contemptuous attitude toward fulfillment of the commandments.[8] "These are heretics and destroyers of the Torah," Delmedigo indignantly declares, "and it is precisely they who have brought it about that the common multitude, which cannot distinguish between ostensible scholars and true sages, removes itself from all science and knowledge whatsoever."[9]

With the same indignation Delmedigo also speaks of the compromisers and peacemakers who refuse to recognize the sharp boundaries which separate religion from philosophy and who, in order to harmonize the two, frequently distort the plain meaning of the Torah. They wish, says Delmedigo contemptuously, to be mediators between theologians and philosophers, but they themselves are neither theologians nor philosophers. They think that they make wisdom or science beloved in the eyes of the people by their compromises but in reality they only discredit it.[10]

To be sure, Delmedigo further declares, philosophical theories are desirable when they facilitate grasp of the foundations of the Torah, for the latter is indeed beyond reason but not contradictory to it. "The divine Torah by no means demands of us that we believe in what is inconsistent with the laws of logic. Human reason, after all, derives from the Creator; hence, it cannot be considered a sin to recognize only what is not contrary to reason."[11] And

7. Completed in January, 1491. First printed in 1629.
8. *Beḥinat Ha-Dat*, 72.
9. *Ibid.*, 73.
10. *Ibid.*, 18. Cf. *ibid.*, 52.
11. *Ibid.*, 14.

indeed we see, Delmedigo adds, how our Torah, which leads man on the way of truth, is not content merely with giving us ethical laws and principles on how to conduct ourselves in life but also teaches us profound truths embracing the whole extent of the world.[12] To penetrate the depth of these truths by way of inquiry and speculation is within the ability only of the select few whose philosophically schooled reason knows how properly to utilize the persuasive power of logical arguments and theories. But, Delmedigo insists, even those philosophically thinking chosen few firmly believe in the principles of the Torah, not merely because their truth is demonstrated through speculation, but above all because they are confirmed through tradition and the holy prophets. "In this particular," he adds, "there is no division of opinion between the philosophically thinking and the plain believer belonging to the multitude; both alike believe without any doubts in the word of the Torah."[13] Where, however, the commandments of the Torah are not consonant with purely philosophic theories, Delmedigo further says, he does not consider it necessary to make any compromise between the meaning of the Torah and philosophy but is content to rely entirely on the truth of tradition and prophecy.[14] True believers must, in any case, give credence to the miracles of the Torah; so it is better to remain faithful to the plain meaning of the text than to interpret it by way of allusion, as the philosophizers do.[15]

It is easy to see that these arguments of Delmedigo's are by no means novel. As the Hebrew saying goes, *kevar dareshu vo rabim* (many have already preached about this). When he attacks the "philosophizers" and compromise-makers, and insists upon the barrier which separates religion from philosophy, he merely repeats (and quite frequently in a rather unconvincing way) the arguments of Joseph Ibn Kaspi, Hasdai Crescas, Joseph ben Shemtov, and others. The thoughts that the author of *Beḥinat Ha-Dat* expresses with regard to the Talmudic Aggadah[16] are already thoroughly developed in Hillel of Verona's *Tagmulei Ha-Nefesh.*[17]

Only in regard to one question does Delmedigo utter original and quite independent ideas. This is on the value and significance

12. *Ibid.,* 65.
13. *Ibid.,* 56.
14. *Ibid.,* 17.
15. *Ibid.,* 49.
16. *Ibid.,* 56.
17. See our history, Volume II, pp. 196–200. Delmedigo borrowed much not only from Jewish writers but also from Christian authors. A. Huebsch, in his article (*MGWJ,* 1882, pp. 555–62; *MGWJ,* 1883, pp. 28–46), has shown decisively that a considerable part of *Beḥinat Ha-Dat is*

of the *hochmat ha-nistar* (hidden wisdom), the teaching of the Kabbalah. He points out numerous inconsistencies and antithetical views among the Kabbalists; this, he insists, is the best proof that this doctrine is not founded on true tradition transmitted from generation to generation.[18] He also ventures to express clearly and distinctly the "heretical" idea that Rabbi Simeon ben Yohai was not the author of the *Zohar;* as proof he notes the fact that in the *Zohar* numerous sages who lived considerably after Simeon's time are quoted.[19]

He has no doubt, Delmedigo adds, that among the Jewish people there will be some who will make a great outcry on account of this and declare him a heretic and an atheist who denies God's word; but he is firmly persuaded that they are mistaken and very far from the truth.[20] But there were many not only within the Jewish community who were extremely indignant at Delmedigo's battle against the Kabbalah; it was also very displeasing to his pupil and friend Pico della Mirandola. The latter was an ardent admirer of Jewish mysticism, and was firmly persuaded that treasures of profound mysteries are concealed in it. It was his fervent wish to penetrate these treasures, but he was persuaded that Delmedigo could not be the guide and doorkeeper who would open the hidden gates of the fantastic, wondrous palace for him. He managed, however, to find the desired guide in the person of the ardent Kabbalist Yohanan Alemanno.[21]

Yohanan Alemanno (1435–1527) is a very unique personality. He was descended from the Golei Tzarefat, the Jews expelled from France. Raised and educated apparently in Germany, he later led a wandering life, spending a rather long time in European Turkey. From Constantinople he went to Italy, where he lived for a while with the philanthropist and maecenas Yehiel of Pisa, with whom Isaac Abravanel carried on a friendly correspondence.[22] At that time Alemanno became acquainted with Pico della Mirandola, on whom he made a deep impression. A man of encyclopedic knowledge, well versed in Greek-Arabic philosophy, Alemanno was also

---

    simply an extract from Averroes' work *Façial maqal* which in Hebrew translation bears the title *Sefer Hevdel Ha-Ne'emar Be-Mah She-Bein Ha-Torah Veha-Hochmah Veha-Devekut.*

18. *Behinat Ha-Dat,* 45a.

19. *Ibid.,* 42–43. See also *ibid.,* 68–69.

20. *Ibid.,* 70.

21. Perles conjectures that Alemanno and Johannes Widmanstadt's teacher Datilus are the same person.

22. An interesting letter from Abravanel to Yehiel of Pisa is published in *Otzar Nehmad,* II, 65–70.

a fervent mystic and enthusiastic follower of the Kabbalah. It is for this reason that Heinrich Graetz, the bitter enemy of the Kabbalah, judges his works as ridiculous and petty ("spiritless writings filled with confusion"). But the more objective Moritz Steinschneider, when speaking of Alemanno, notes that "his peculiar attitude toward mysticism and Arabic philosophy, the extraordinary range of his reading, and his personal situation make him one of the most interesting phenomena of the Renaissance."[23] Even as a distinguished old man Alemanno still read his lectures on the "esoteric wisdom" with great fervor before a large audience, one of whose most enthusiastic members was Pico della Mirandola.

Alemanno's major work, *Ḥeshek Shelomoh*,[24] has remained in manuscript; only the first part was published under the title *Shaar Ha-Ḥeshek*.[25] This work, in which he presents his mystical-philosophical world outlook, is written in the form of a commentary to the Biblical Song of Songs. Alemanno was convinced that King Solomon was the greatest thinker who ever lived among all the peoples of the world. He places him not only above Plato and Aristotle but, in certain respects, even above Moses.[26] Solomon, Alemanno asserts, possessed such marvelous wisdom that the profundity of his words is grasped by each individual according to his level of understanding. And the highest degree of wisdom is attained by Solomon in his Song of Songs. (Here the interesting point that many of the ideas Alemanno expresses in his works are also in Jehudah Abravanel's *Dialoghi di amore* is worth noting. Since Alemanno's work was written fifteen years before the *Dialoghi*, one must conclude that he had a definite influence on Abravanel.)

Alemanno asserts that Solomon was the first to penetrate into the mystery of the divine nature, which is beyond boundary and end and cannot be contained either by the celestial vaults or by

23. *Verzeichniss der hebräischen Handschriften der königlichen Bibliothek zu Berlin*, II, 5; *Hebräische Bibliographie*, XXI, 130–32.
24. This work was written by Alemanno when he was fifty years old (see *Hebräische Bibliographie*, V, 28). On another work of Alemanno, see G. Scholem's report in *Kiryat Sefer*, V, 273–77.
25. Printed in Leghorn in 1690 with numerous notes by the editor, Jacob Moses Ḥayyim Baruch; reprinted in Halberstadt in 1862.
26. *Shaar Ha-Ḥeshek* (1690 edition), 14: "In this King Solomon, peace be upon him, was wiser than Moses our teacher, peace be upon him." When he points out that Solomon was expert in all the sciences Alemanno relies quite frequently on non-Jewish sources, among them on a work by Apollonius of Tyana which he called *Melachah Muskelet*. This work, Alemanno notes, was translated from Latin into Hebrew by an author of the fourteenth century named Solomon ben Nathan Orgeri.

the infinite distances of the myriads of stars and planets. God is omnipresent, and yet one definite and delimited point, the sanctuary built by Solomon, becomes the *bet ha-behirah*, (the chosen house), where God's glory and splendor rest. In God no alteration ever takes place; nevertheless, as Solomon indicates, God accepts "every prayer and supplication" (I Kings 8:35); to His throne of glory every petition and cry for help from all corners of the earth rise.[27]

While Jehudah Abravanel considers love the foundation of the world, Alemanno declares its basis to be *heshek*, ardent desire. In knowing God by way of true reverence, he affirms, speculative reason plays only a secondary role. Its light is pale and diffuse. But dazzlingly bright, like the rays of the sun, are the prophetic fervor, the mystic intuition, and the level of transcendence of corporeality that man reaches not with the aid of detached weighing of opinions and logical theories but with the flame of impetuous desire, with the sweetness of trembling ecstasy, which attain to "divine madness."[28] And in this consists the secret of Hosea's words, "the prophet is a fool, the man of the spirit is mad" (Hosea 9:7).[29]

The intimate experiences of the soul, born in passionate enchantment, are incomparably stronger, Alemanno asserts, than everything we perceive with our ordinary senses.[30] In the moment of revelation, which is attained through ecstasy, we see the world in an altogether different form than when we consider it with our sober reason. Before our enlightened eyes is revealed such a harmonious wholeness and regularity as appears wild and strange to ordinary reason. And precisely in these moments of "madness" do we understand the true nature of being and becoming, which remains veiled to logically thinking reason and to scientific, investigative thought. The rational world comprehended by common sense is merely a weak reflection of the other, the only real world, which discloses itself in the moment of sudden illumination when man attains the state of "divine madness."

It is written, "And thou shalt love the Lord thy God with all thy heart, with all thy soul, and with all thy might." This, indeed,

27. *Shaar Ha-Heshek*, 25.
28. It is difficult to say whether Alemanno was familiar with Plato's dialogue *Phaedo*, in which religious-prophetic ecstasy is declared to be the highest of the four degrees of divine madness. It has also not been established whether Alemanno was familiar with the concept of "divine intoxication" encountered so frequently in the work of the Jewish neo-Platonist Philo of Alexandria.
29. *Shaar Ha-Heshek*, 33a.
30. *Ibid.*, 46b.

is the only way that leads man to true bliss, for only through this love can he come to passionate ecstasy, to "divine madness." In fact, it is in this, says Alemanno, that we see the difference between the "sweet singer of Israel," King David, and his son Solomon. In the Psalter love for God is celebrated. Marvelously beautiful and pure is this love, but it does not lead to the supreme goal: man's union with God. At first Solomon followed this path, which his father had shown him. But he soon realized that this is merely the preliminary stage, the first level, which leads to the highest degree of mystical beauty: the ecstatic revelation of "divine madness." And it was this profound mystery that Solomon revealed to us in his Song of Songs.[31]

In Alemanno's view, everything that occurs in the supernal worlds—the circuit of the spheres and the movement of the planets—is merely a disclosure of the ardent drive for union with the source of perfection, with divinity.[32] The greater the separation and the further the distance from divinity, the greater is the corporeality, the grosser the forms. But even at the lowest levels the crudest material is filled with the drive to raise itself stage by stage to the distant heavenly heights. Whence comes this impetuous drive? What is the source of this marvelous power that raises and inspires the petty and lowly, and lets the divine, exalted beauty of the celestial spheres fall on everything that lives and springs forth on the earth? It is *ḥeshek*—passionate desire, flaming ecstasy.[33]

Desire is the dynamic power which brings all things to the loveliest harmony and the superlative level of perfection.[34] Everything that exists, the exalted and heavenly as well as the earthly and material, overflows with it, for in the same measure as the lowly longs and strives to the higher and more perfect, the exalted strives toward the earthly and lowly, imbued with the desire to illuminate the lowly with its light and thereby disclose the magnitude of its perfection.[35] "As much as we strive toward God and His perfection, so does divinity strive toward us in order to endow us with its perfection."[36]

These two mighty desires—the desire to receive and to be endowed, on the one side, and the longing to give and bestow, on the other—are the two central pillars on which the whole divine

31. *Ibid.,* 33–34.
32. *Ibid.,* 38b.
33. *Ibid.,* 39.
34. *Ibid.,* 38b.
35. *Ibid.,* 39a.
36. *Ibid.,* 34b.

structure, the infinite universe, is reared.[37] Desire and ecstasy are
the divine breath which permeates the whole world, unites everything from one end to the other, binds divinity together with
nethermost Sheol, and compels those who scrabble in the deepest
abysses of hell to strive toward the heavenly palaces.[38]

The focal point in all of the infinite universe is man. This fundamental idea, however, is explained by Alemanno in neither a philosophical nor a religious-psychological way, but with the aid of
"combinations of letters" and all kinds of *notarikon*. Not without
reason does he refer frequently to Abraham Abulafia[39] and Joseph
Gikatilla.[40] Like Abulafia, Alemanno speaks of seven ways to wisdom and of seven levels of perfection. The "acquired intellect,"
the abstract ideas (*muskalot*) which man attains through philosophical speculation and inquiry, is only the second level of perfection. A significantly higher level, the fourth, according to
Alemanno, is the inward feeling disclosed in the inspired word
of sincere prayer.[41] The fifth level is attained only through combinations of letters, "as the *Sefer Yetzirah* and many later Kabbalists, chief among them Abraham Abulafia, explained to us." The
letters, Alemanno asserts, are not inanimate signs but living symbols
in which a tremendous, mysterious power inheres. Through com-
bining the letters of the divine names, one may penetrate into the
sacred mysteries of the Torah which no philosopher can grasp.
Through combination of the letters of His holy name God Himself
created the world.[42] And yet, no matter how great and profound
these mysteries are, there is an even more exalted degree of perfection, namely, when the letters and words are embodied in deeds,
veil themselves in the garment of commandments. It has already
been shown by Menahem Recanati, Alemanno insists, that man,
with his performance of the commandments and good deeds, brings
it about that the "influence" of the heavenly "chariot" is spread
over the terrestrial world. Through the commandments of the
Torah man unites the material and the spiritual worlds; and just
as the spheres and planets with their harmonious movements reveal
the cosmic thought of the supreme wisdom, so the commandments
of the Torah, when embodied in man's actions, are the revelation

37. "These are the two columns on which the house of the Lord is established" (*Shaar Ha-Heshek*, 39b).
38. *Ibid.*, 39a.
39. *Ibid.*, 35b.
40. *Ibid.*, 37b.
41. *Ibid.*, 34b.
42. *Ibid.*, 36b.

of his understanding of God and thereby become the symbol of his immortal spirit.[43]

This zealous Kabbalist and enthusiastic preacher of "divine madness" introduced Count Pico della Mirandola into the inner sanctum of the mysteries of the Kabbalah. At Alemanno's suggestion, his Christian pupil translated Recanati's commentary to *Hochmat Ha-Nefesh* by Eleazar of Worms (in the Latin translation, the work is entitled *Scientia animae*) and Shemtov Falaquera's *Sefer Ha-Maalot*. In 1486 Pico published his well-known work *Conclusiones philosophicae, cabalisticae et theologicae*, in which the fundamental problems of God, world, and man are treated. In this work he endeavors to show that the Kabbalah is consonant with Christian doctrine on numerous questions.

Not for this reason alone, however, was Pico so intensely interested in the wisdom of the Kabbalah. An especially powerful impression was made on him by the fact that the Kabbalist books strongly emphasize the universal role of the human personality in the cosmos as a whole. There is no doubt that this basic principle of Jewish mysticism had a great influence on Pico's "Oration on the Dignity of Man," renowned as one of the loveliest monuments of the Renaissance.

Pico della Mirandola was by no means the only Christian scholar interested in Jewish mysticism. In fact, Pico himself taught the "esoteric wisdom" to the famous German humanist Johannes von Reuchlin (1455–1522), who later in his work *De arte cabalistica* attempted, like Pico, to demonstrate that the Kabbalah is in complete harmony with the foundations of Christianity. Pope Sixtus IV even ordered several Kabbalist books translated from Hebrew into Latin, because this might, in his view, be very useful to the Church.

Among Yoḥanan Alemanno's auditors was the German scholar Johannes Albrecht Widmanstadt, who spent several years in Italy. But Alemanno was then quite old; hence Widmanstadt, together with Cardinal Egidio da Viterbo, applied to the philosophically learned Kabbalist, Baruch of Benevento,[44] to teach them the litera-

---

43. *Ibid.*, 45a.
44. In one of Widmanstadt's manuscripts the following note appears: "audivi Baruch Beneventanum optimum cabalistam, qui primus libros Zoharis per Aegidium Viterbiensem Cardinalem in christianos vulgari" (see Perles, *Beiträge*, p. 180). On Benevento's broad philosophical knowledge see Paulus Emilius' letter in the introduction to the Augsburg edition of the Judeo-German translation of the Pentateuch (see *MGWJ*, 1876, pp. 363–65).

ture of the Kabbalah. Widmanstadt was also on friendly terms
with the Jewish translator and scholar Jacob ben Simeon Mantino
(1490–1549), who played such an unlovely role as the ruthless
prosecutor in the tragic fate of the brilliant and richly imaginative
mystic Solomon Molcho. Quite uncongenial as a person and communal leader, Mantino nevertheless had considerable merits in the
realm of science. A physician in Bologna in his younger years,
later court physician to Pope Paul III, professor in the medical
faculty of the University of Rome, and member of the rabbinic
court of the Roman community, Mantino, while extremely busy
with his medical practice, nevertheless found time to devote himself
to scientific pursuits. At the request of his Christian friend the
bishop of Verona Gianmateo Ghiberti, and others, Mantino translated from Hebrew into Latin many commentaries by Averroes
on the works of Plato and Aristotle, as well as Maimonides'
Shemoneh Perakim, and participated in the publication of *A Guide
for the Perplexed* in Latin.[45]

Highly reputed in the Christian world at that time also was Mantino's contemporary Abraham ben Meir de Balmes (c. 1440–c.
1523). Active as a prominent physician, de Balmes also devoted
himself considerably to Judaic scholarship and delivered lectures
at the University of Padua before large Christian audiences.[46] At
the request of Cardinal Domenico Grimani, who aided Reuchlin
in his battle against the Dominicans and the apostate Johannes
Pfefferkorn, de Balmes translated numerous works of Averroes,
Ibn Badjdja, and others from Hebrew into Latin.

De Balmes, however, acquired his reputation not as a translator
but mainly as the author of an important work, *Mikneh Avraham*
(published in 1523), on Hebrew philology, a field which greatly
interested the humanistically-minded Christian scholars of that era.
We have noted that Pico della Mirandola was so proficient in Hebrew that he could translate directly from it into Latin. In this
respect he was not at all exceptional. The great interest which
the ancient world and the classical writers of Greek and Latin
literature evoked in the Renaissance era also brought it about that
the humanists turned their attention to the second major source

---

45. The author of *Shalshelet Ha-Kabbalah* is mistaken when he speaks
of Mantino as the translator of Maimonides' *Guide for the Perplexed*
into Latin. For more about Mantino, see Vogelstein and Rieger,
Geschichte der Juden in Rom, pp. 94–97; Steinschneider, *Hebräischen
Übersetzungen,* and in *Hebräische Bibliographie,* pp. 44, 86; Graetz,
Geschichte der Juden, Vol. IX; *REJ,* VII, 283 ff.
46. Among Abraham de Balmes' disciples who studied Hebrew with him
was the novelist Francesco Maria Malza.

of ancient civilization, the language of the Bible. To be sure, this was not the only factor. Various motives were involved in the strong interest of Christian scholars in Hebrew. Already in the first half of the fifteenth century, the Florentine scholar and political leader Giannozzo Manetti noted that to be able successfully to conduct polemics against Jewish scholars on questions of dogma and faith, one must be well acquainted with the Hebrew language and Jewish literature. It was this Manetti whom Pope Nicholas V commissioned to translate anew the entire Bible from the original into Latin. But many humanists had more secular motivations. They were convinced that Hebrew was the key to whole treasures of knowledge in various realms. "Long before Reuchlin," notes the eminent historian of the Renaissance era Jacob Burckhardt, "the humanists considered it extremely important to study the Hebrew language." Reuchlin himself, who became interested in the Kabbalah and Hebrew literature under the influence of Pico della Mirandola, learned the language of the Bible thoroughly under the direction of the Jewish scholar Obadiah ben Jacob Sforno.[47] Reuchlin was the first to introduce Hebrew into the curriculum of university studies. As professor of Greek and Hebrew at the University of Tübingen, he produced a whole school of Christian Hebraists. In his *De verbo mirifico* Reuchlin sings the praises of the "divine" Hebrew language. In it Berechyah, a Jewish Talmudist, and Capnion, a Christian scholar, carry on a conversation with a Greek philosopher, and all three finally conclude that not only are the Hebrew language and the wisdom of Israel the acme of knowledge but that even in the Hebrew alphabet, in every letter and crownlet, profound and wondrous mysteries are concealed. For Christian learned circles interested in Hebrew Reuchlin composed his textbook *Rudimenta hebraica* (1506), the first Hebrew grammar written by a Christian. Reuchlin was certain that with this work he had created for himself an eternal memorial (*exegi monumentem aere perennius*). In fact, however, his textbook is very far from perfect. It contains only the most elementary principles of grammar and a very incomplete list of Hebrew words. Such a work could quench the thirst of the humanists for Hebraic knowledge only to a limited degree. Jewish savants then came to their aid.

It was, in fact, under the influence of humanist ideas that interest in Hebrew philology grew among the Italian Jews themselves. Here a tendency is discernible which is reminiscent of that early period of Spanish-Jewish culture when Jewish scholars, under the

47. On Obadiah Sforno, see Chapter 4 of this volume.

influence of the great Arabic philologists, enthusiastically under-took an exploration of the language of the Bible. The more the humanists immersed themselves in the world of classical antiquity, the more enchanted they were by the splendor of pagan culture. The literary monuments of Greek and Latin antiquity became for them the source of all human wisdom and knowledge. The most popular writers among the intellectual readers of the day were the classical poets, historians, and orators. No time or trouble, not to speak of expense, was spared to revive and explore Graeco-Roman antiquity as completely as possible. Hence, it is not at all surprising that the fifteenth century was so full of exciting dis-coveries in the field of ancient literature. Both spiritual and secular princes and officials employed numerous scribes and copyists to transcribe and translate old manuscripts for them.

The intense interest in the ancient literature of Greece and Rome in the fifteenth century reached the point where the İtalian intelli-gentsia began to neglect their own national literature. In the hu-manist circles the idea that Latin must remain the only universally recognized literary language became ever more prevalent. Even the fact that the great Dante wrote his immortal work in the Italian vernacular was deplored. Cicero was regarded as the exemplary writer of literary prose, and many humanists considered it a point of honor not to use any expression not found in this "unattainable model" of classical Latin prose. The loftiest ideal of the humanists was to create a neo-Latin poesy, to employ the language of Cicero and Plautus for poetry and oratory. Under the influence of the great orator of ancient Rome, rhetoric came to occupy an extremely important place among the humanists, and their greatest pride was the ability to present in public a Latin eulogy constructed accord-ing to the principles of ancient oratory. It was at that time also that the learned Lorenzo Valla wrote his philological works, *De lingae latinae elegentia* and others, in which he endeavored to ex-pound scientifically all the unique qualities and beauties of Latin and its verbal treasures.

All this had a strong influence on Jewish intellectual circles as well. Moses ben Shemtov Ibn Ḥabib, a native of Lisbon but from his youth a resident of southern Italy, in 1486 completed his text-book *Darchei Noam*, in which he deals with the forms of Hebrew poetry, employing the principles of Aristotle's *Poetics*. Ibn Ḥabib attempts to show that rhyme and meter were already accepted in Hebrew poetry in Biblical days.[48] He also composed a Hebrew

48. See *Darchei Noam*, 13a (according to the Venice edition of 1546): "I call heaven and earth to witness that when I was in Valencia . . . all the people who were at the gate and the elders told me that there

grammar, *Perah Shoshan*, but the outline only of this work was published (together with *Darchei Noam*) under the title *Marpe Lashon*.

More typical of contemporary currents is another philologist, Jehudah ben Yehiel, better known by the name Messer Leon. About his life we have very little information. We know only that his father was a physician and that he himself also studied medicine.[49] He resided for a time in Mantua as rabbi of the community, but because of a sharp controversy that broke out between him and the famous Talmudic scholar of that era, Joseph Colon, both parties to the dispute had to leave Mantua at the command of its duke (1475). Messer Leon thereafter lived in Padua, Ancona, and Naples, where he died some time after 1490.[50]

Messer Leon is one of those extremely interesting personalities who, while standing on the threshold of a new era and finding themselves under the influence of two civilizations, do not allow themselves to be led blindly by the new currents but attempt to synthesize the old with the new and to give the still valuable older content newer and more contemporaneous forms. Messer Leon was a competent scholar in Greek-Arabic philosophy,[51] wrote

---

was the tombstone of a general of Amaziah, the king of Judea. And when I heard this, I hastened to see this tombstone, which was of stone at the top of a hill. After much trouble I read the inscription that was chiseled on it and it was in the form of a poem:

> *Seu kinah*
> *Be-kol marah*
> *Le-sar gadol*
> *Lekaho Yah.*

> Lift up a lamentation
> In a bitter voice
> For the great general
> Whom God has taken.

"And I could read no more because it was rubbed out, but the second poem ended with the words 'of Amaziah.' Then I became convinced that rhymed poems had existed from the time our forefathers were on their own land." In modern times one scholar has conjectured (though on very flimsy grounds) that the tombstone Ibn Habib describes was that of the famous poet Solomon Ibn Gabirol (*Ha-Shiloah*, I, 228).

49. His son David relates that Messer Leon composed a medical work in Latin.
50. Jacob Provinciali's letter to Messer Leon's son, which was written in 1490, refers to Messer Leon as someone still living.
51. To be sure, only from the Hebrew and Latin sources, for it is very doubtful that Messer Leon knew Arabic.

commentaries on the works of Averroes,[52] and composed a text-book on logic, *Michlal Yofi*, in the introduction to which he issues forth quite sharply both against the *mitpalsefim* (philosophizers) and against the "foolish" mystics, of whom he says that "they like best what is most wildly impossible and worthless." At the same time the breath of the Renaissance era is discernible in his work. He diligently studied the works of Cicero, Quintilian, and their commentators, and on solemn occasions delivered lofty eulogies and festal addresses constructed according to the most rigorous principles of ancient rhetoric. Messer Leon, however, was a child not only of the youthful Renaissance but also of the old people of Israel. A fine stylist and scholar of the Hebrew language,[53] he could not agree with the view, so popular among the humanists, that Cicero was the supreme model of oratory and perfect prose style. He wished to show that in the realm of style and oratory the prophets and Biblical historians must be acknowledged as the supreme masters. To this end he composed his work *Nofet Tzufim*.[54]

This rabbi of Mantua was the first Jewish scholar who dared to consider the Bible not merely as "sacred scripture," a divine and holy work, but also as one of the most remarkable of literary monuments, a collection of supreme artistic achievements. Messer Leon adopts Quintilian's view that the truly perfect orator must also be a man of pure morality, that he must have, in addition to an eloquent tongue, the highest spiritual qualities. For this reason, he concludes, the greatest orators were the best and noblest representatives of the Jewish people: the Biblical prophets.[55]

Like the majority of Jewish scholars in the Middle Ages, Messer Leon was firmly persuaded that all wisdom and scientific knowledge derive from the Jews. In the days of the prophets, when the divine spirit rested on Mount Sinai, he declares, Jews were the bearers of human knowledge, and their sacred Torah was the source of all the sciences. They were above all other peoples culturally, and not without reason was it then said of them, "This great nation is a wise and understanding people." However, since, because of their numerous sins, the word of their prophets was

52. For more about these unpublished works of Messer Leon, see Steinschneider, *Hebräischen Übersetzungen*, pp. 77–86.
53. He gave lectures on Hebrew philology before a circle of young people, and to this end composed a special textbook in 1454.
54. Composed after 1454, because in it his work *Livnat Ha-Sapir*, which he completed in that year, is mentioned several times. We have utilized the very rare Mantua edition (published before 1480), but since the pages are not numbered we shall quote it henceforth according to the second edition which Jellinek published in 1863.
55. *Nofet Tzufim*, 11; cf. *ibid.*, 3, 184 ff.

silenced and the wells of their wisdom dried up, they can no longer penetrate into the profundities of the holy writings. The situation has changed to such an extent that we now very frequently observe the following phenomenon: only after we become familiar with various branches of knowledge from foreign sources are our eyes opened, and treasures of wisdom and beauty which were heretofore veiled are disclosed to us in the Bible. This very thing, Messer Leon adds, actually happened with him. Only after he had learned the nature and significance of rhetoric from foreign sources[56] did he begin to look upon the Bible with altogether different eyes and observe in it things such as he previously had no conception of; only then did he begin to appreciate the rhetorical artistry and inimitable stylistic beauties of the Bible, in comparison with which those of other literatures and peoples are like little grasses compared with the cedars of Lebanon. Messer Leon further relates how only after he had become familiar with the work of Quintilian and Cicero did he understand that the Hebrew prophets were also brilliant orators and supreme masters of fervent style,[57] and he speaks indignantly of the "ostensibly wise among our people" who maintain that we have no reason to seek wisdom from foreign sources. They think they are thereby fulfilling the Biblical verse, "He will magnify the Torah and make it glorious" (Isaiah 42:21). But they are mistaken; with their talk they merely degrade the Torah, for they place obstacles on the way leading to the thorough investigation of its invaluable treasures.[58]

Messer Leon endeavors to teach his readers the fundamentals of rhetoric, the unique laws and principles of rhythm and harmony by which all passionate style is distinguished. He attempts to explain in popular form how a man may manage, with the aid of symbols, signs, and similes, to transmit to another the immensely rich variety and color of human feelings and moods. In *Nofet Tzufim* this is illustrated exclusively through quotations from the Bible. Not only the visions of the prophets but even the words of God Himself are quoted by Messer Leon as models of exalted and beautiful style. While earlier commentators, especially the Kabbalists, saw in every superfluous letter, in every repeated word

56. Of "foreign sources" Messer Leon quotes mainly Quintilian, Cicero (to whom he refers sometimes by his patronymic but often by his first name, Tullius), and also a commentator of Cicero's, Vittorino. Quite frequently Messer Leon also refers to a "short textbook" which Aristotle allegedly wrote especially for his pupil Alexander of Macedon (*ibid.*, 65, 88, 99).
57. *Nofet Tzufim*, 184, 192 ff.
58. *Ibid.*, 49.

or expression that occurs in the Torah, profound allusions and stupendous mysteries, the author of *Nofet Tzufim* declares all these things simply stylistic adornments, and notes that this must be so according to the principles of rhetoric and the laws of oratorical art.[59]

In this connection Messer Leon insists that familiarity with the laws of elegant style and poetic art forms, and the proper use of the principles of rhetoric, may serve as aids in the exegesis of the Biblical text. He gives as examples numerous expressions and descriptions from the Bible[60] which seem obscure and incomprehensible because they are not considered from the standpoint of rhetorical art and because we forget that we have to do here with products of passionate style and poetic creation, in which special laws obtain.

It is extremely characteristic of contemporary moods in Italian Jewry that Messer Leon's *Nofet Tzufim* was one of the first Hebrew books to be printed. The cultured physician Abraham Conat, who in the late 1470's established a Hebrew press in Mantua,[61] was so charmed by Messer Leon's work on rhetoric that he considered it his prime duty to acquaint wider circles with it as quickly as possible.[62]

In 1454 Messer Leon composed a textbook of Hebrew grammar for his pupils. This work was widely disseminated among Jews. At the end of the fifteenth century, however, the more interest in Hebrew grew in Christian learned circles, the more the desire arose among Jewish scholars to come to the aid of their Christian colleagues and create for them "helping books" that would facilitate their acquisition of a knowledge of the language. To this end, Messer Leon's pupil, Abraham de Balmes, composed his previously mentioned grammatical work, *Mikneh Avraham*. The author himself notes that he wrote his work not only for Jews but for "other peoples" as well, and for this reason the work was published (in Venice, 1523) with a Latin translation, and the Hebrew text was printed with vowel points so that non-Jews would not stumble in reading it.

De Balmes' work is undoubtedly an important phenomenon of that era. The author of *Mikneh Avraham* attempts to ground the structure of the Hebrew language philosophically, gives a historical-critical overview of the development of Hebrew grammar, and in this connection rejects many views of previous grammarians

59. *Ibid.*, 193.
60. See, for example, *ibid.*, 26, 90, and 170–71.
61. See Zunz, *Zur Geschichte und Literatur*, p. 249.
62. See his addendum at the end of *Nofet Tzufim*.

which he considers unfounded.[63] De Balmes, incidentally, is the first among Jewish philologists to distinguish syntax as an altogether independent part of grammar.[64]

Characteristic of our author is the manner in which he attempts to ground scientifically both the accepted view that Hebrew is the "chosen language" and the doctrine of the Kabbalists that a hidden power inheres in the words of the Bible and in "combinations of letters." He bases himself on the lovely Biblical legend which relates that God brought before Adam all the creatures of earth and all the birds of heaven so that he might give them names. "And whatsoever Adam called each living creature, so was its name" (Genesis 2:19). There is no doubt, de Balmes insists, that every designation which Adam gave in Hebrew,[65] and to which the Creator Himself assented, expressed fully the true nature of each creature. "For this reason," he declares, "we call Hebrew the holy tongue, i.e., the separated and chosen, which creates and defines." In it man first created his concepts and ideas, and its designations and names therefore express more clearly the true nature of things than is the case with all other languages.[66]

Mikneh Avraham is written with great scholarship but in difficult, cumbersome language. It was therefore not particularly accepted by the public, especially the circles which needed it most, the Christian Hebraists.[67] The real teacher and guide of the Christian humanists in the realm of Hebraic knowledge was de Balmes' younger contemporary, Elijah ben Asher Ha-Levi Ashkenazi, better known as Elijah Baḥur or Elijah Levita.

About Elijah Levita's youth we have very slight information. We know only that he was born in the village of Ipsheim not far from Nuremberg. On the question of the year of his birth there is something of a scholarly controversy. Most biographers indicate the year 1472, relying on the introduction to the second edition of his *Sefer Ha-Baḥur* which appeared in 1542 and in which Elijah says of himself, "and I am now as a man of seventy years."

63. He issues forth with special frequency against Rabbi David Kimḥi. In *Mikneh Avraham* we encounter quite frequently expressions such as the following: "These are things . . . which many of the grammarians believed and which are unacceptable to me . . . and in this Rabbi David Kimḥi and his friend were confused."
64. See Gate Seven in *Mikneh Avraham* ("Shaar Ha-Harkavah Veha-Shimmush").
65. De Balmes also attempts to present "scientific" arguments supporting the idea that the vernacular of the first human generations was Hebrew.
66. *Mikneh Avraham*, Gate One.
67. On the dissatisfaction of the Christian Hebraists with the work of de Balmes, see Perles, *Beiträge*, pp. 37–39.

But we are dubious about this date and believe that Elijah was born in 1468. On the last page of the book on Jewish religious laws, *Shaarei Dura*, which appeared in 1548, Elijah, who was proofreader of the edition, indicates explicitly that he is eighty years old,[68] from which it follows that he was born in 1468.

Elijah was the youngest of nine sons. When and under what circumstances he came to Italy is not definitely known. Most probably the same factors that impelled so many German Jews to migrate to southern Italy, the constant persecution of Jews in the Germanic lands, also brought him there. It is clear that Elijah did not obtain any great knowledge of Hebrew philology in Germany. The German Jews generally had little familiarity with grammar, and among the Spanish and Italian Jews of that era they were regarded not without cause as "stammering" and "heavy-tongued."[69] Hence there is no doubt that the fact that Elijah became the "great grammarian" (*medakdek*) is due to the Italian school. At the end of the fifteenth century we already find him in Venice, and in 1504 he was in the old cultural center of Padua, immersed in philological studies[70] and surrounded by pupils. His first philological work was a commentary to Moses Kimhi's grammar, *Mahalach Shevilei Ha-Daat*, which became, thanks to his additions and explanations, extremely popular in Christian circles. It went through numerous editions,[71] and the well-known Hebraist Sebastian Muenster, who himself admitted how indebted he was to Elijah Levita,[72] issued *Mahalach Shevilei Ha-Daat* with a Latin translation (Basel, 1531, 1535).

68. On this see also *Tziyyon*, 1841, p. 199; *Literaturblatt des Orients*, 1843, p. 14; *ibid.*, 1847, p. 58.
69. Isaac Abravanel, in his well-known letter to Saul Cohen Ashkenazi, expresses his astonishment that the latter is exceptional among the other Ashkenazim and writes Hebrew so beautifully (*Teshuvot*, 11a). The Italian Joshua Soncino writes in the same way: "And all the Ashkenazim by nature are stammerers and heavy of mouth and tongue; they have not the capacity to express with their lips or to write with pen the profundity that lies in their hearts, and only he who listens carefully to them will understand them" (see *Kore Ha-Dorot* [Venice edition], 29a).
70. Elijah Levita himself notes that he devoted very little attention to the Talmud. See the second introduction to his *Tishbi:* "For my sins, most of my years have already passed and I have not studied well the discussions of Abbaye and Rava, and I devoted myself to the sages little."
71. The first edition of Kimhi's grammar with Levita's supplements appeared in Pesaro in 1508. Levita's own handwritten manuscript with his supplements to Kimhi's grammar is in the Asiatic Museum in Leningrad.
72. See Perles, *Beiträge*, pp. 32, 39.

In 1509, when Padua passed into the hands of enemy armies, Elijah lost his entire fortune and, stripped and penniless, returned to Venice. A few years later, in 1514, he settled in Rome, where he became friendly with a scholarly and prominent Catholic cardinal, Egidio da Viterbo. This friendship of many years played a most important role in Elijah's scientific activity.[73] Egidio first sought Elijah's acquaintance so that the latter might introduce him to the "hidden wisdom" and facilitate his knowledge of Hebrew Kabbalist works. Still preserved is Elijah's copy, in his own hand, of the three Kabbalist books of Eleazar of Worms, *Sodei Razaya*, *Hochmat Ha-Nefesh*, and a commentary to the *Sefer Yetzirah*, which the Jewish scholar transcribed in 1515 especially for his pupil and patron, Egidio.[74] The obdurate controversy between Reuchlin on the one side and the apostate from Judaism Pfefferkorn and the Dominicans on the other, which then created such a tremendous sensation, further intensified interest in the Hebrew language and literature within learned circles. The intellectually curious Egidio was therefore especially desirous that his Jewish friend devote himself entirely to Hebrew philology and compose, first of all, a handbook of the Hebrew language.[75] To give Elijah the material requirements necessary to devote himself to scientific work, Egidio da Viterbo settled him in his own palace (1517) and provided him with all his needs.[76] Egidio also took care to remove another obstacle which might hinder Levita's scientific work: he obtained permission from the pope to establish a Hebrew press in Rome for the special purpose of publishing his friend's works.

Elijah Levita sat "in the tent of Torah" and wrote one work after another. In 1517 his famous grammar, *Sefer Ha-Baḥur*, appeared in Rome, and immediately afterwards he published his *Luaḥ Be-Dikduk Ha-Pealim Veha-Binyanim* and his textbook on foreign

---

73. Levita himself describes at length his cordial relationships with Cardinal Egidio in the third introduction to his *Massoret Ha-Massoret*. He insists that he himself learned much from his cultured pupil: "And so we took counsel together; my spirit influenced him, and I also derived from him many good and pleasant things which are consonant with the truth" (*ibid.*, 8–9; we quote according to the first Venice edition). In the third introduction to his *Tishbi*, Levita notes that for his knowledge of Greek he is entirely indebted to Egidio: "And some will marvel at the fact that I introduce Greek in many places, believing that I am not familiar with the language; but they do not know that I obtained all this from the cardinal with whom I lived for thirteen years" (we quote according to the first edition of *Baḥur*).
74. See *Iggerot Shadal*, VI, 1020–21.
75. See the introduction to the first edition of *Baḥur*.
76. Introduction to *Tishbi* (1538), 9.

and complicated words in Hebrew, *Sefer Ha-Harkavah*.[77] Thereafter Elijah worked for some years on two large philological
works, on a Bible concordance entitled *Sefer Ha-Zichronot*, and
on *Meturgeman*, a dictionary of all the Aramaic words in the Talmud. The turmoils of war, however, suddenly interrupted his
scholarly activity. The armies of the emperor Charles V smashed
into Rome (1527), and in the pillage which ensued Elijah lost
not only his entire fortune but also some of his already completed
manuscripts.[78] He then spent two difficult years in wandering. In
1527 we find him in Pesaro, where he published, through the
Soncino press, his philological work *Pirkei Eliahu*.[79] From there
he wandered to other cities until he settled in Venice in 1529.
There he was supported at first by his faithful friend Egidio da
Viterbo, who again took care that the Jewish scholar should have
the opportunity to devote himself to his scientific work.[80] Elijah
also obtained support in Venice from the French ambassador,
George de Selve, who studied Hebrew with him.[81] In 1538 he
published in Venice his famous work *Massoret Ha-Massoret* in
which he expresses the, for that time, extremely radical idea that
the vowel points and accent marks in the Biblical text are not a
"law of Moses from Sinai"; they were completely unknown not
only in Ezra's time but even in the days of the Talmud, and are
a later achievement of the Masorites who lived in Tiberias after
the close of the Talmud.[82]

77. The first edition of *Sefer Ha-Harkavah*, with various supplements,
was published by Levita himself in 1546.
78. See *Massoret Ha-Massoret* (1538), 10, as well as the introduction to
Sefer Ha-Zichronot.
79. Benjacob is mistaken when he notes that Soncino published *Pirkei
Eliahu* in 1520. At the end of the second (Venice) edition (1546)
the following note is printed: "And so these chapters are published
for a second time—chapters which Elijah, the great grammarian, composed, adding some choice things which were not known to him when
he first had them printed in the city of Pesaro by Soncino in the
year 1527."
80. Levita tells of this at length in the interesting supplement to be found
in his handwritten *Meturgeman* (see *Magazin für jüdische Geschichte*,
II, 68).
81. See Brüll, *Jahrbücher für jüdische Geschichte und Literatur*, IV, 181,
and Levita's letter of thanks to de Selve in the introduction to his
Sefer Ha-Zichronot.
82. Third introduction to *Massoret Ha-Massoret* (1538), 11–15: "I reckon
that the vowel points and the musical notations did not exist before
Ezra or in the time of Ezra or after Ezra until after the close of
the Talmud. And I can demonstrate this with clear and convincing
arguments" (page 22); "therefore I say that it is clear to me that
the vowel points did not exist in the days of the sages of the Talmud

This evoked great displeasure in orthodox Jewish circles, which saw in Elijah's conclusion genuine heresy. On the other hand, his scientific investigation made a great impression on the Christian learned world. The work was immediately reprinted in Basel, with Muenster's Latin translation of all three of Levita's introductions. All the later Christian Hebraists—Buxtorf, de Rossi, and many others—made use of *Massoret Ha-Massoret*. In 1772 Christian Gottlob Meyer published a German translation of the work, and in more recent times (1867) Christian David Ginsburg published an English translation, together with a biography of Levita.

In Venice Levita also completed his concordance, *Sefer Ha-Zichronot*, on which he had worked for more than twenty years.[83] His later philological works were published by Levita in Isny: *Meturgeman* (1954), a Yiddish-Hebrew dictionary entitled *Shemot Devarim* (1542),[84] and *Tishbi*, an explanation of 712 words that occur in the Talmud and Midrashim.[85]

The last two works mentioned have a relationship not only to Hebrew philology but also to Old Yiddish. Of Elijah's achievements in this realm, we shall have occasion to speak at length in the volume of our work in which Old Yiddish literature is treated. There we shall see Elijah from an altogether different aspect—not the dry philologist but the entertaining writer of romances, the creator of the *Bovo Buch* and other knightly tales. In the meantime

---

until the time of the Masorites who lived in Tiberias, and it is from them that we received all the vowel points" (23–24). See also Levita's *Tov Taam*, introduction, as well as Chapter 2, page 9.

83. See the introduction to *Massoret Ha-Massoret* (1538), 27. This work was to have been printed in Paris through the good offices of de Selve, but because of some unknown obstacles it was not published and has not been printed in its entirety to the present day. Published are only Levita's letter of thanks to de Selve in the introduction (*MGWJ*, XII, 96–108) and the rhymed introduction (*Letterbode*, VII, 146–47). In 1875 B. Goldberg was supposed to publish the entire concordance, but only the first fascicle (to *Agma*) appeared.

84. This little dictionary is now extremely rare, and we have not seen it. Information about it is provided by Perles, *Beiträge*, pp. 131–38, and Max Weinreich, *Shtaplen*, pp. 83–86.

85. Most of the copies of *Tishbi*, which appeared with a Latin translation in 1541, have been preserved with some pages torn out. This was brought about by the word "Jesus" which is also explained in *Tishbi*. Levita's commentary on this word did not please the later Christian censors. In the copy of the Isny edition which we employed the entire sheet in which the suspect word is printed has been torn out. In the copy of the Basel edition, which we have seen, only the columns containing the Hebrew and Latin text dealing with the word Jesus have been excised.

here we shall give only an estimate of Elijah the grammarian, the author of *Massoret Ha-Massoret*.

Elijah Levita was not an original scholar with whose work a new chapter in the development of his scientific field begins. He cannot, in any case, be compared with the first-rate Jewish scholars of the eleventh century who laid the foundations of Hebrew philology. He was merely an extremely diligent and competent craftsman, endowed with the talent of the excellent popularizer. In addition he was a sociable and congenial person, and, by his personal qualities, best fitted for the important and, in a certain respect, historic role that he fulfilled: familiarizing the Christian learned world, among whom the humanist tendencies had aroused great interest in the language of the Bible, with Hebrew philology and the characteristics of the Hebrew language. Elijah did not seek new paths and did not attempt, as did de Balmes, to criticize the old. On the contrary, he faithfully followed the Kimhis, and one of his last works was a new edition of David Kimhi's grammar, *Michlol*, with additions and explanations (*nimmukim*). Because he was so well suited to the tasks of his time, he was very popular in his generation and extremely well liked in humanist circles.[86] With complete justification Elijah, who by nature was a modest person and far from given to boastfulness, says of himself: "I can publicly declare that it would be difficult to find another author who has had the privilege of seeing his works printed so frequently while still alive and of being so widely accepted among readers. . . . My name is widely known both among Jews and Christians, and all wish to be my pupils."[87] Along with this, however, Elijah deems it necessary to emphasize: "I swear by my Creator that for all this I am indebted to a Christian pupil of mine who marked out this way for me."[88]

Levita's reputation was carried far beyond the boundaries of Italy. He was even offered a chair at the University of Paris,[89] but he did not wish to live in France, where there had been no Jewish settlement since the expulsion of 1395. He also declined

86. In Levita's previously mentioned handwritten manuscript an interesting notice about the honoraria which he received from his Christian pupils for his Hebrew lessons is contained.
87. Second edition to *Massoret Ha-Massoret*.
88. *Ibid.*
89. Under the influence of the Reformation the Catholic Church also modified its strict prohibition against translating the Bible into the vernacular. In France, too, interest in the original of the Biblical text grew, and ten years after the appearance of Martin Luther's translation of the Bible the French translation of Pierre Olivetto was published.

all other invitations to lecture in Christian academies.[90] On the other hand, Elijah gladly responded to invitations from Christian proprietors of Hebrew presses to occupy the post of chief proof-reader and make-up man, because, with his fine sensitivity, he saw in this occupation a highly important cultural function. To make this clearer, it is worth dwelling on the significant cultural role which the Hebrew presses of Italy played in the Renaissance era.

Of all Jewish communities, the Italian was the first that sought to employ Gutenberg's brilliant invention. Thirteen years after the first press with movable type was established in Strasbourg (1460), two Hebrew presses were founded in Italy, one in Reggio di Calabria and the other in Pieva da Saca. The paean at the end of the first printed Hebrew book, Rabbi Jacob ben Asher's *Arbaah Turim*, provides a clear notion of the ardent enthusiasm with which the Italian Jews approached the "sacred work" of printing books:

I am the art that is the crown of all the arts. I myself am hidden, but in me all secrets are concealed. Without pens, my script is clear to all; without scribes do I create books. In a moment I am dipped in ink. Without rulers, yet my script is evenly formed. It is remarkable that the prophetess Deborah celebrated the staff of the scribes. If she were to see me, she would carry me as a crown on her head. This is written as a memorial in the year 5235 [1475 C.E.], according to the Hebrew reckoning.

The first Hebrew book that was "written without pens" is printed so magnificently that it could serve as a model even today. At the same time (around the year 1475) the physician Abraham Conat, previously mentioned, founded a press in Mantua. At the end of several of his editions he declares proudly: "I am he who writes with many pens and yet not miraculously. I have taken pains to disseminate knowledge of Torah in Israel and have per-fected myself in the art of printing, to set one column after another in even rows."[91] But it was not only the publishers who regarded themselves as disseminators of culture. In many old editions of the first presses are printed declarations of the typesetters and proof-readers, who emphasize that their work, the printing craft, is truly

90. See the third introduction to *Tishbi:* "For many times I was called by numerous princes, great men, cardinals and rulers—even from the city of Paris in France by the command of the king—but I did not listen."
91. See the end of the Mantua edition of *Josippon.*

a "holy work," and that through it they have the privilege of "spreading books in Israel and benefiting many."

At the beginning of the 1480's[92] the Soncino family, which holds the most honored place in the history of Hebrew printing, began its fruitful cultural labors. It established presses in various Italian cities (Soncino, Brescia, Casale-Maggiore, etc.) and later also in Constantinople and Salonika.[93] The major representative of the family, Gershom (Geronimo) Soncino, declares proudly: "I have published numerous books which provide knowledge of our sacred Torah, besides twenty-three tractates of the Talmud with Rashi and *Tosafot* which are eagerly employed in the Talmudic academies."[94] "For out of Zion shall go forth the Torah, and the word of the Lord from Soncino"—this became the favorite motto of the Soncino press.

Together with the press owners, the proofreaders, on whom the very important and responsible task of criticizing and correcting the text actually fell, played a highly significant role in the first Hebrew presses. In most of the editions of the oldest presses the proofreaders lament, in their epilogues or addenda, the great scarcity of manuscripts. It was often necessary to undertake a long journey to obtain a needed manuscript, and it not infrequently turned out that the manuscript obtained with such difficulty was so full of errors that it was virtually impossible to make use of it.[95] Gershom Soncino travelled through France and other lands and collected rare manuscripts which he later published.[96] It would happen quite often that the publisher, when approaching the task of printing an old work, had before him only a single handwritten copy of the work, a copy which had many blank places. The publisher then had no alternative but to leave empty space so that the reader might afterwards have the possibility of filling in the missing lines at the appropriate opportunity. It would also happen that, while in the process of printing, the publisher managed to obtain a better copy of the work in question. He would then print

92. In the 1470's a Hebrew press was also established in Naples. This press published many important Hebrew works, among them Maimonides' *Guide for the Perplexed*. On the title pages, however, neither the date nor the place of publication is noted. Chwolson mistakenly noted that this press was located in Rome (see *ZHB*, VII, 26).

93. For a discussion of the Soncino presses in Turkey, see *ZHB*, IX, 21–25.

94. We quote from Chwolson's well-known work on the first Hebrew presses (*ZHB*, VII).

95. See *ibid*.

96. See Soncino's introduction to his Constantinople edition of David Kimḥi's *Michlol*.

the omitted passages at the end of the book or insert them in some suitable place.[97] But when several manuscripts of the same work, but in different versions, were at hand, the proofreader had to choose, on the basis of his own judgment, the correct text. The proofreaders not infrequently reminded their readers of this point: "I have here corrected and added according to my understanding." Along with this, they would proudly add how, with great effort, they managed to "purify the manuscript of numerous mistakes."

Very interesting in this respect is the long epilogue of a proofreader of that era, in which he complains that he is frequently obliged to print manuscripts containing a great many errors and incidentally describes how he would correct the text:

Says Jacob ben Ḥayyim Adonijah Linel: Having completed the setting of the type of *Seder Tohorot* [one of the six orders of the Mishnah], I deem it necessary to defend myself, for people are still little accustomed to such things, and the manuscripts are full of errors; in addition, they are very rare and difficult to obtain. Let every reader realize that God alone knows how much effort and toil I expended in completing the setting of this book, because I had at hand only one copy of *Kelim* to *Negaim* [tractates contained in the *Seder Tohorot*], and the copy was full of errors, despite the fact that it had been given to me with the assurance that the text had been read through and corrected. . . . In the *Tosefta* particularly there was not a single place that was free of mistakes. . . . So, following my humble judgment, I read everything through, considered and clarified it from all sides, until every passage became clear and comprehensible. Where, in my view, there were still things lacking, I added according to my judgment, and where this was not possible, as, for example, in the *Tosefta* to *Kelim* . . . I left the missing passage unfilled. In several places where the text seemed to me erroneous and incomprehensible I corrected it according to my understanding.[98]

We here see quite clearly that the proofreaders actually functioned as editors, took on themselves the responsible task of correcting and critically illuminating the text—a task which requires, besides great scientific knowledge, a critical sense, a fine tact, and a special kind of prudence. Hence it is not at all surprising that the proofreaders would very often erroneously interpret passages which were incomprehensible and in which mistakes had been made by copyists. From the "correction" of the proofreaders the text would thus become even more corrupt and confused, as Elijah

97. See Chwolson, *op. cit.*, p. 12.
98. Mishnah, *Seder Tohorot* (Venice edition, 1546), 163b.

Levita in fact complains.[99] There was also another problem. The proofreaders were not content with the role of editors but also became censors. At times, out of piety and religious motives, they would deliberately and tendentiously alter the text. Daniel Chwolson provides interesting details about this. Maimonides, for example, indicates in his *Mishneh Torah* that even in the times of the Messiah the "orders of creation," i.e., the laws of nature, will not be changed, and he declares incidentally that what is written in the Book of Isaiah about the wolf dwelling with the lamb, the leopard lying down with the kid, and the lion eating straw like the ox, is merely a "parable and a riddle." The pious proofreader threw this "heretical" statement out and, in place of it, inserted in Maimonides' text his own polemical discussion of twenty-three lines *against Maimonides,* without the slightest indication that the whole discussion does not belong to Maimonides' text but to himself, the later controversialist.[100]

Given so slight a feeling of responsibility on the part of many proofreaders, the great cultural significance of the fact that heading some of the Hebrew presses were such learned and cautious craftsmen as Elijah Levita becomes clear. In this connection, it is interesting that Levita was mainly engaged as a proofreader in Hebrew presses belonging to Christian proprietors. It must be borne in mind here that the first Hebrew presses in southern Europe, in Italy and Spain, existed only until the 1490's. The great expulsion of the Jews from Spain and Portugal, then the French-Italian war of that period, destroyed most of them. In the period from 1494 to 1506 the Soncino press was the only Hebrew press not merely in Europe but in the entire world. In the first quarter of the sixteenth century, with the growing interest in Hebrew literature, a new era in the history of Hebrew printing began. Christian entrepreneurs, mainly merchants of Venice, established great Hebrew presses.[101] "For many years," writes Chwolson, "wealthy and prominent Venetian merchants expended large sums of money to attract the best proofreaders and to raise their splendid presses to such a level that their remarkable editions to this day enchant the connoisseur of finest taste."

The Christian proprietors were not concerned with profits alone. They regarded their presses not only as a good business but as a "holy work." They were not merely merchants but humanists

99. In his introduction to *Massoret Ha-Massoret* (1538), 18.
100. Chwolson, *op. cit.,* pp. 15–16.
101. S. D. Luzzatto notes (*Iggerot Shadal,* 1129–30) that the Hebrew presses in Venice were in Christian hands because Venetian ordinances forbade Jews to engage in book publishing.

as well. In this connection the following statement of the proof-reader Jehudah ben Isaac Ashkenazi, who worked for the press of the wealthy Venetian Marco Antonio Giustiniani, is interesting:

My noble patron, who is such a great lover of our people and our holy language and greatly appreciates the studies which reside in the tent of Torah and strengthen its pillars and foundation stones, requested that I spare no expense and see to it that as many useful books as possible be printed. . . . Not to become rich and obtain greater profits did my patron appoint me as director of his press, but out of the desire to act for the sake of God's name, and to aid those who are eager for God's word but are not in a position to purchase the necessary books because they are too expensive. . . . The highest goal of my lord was to benefit many.[102]

The first Christian merchant to found a Hebrew press was the wealthy Venetian Daniel Bomberg (died 1549).[103] Bomberg invested a large fortune in this establishment, which was renowned as one of the richest and most beautiful of that era. To obtain some notion of the size and compass of his press, it suffices to note that the splendid Bomberg edition of the Hebrew Bible (*Mikraot Gedolot—Biblioteca Rabbinica*) with the commentaries of Rashi, Ibn Ezra, David Kimḥi, and Gersonides was completed in 1517 in the course of a few months.[104] Bomberg invited the best proofreaders into his business. As soon as Elijah Levita settled in Venice in 1529, he at once engaged him as chief proofreader. Levita held this position until 1538 when Bomberg, who found himself in a critical financial position, had to close his press temporarily. Shortly afterwards, in 1540, Levita was invited by another Christian, the learned Hebraist Paulus Fagius (1504–49), to become director of the Hebrew press which he had established at Isny in Würrtemberg. Levita, who had great respect for Fagius' scholarship,[105] gladly accepted this position. Only in 1544, feeling debilitated with age, did he decide to return to his favorite city, Venice,

102. See *Seder Tohorot* (Venice edition, 1546), 163b.
103. For a discussion of the Bomberg press, see A. Freimann, *ZHB*, X, 32–36, 38–40, and 79–88; A. Berliner, *Jahrbuch der jüdischer literarischer Gesellschaft*, III.
104. The Bomberg Press also published, with the authorization of Pope Leo X, the whole Babylonian and Palestinian Talmuds for the first time (1521–22).
105. See his introduction to *Tishbi:* "And indeed it is fitting that he [Fagius] should be called by his people as we call our teacher, Moses ben Maimon. As we say, 'From Moses unto Moses there arose none like Moses,' so they may say about him, 'From Paul to Paul there arose none like Paul.' "

and there "await his approaching death together with his aged wife."[106] But even in his final years in Venice, Levita was still engaged in extensive literary activity and also participated in the proofreading of Bomberg's last editions.

Testimony to the great impression that Elijah Levita produced on his generation is provided by the inscription on his tombstone, where there is a reference to the Biblical account of the prophet Elijah's ascent to heaven in a storm.[107] Nevertheless, many rabbis complained of Levita because he disclosed the secrets of the Torah to Christian scholars and lived for a long time with Cardinal Egidio da Viterbo in the latter's palace.[108] "Yes, it is true," Elijah defends himself,

I spent ten years with the cardinal . . . I studied with Christians. . . . But know that, despite all this, I remained a pious Jew and have no feeling of guilt. The prohibition applies only to the secrets of the Kabbalah, which may not be revealed to strangers but to the elect few alone; however, I taught both Jews and Christians merely the principles of Hebrew grammar.[109]

And he refers, in this connection, to previous generations and to numerous rabbis of his own day who also "study with Christians."[110]

106. See the introduction to his *Meturgeman*. The closing lines are tenderly simple:

My God, I pray Thee, grant grace and truth to me and to my wife,
That she may not be a widow nor I a widower.
Let us die together, and in Paradise in her bosom I will sleep
Until the time of the end arrives when we shall rise to eternal life.

107. This inscription is also referred to in the introduction to *Kissot Le-Bet David* (1646).
108. Elijah Levita himself tells of this in the introduction to his *Massoret Ha-Massoret*: "And about this there was a great outcry against me, and it was not accounted to me for righteousness. Some of the rabbis did not greet me cordially and said woe to my soul for teaching Torah to a gentile."
109. This statement is not entirely accurate. In point of fact, Levita familiarized some of his Christian pupils not only with Hebrew grammar but with the Kabbalah. Cardinal Egidio da Viterbo, for example, owed his information about Jewish mysticism entirely to Levita. Levita himself thought very little of the Kabbalah, and brands as "foolishness" belief in Lilith and the destroying angels: "It is repugnant to me to write about this, for I do not believe in all these foolish tales."
110. One of these rabbis was the rabbi of Rome, Michael ben Shabbetai (Zematus Judeus), who also acquainted Egidio and Widmanstadt with the mysteries of the Kabbalah (see Vogelstein and Rieger, *Geschichte der Juden in Rom*, II, 92; Perles, *Beiträge*, p. 186).

"You should also know," Elijah points out, "that a great benefit accrues from my studying with Christians. I swear to you that the Christian scholars whom I or others have familiarized with Jewish studies are all reliable and honorable men and, to the extent of their powers, do favors for Jews."

It is true that Elijah's closest friend, Cardinal Egidio da Viterbo, was indeed a friend of the Jews and even made an attempt to prevent publication of the papal bull concerning the introduction of an Inquisition tribunal against the Marranos. But it must also be noted that in the humanist-theological circles with which Elijah Levita was in friendly association a definite hostility toward Judaism was discernible, and this attitude not infrequently found expression in tracts and lampoons. In this respect the German humanists were especially active. One of Levita's devoted disciples and admirers, Sebastian Muenster, who translated several of his works into Latin, published in Basel (1539) in Hebrew and Latin a tract about the advent of the Messiah in the form of a disputation between a Christian and an "insolent Jew" (*Yehudi ḥatzuf*).[111] At almost the same time another pupil and friend of Levita's, the previously mentioned Paulus Fagius, published in Isny in 1542, in Hebrew, together with his own Latin translation, a sharp tract against Judaism, *Sefer Emunah*, written by an apostate missionary.[112] Two years later he issued, with conversionist intent, a Yiddish translation of the Pentateuch with an extensive introduction filled with contemptuous statements about Jews and Judaism.[113] Not without reason does Elijah Levita deem it necessary to indicate in the introduction to his *Sefer Ha-Zichronot* that a concordance such as this is, besides everything else, extremely useful and important for those who must carry on disputations with opponents of Judaism.[114]

111. This work is extremely rare. We have utilized the copy in the Asiatic Museum in Leningrad.

112. Steinschneider notes (*REJ*, V, 59) that several years earlier Sebastian Muenster published a significant part of this tract in *Lex Dei vora*. Apparently Fagius himself did not know who the author of *Sefer Emunah* was, for at the end of his book the following appears: "I, the humble and young translator, apologize to every reader of this book and ask that if he find some mistake in it he judge me in the scale of merit, for I translated it as I found it." On the theory that the author of *Sefer Emunah* was Paul Bonnefoy, an apostate who lived in the first half of the fifteenth century, see Steinschneider, *REJ*, IV, 78.

113. See M. Weinreich, *Shtaplen*, 100–102.

114. "That this book may serve well as a weapon and be very useful in disputations with the opponents of our faith, and this in two ways: one, since they are accustomed to debate with us and bring arguments from Biblical verses . . . he who familiarizes himself with this book

The Italian scholars of that time would also not infrequently issue forth with polemic debates. On becoming familiar, under the influence of the humanist circles, with Hebrew literature, the Christian theologians realized with astonishment that in Jewish mysticism an honored place is accorded ideas having a definite affinity to Christian religious views. This strengthened their missionary ardor, and they carried on long debates with Jewish scholars to show them "with signs and wonders" that the *ḥochmat ha-nistar* (hidden wisdom) agrees with Christian doctrine. A very typical portrait of such disputations is given us by the Italian scholar Carolus Bovilus in the introduction to his work *Dialogi de trinitate* (1515), in which he describes his polemic with the papal court physician, Bonet de Lattes (Jacob ben Immanuel),[115] who acquired fame with his invention of an astronomical instrument making possible the determination of the position of any planet or star at any given moment.[116]

In this connection the following point is interesting: precisely at the time when these unique theological debates were being carried on and Muenster and Fagius were printing their missionary works, Joseph ben David Ibn Yaḥya's *Torah Or*,[117] in which the author attempts to reveal "the light that is in the Torah" and the chosenness of the Jewish people, appeared. Joseph Ibn Yaḥya was the scion of a very prominent family which played a significant role in Portugal and Spain. As early as the eleventh century one of the Ibn Yaḥyas, David Yaḥya ben Yaish, was very popular in Lisbon among both Jews and Christians, and the Portuguese king Alfonso V bestowed an honorary title on him for his heroism.[118]

---

will know how to do the same. The second way is known, for most of the controversy between us and them is on the question of the Messiah, whether he has already come or is yet to come, and on the duration of the exile, the redemption, etc."

115. Bonet was greatly favored by Pope Leo X. When the controversy between Johannes von Reuchlin and the Dominicans began, Reuchlin applied first of all to Bonet with the request that he defend him before the pope. Indeed, it is because of Bonet that the obdurate struggle ended with Reuchlin's victory (see Guttmann, *MGWJ*, 1899, pp. 223–58; Vogelstein and Rieger, *Geschichte der Juden in Rom*, pp. 81–83).

116. Bonet described his discovery in the work *De annuli astronomici* (Rome, 1493), which Jacob Faber (Jacobus Faber Stapulensis) published in 1500 (Guttmann, *MGWJ*, 1899, p. 260).

117. Completed at the end of 1537, printed in Bologna in 1538.

118. Joseph ben David gives his entire pedigree in the preface to *Torah Or*. See also the introduction to his son's well-known work *Shalshelet Ha-Kabbalah*.

Joseph ben David Ibn Yaḥya's grandfather Joseph ben David, a prominent communal leader in Lisbon, fled from Portugal in 1494, when he was seventy, out of fear of the forcible conversion decree which the Portuguese king João II had issued. After many trials he arrived in Castile, and there, in the kingdom of the pious Catholic Ferdinand, was promptly seized and condemned to burning at the stake. Thanks to the intercession and protection of the duke Alverez of Braganza, he was freed and received permission to leave Castile. He set out for Italy but was destined not to find rest there either; as he was about to enter Pisa, he and his entire family were captured by the French army which was then besieging the city. For a large ransom he was freed and settled in Ferrara. His afflictions and trials, however, were still not over. He was charged with propagandizing among the Marranos and urging them to return to Judaism. For this he was put under arrest and cruelly tortured. Once again, the old man managed to obtain his liberty through a large ransom. Exhausted by his tortures, he died soon afterward.[119]

Joseph ben David Ibn Yaḥya, the author of *Torah Or*, was himself in danger of death when he was still being carried in his mother's womb and was saved in the most remarkable way. In 1494 his mother, who was then pregnant with him, escaped from Lisbon disguised in men's clothing together with her husband and father-in-law. In Pisa, when they were surrounded by the French soldiery, the pregnant young woman, to save herself from being violated by profligate soldiers, jumped from a high tower but miraculously survived unharmed. She went to Florence and a few months later gave birth to the future author. "Even before I saw the world," relates the author of *Torah Or*, "God already performed great wonders for me."[120]

All these tragic experiences had a profound influence on his world outlook. Pious and reverent himself, he issues forth sharply against Maimonides because the latter "allowed himself to be led astray by the philosophers with their speculations" and came to the "thoroughly false" conclusion that only the philosophically educated can hope for immortality since only through philosophical inquiry, through sharpening and training his mind with abstract concepts, does a man create a bond between himself and divine

119. Graetz' report that Joseph ben David did not survive the fearful tortures and died in captivity is not correct. See the introduction to *Torah Or*.
120. All the troubles and terrors of the pregnant woman, however, had a very deleterious effect on her child. Joseph ben David was weak and sickly all his life and died at the age of forty-five, in 1539.

providence. This, Ibn Yaḥya insists, means that according to Maimonides only the elite few are blessed with immortality, but the great majority of the community, not to speak of women and children, are erased from the book of memory, no matter how pious they may be and how faithfully they fulfill God's commandments.[121] Ibn Yaḥya sees in this idea the greatest heresy and atheism. He believes with perfect faith in the statement of the Talmudic sages that "all Israel has a share in the world to come." He is firmly convinced that "the fundamental principle of the divine Torah is the belief in reward in the future world,"[122] and that the advent of the Messiah and the resurrection of the dead are the revelation of divine justice "in order to compensate Israel for all the terrible sufferings, afflictions and persecutions which its unfortunate children endured in exile for the sake of God's name."[123]

It is interesting to note that Ibn Yaḥya, when polemicizing against Maimonides, sets over against him Jehudah Halevi, the author of the *Kuzari*. We noted in the first volume of our work (Chapter Five) that Jehudah Halevi was not content with underscoring the national character of the Jewish faith. He also endeavored to explain that Judaism can display its great moral influence and manifest in full measure its educative power chiefly in regard to the Jewish people, for only among them did the ethical principles of the Torah of Moses pass from generation to generation and work ceaselessly on a long chain of generations, training their moral sentiment in a purely ethical environment. Thanks to this religious-ethical milieu, to the hallowed tradition which passed as a legacy from one generation to another through thousands of years, the Jews became the "chosen" people. Hence, Halevi insists that even when someone of the nations of the world "joins us" he still "does not become equal to us."

This idea about the chosenness of the Jewish people obtains in Ibn Yaḥya a cosmic significance. The Jewish people, he explains, is a unique and unparalleled category in the order of creation.[124] "God," *Torah Or* teaches, "created seven levels of creatures: angels, spheres, the people Israel, human beings, animals, plants, and minerals."[125] The people Israel is "the crown of mankind." Maimonides' doctrine about immortality, says Joseph Ibn Yaḥya, is correct only in regard to other nations, for their souls are under the dominion of the earth spirit, the "active intellect." Israel, how-

121. *Torah Or*, 5a (we quote according to the edition of 1538).
122. *Ibid.*, 4a.
123. *Ibid.*, Chapter 41. See also *ibid.*, Chapter 78.
124. *Ibid.*, Chapter 11.
125. *Ibid.*, Chapter 37.

ever, is in direct union with the Creator Himself,[126] and each individual Jewish soul is immortal by its very nature, for "it is taken directly from beneath the Throne of Glory."[127] Neither the active intellect nor any other of the spheres is the prototype of Israel but the divine Torah itself.[128]

Ibn Yaḥya, therefore, in complete opposition to the missionary-minded humanists, has very little enthusiasm for the idea of bringing persons of other religions into Judaism, for the soul of the stranger who has been converted and accepted in the Jewish faith can still not easily change its nature and immediately obtain the moral purity and divine refinement with which the Jewish soul is endowed as a result of its immensely rich national-historical and spiritual-cultural legacy.[129]

Torah Or is only the first part of Ibn Yaḥya's projected work. The two further parts are *Derech Ḥayyim*, on the Torah that is in heaven, and *Ner Mitzvah*, on the mysteries concealed in the precepts of the Torah of Moses.[130] In later years when, as we shall see, reaction grew in Italy and Jewish books came to be persecuted, the manuscripts of both of Ibn Yaḥya's works were burned at the command of the censor because of their allegedly pernicious tendency.[131] But while Ibn Yaḥya was still alive, the Jews in Italy could give free utterance to their thoughts. The true spirit of humanism is disclosed in the fact that in religious debates the Jewish side could express its views without hindrance and issue forth with its criticism of the dogmas of the Catholic Church with impunity. In this respect the religious disputations which Elijah Levita's older contemporary Abraham ben Mordecai Farrisol carried on are extremely interesting. Of this we write in the next chapter.

126. *Ibid.*, Chapters 16, 17, and 42.
127. *Ibid.*, Chapter 62.
128. *Ibid.*, Chapter 33.
129. *Ibid.*, Chapter 62.
130. See the introduction to *Torah Or*. On Ibn Yaḥya's commentaries to books of the Bible see Carmoly, *Divrei Ha-Yamim Le-Venei Yaḥya*, pp. 31–32.
131. His son tells of this in his *Shalshelet Ha-Kabbalah*. Not long ago Cecil Roth found a considerable part of Ibn Yaḥya's *Derech Ḥayyim* in a copy handwritten by the author of *Shalshelet Ha-Kabbalah* (see *Kiryat Sefer*, III (1927), 236–40).

CHAPTER THREE

Historical Literature in the Fifteenth and Sixteenth Centuries

BRAHAM ben Mordecai Farrisol, a native of Avignon (born in 1451), moved as a twenty-year-old to Mantua, where he became friendly with Messer Leon. Two years later he settled in Ferrara. Having a beautiful voice, he became the *hazzan* or cantor of the local congregation.[1]

At the same time the young cantor, thanks to his broad culture, became very prominent at the ducal court of Ercole d'Este I. The freethinking and intellectually curious duke liked to carry on discussions with the well-informed Farrisol and listened with great pleasure to the religious disputations which the latter conducted in his presence with the monks of various Catholic orders. "At the request of my lord, Duke Ercole, his wife and his brothers," relates Farrisol, "I had frequent occasion to carry on religious debates in their presence with two Christian scholars, the Dominican monk Ludovic of Valencia and the Franciscan friar Malepinto." The duke was so interested in these disputations that he proposed to Farrisol that he write them up at length in Hebrew and also make

1. See *Iggerot Shadal*, 434.

an abstract in Italian so that the opposing side might be able to reply to it. The unpublished manuscript of Farrisol's polemic work has been preserved in two versions under two different names, *Magen Avraham* and *Vikkuaḥ Ha-Dat*. As far as may be conjectured from the published headings of the seventy-four chapters of which the work consists,[2] and also according to the reports of those who have familiarized themselves with the manuscript itself,[3] Farrisol's *Magen Avraham* has little originality. Most of his arguments and replies are derived from other Jewish polemicists of his age, especially Rabbi Simeon bar Tzemaḥ Duran.

On the other hand, Farrisol appears as a genuine innovator in another work through which he acquired fame. He knew of the exciting discoveries that were made overseas in his generation. Christopher Columbus discovered a new world and courageous seafarers circumnavigated the uncharted southern coasts of Africa and established a new route to India. Farrisol was the first among Jewish scholars who properly appreciated the value of cosmography. "Instead of wasting time reading love stories and knightly romances and all kinds of other utterly false tales," writes Farrisol,

I consider that it would be far more useful to become familiar with the extremely interesting science which among other peoples bears the name cosmography. I therefore set myself the task of giving the most accurate information possible about the characteristics of various climes and about the history of human settlements. I shall describe all kinds of rivers, mountains and forests, the various lands and the distant islands, the recently discovered new world and the wonders of the old world.[4]

To this end Farrisol in 1524 wrote his *Iggeret Oreḥot Olam*, which was reprinted numerous times[5] and was translated into Latin by Thomas Hyde (1691) under the name *Tractatus Itinera Mundi*. In his work Farrisol made use both of older sources and of the newer works of Amerigo, Bergomas, and others. The most interesting thing, however, is the author's attempt to utilize the Bible itself as a major source for cosmography. In Scripture, wherein not only Kabbalists but even philosophically-minded rationalists saw profound allegories and great revelations, Farrisol's sober and clear mind[6] perceived only the earthly and concrete. Even the Garden of Eden spoken of in Genesis is sought not in the heavens but

2. Steinschneider's catalogue of Berlin manuscripts (1878), pp. 109–10.
3. See Kirchheim, *Literaturblatt des Orients*, VI, 7.
4. See the introduction to *Iggeret Oreḥot Olam*.
5. We have employed the Oxford edition of 1691.
6. Farrisol says of himself: "I am of those who have little faith in vanities and follies."

on earth,[7] and the author insists several times that the Torah takes pains, in connection with every geographical point it mentions, to note its precise boundaries.[8] "I know very well," he adds contemptuously, "that the ignoramuses and vulgarians will in no way be able to understand this."[9] Farrisol was the first in Hebrew literature to describe the new route to India which the Portuguese had established and to provide information about the islands of the newly discovered world.

A younger contemporary of Farrisol's, the talented Joseph ben Joshua Ha-Kohen (1496–1575), also familiarized the Hebrew reader with this new world and the other great discoveries of the era. Like Farrisol, Joseph Ha-Kohen considered it necessary to stress the importance of cosmography and geography. In 1555 he translated into Hebrew Joan Boemus' geographic work *Omnium gentium mores leges et ritus*, published in Augsburg in 1520, under the title *Matziv Gevulot Ammim*. To this work he added a chapter in which, relying on the Bible and other Jewish sources, he describes the condition of the earth before and after the Deluge. "Whoever wishes to familiarize himself with all the lands of the world," he declares, "should read my book." Joseph also wanted to acquaint the Jewish reader with the new world which Columbus and his successors had discovered, and to this end decided to translate the major work of the Spaniard Francisco Lopez de Gomara, *La Histoire générale de las Indias*. He completed the translation as two separate works. The first, *Sefer Ha-India Ha-Ḥadashah*, deals with "Spanish India," i.e., the American continent in general and Peru in particular. "Behold, here is a book," he declares in the introduction, "which will familiarize you with India and the distant islands." The second book bears the title *Sefer Hernando Cortez*. "Listen attentively," the author says, "I will tell you of Cortez, his deeds, sufferings, and troubles. This is the man who carried on war against Mexico and with his great cleverness conquered it."

This work has remained in manuscript.[10] Also unpublished is another geographic work by Joseph Ha-Kohen that was found in manuscript in Baron Günzburg's library.[11] The only two works

7. *Iggeret Oreḥot Olam*, Chapter 30.
8. *Ibid.*, Chapter 10.
9. Farrisol also translated several works of Aristotle and Porphyry from Latin into Hebrew. In addition he wrote commentaries to the Pentateuch (*Pirḥei Shoshanim*), Job, and Ecclesiastes.
10. We have employed the reports of Steinschneider in his catalogue of the Berlin manuscripts and the work of Isadore Loeb in *REJ*, XVI, 29–31.
11. Senior Sachs notes this work under the following title in his catalogue (No. 257): *Gelilot Ha-Aretz Veha-Olam He-Ḥadash Mi-Rabbi Yosef Ha-Kohen Baal Emek Ha-Bacha*.

by Joseph which had the good fortune to be published, and thanks to which their author became extremely well known, lead us into another realm which, in that period, especially attracted the attention of Jewish intellectual circles—historiography.

The destruction of the largest Jewish community, that of Spain, and the growth of new cultural centers in European Turkey, North Africa, and the ancient land of the fathers, Palestine, made a profound impression on the Jewish world. In the great sufferings and afflictions which they had just lived through, pious souls clearly perceived the "pangs of the Messiah." Hearts overflowing with their people's sorrows were concerned to gather "the tears into a national vessel" as quickly as possible, to note down all the tragic events in chronicles and genealogical books. To keep them alive in the memory of future generations, it was considered necessary to relate all the troubles and persecutions which their ancestors had to suffer from generation to generation. The closing chord with which these chronicles generally ended was a heartrending description of the catastrophe that befell Spanish-Portuguese Jewry.

The first of these historiographers and chroniclers was one of the exiles of Spain, the well-known author of *Sefer Yuḥasin* Abraham ben Samuel Zacuto. Born in the Spanish city of Salamanca in 1450, Abraham Zacuto acquired considerable renown in his youth as an astronomer and mathematician, and at the age of twenty was appointed professor of astronomy and historiography in his native city. In 1473, at the suggestion of some prominent Christian scholars, Zacuto composed his famous astronomical tables,[12] which were promptly published in Latin and Spanish. The Hebrew text, however, remained in manuscript.[13]

After the great expulsion of 1492 Zacuto, with many other exiles, went to Portugal, where he soon obtained an honored place at the royal court as astrologer and archivist-historian. Columbus and the famous seafarer Vasco da Gama held the Jewish scholar in high esteem. Columbus made extensive use of Zacuto's astronomical tables when he worked out the route of his heroic journey over the uncharted distances of the Atlantic, and in the library of the brilliant discoverer of the new world the Latin edition of Zacuto's tables has been preserved. Vasco da Gama, before setting out on his sea voyage in 1497, also took counsel with the Jewish scholar and bade a friendly farewell to him.[14]

12. *Almanach perpetuum sine ephemerides et tabulae septem planetarum.*
13. The Spaniard Daniel ben Peraḥyah Ha-Kohen published the Spanish translation in Hebrew letters as a supplement to the mathematical work *She'erit Yosef* (Salonika, 1568).
14. See Kayserling, *Die Geschichte der Juden in Portugal,* pp. 121–23.

In the same year a new misfortune befell the Spanish exiles. They were driven out of Portugal, and Abraham Zacuto was again compelled to go into exile. On his wanderer's way he had to suffer a great deal. He was twice captured and, after great trials, managed to arrive in Tunis. But there again he was not destined to find rest for long. Tunis soon fell into the hands of the Spaniards and Zacuto again had to flee to Turkey, where he died in 1515.

In the years that Zacuto spent in Tunis he wrote his historical work *Sefer Yuḥasin* (completed 1504), with which he acquired a high reputation. The author himself notes in the introduction that the many troubles he had to suffer aged him prematurely and broke his spiritual and intellectual powers. This is very clearly discernible in the structure of his work. Zacuto intended to present in his *Sefer Yuḥasin* a systematic historical account in chronological order from the most ancient times until the fourteenth century. In fact, however, his work is merely a collection of various pieces of information and descriptions, taken mainly from older Jewish literary-historical works. Much space is given by Zacuto to the chronology of the Tannaim, Amoraim, and later Torah scholars, and in this he chiefly utilizes Rabbi Abraham Ibn Daud's *Sefer Ha-Kabbalah*. Descriptions of certain events of general or specifically Jewish history are introduced without any order. Some of these, e.g., the description of the famous academies at Sura and Pumbeditha, or the pages which familiarize us with the methods by which the Babylonian exilarch was selected, have great cultural-historical interest. Of significant value also is the information given concerning the author of the *Zohar*.[15]

Zacuto did not publish his *Sefer Yuḥasin* in his lifetime. Fifty years after his death the physician Samuel Shullam of Cairo printed it in Constantinople, but with numerous abridgments and alterations. Only in modern times, in 1857, did Filipowski publish the complete text, following Zacuto's own handwritten manuscript in the library of Oxford University.[16]

The defects of Zacuto's work—a dearth of chronological order and a lack of systematic wholeness—are manifested in even greater measure in the no less popular *Shevet Yehudah*. Of the author of *Shevet Yehudah*, Solomon Ibn Verga,[17] very little is known. Born

15. See *Yuḥasin*, Filipowski's edition, pp. 88–89, 95–96.
16. For textual corrections see I. Loeb, *REJ*, XVI, 223–35.
17. To be sure, Solomon Ibn Verga is not the sole author of *Shevet Yehudah*. His son Joseph, who was a rabbinic judge in Adrianople in the middle of the sixteenth century and composed a work on the Talmud, *She'erit Yosef*, added several documents and descriptions of important events of his own time to his father's work.

in Castile, he had occasion apparently to participate quite frequently in the religious disputations which were then so fashionable. He relates that in 1481 he made a tour, as plenipotentiary of the Spanish communities, to collect funds for the redemption of Jews taken captive in Granada.[18] After the great expulsion of 1492, Ibn Verga went with many other exiles to Portugal. In 1497, after the decree of expulsion was issued in Portugal also, Ibn Verga apparently became a Marrano, and later, living in the vicinity of Lisbon, witnessed the bloody pogrom which the Lisbon mob visited on the forced converts in 1506. A year later, when Portugal opened its borders and permitted the forced converts to leave, Ibn Verga went to Italy, where he spent his last years. It was there that he completed his chronicle, *Shevet Yehudah.*[19]

Had Ibn Verga lived in the days of Alḥarizi and Joseph Zabara, he would doubtless have written lusty parodies, caustic satires, and sharply honed epigrams with great dexterity. But he was born in a time of trouble, lived in a generation of fearful destruction, and himself drank from the bitter cup of exile. Hence, the laughter died on his lips and, instead of singing lusty songs and telling happy tales, he became the historian of the "valley of weeping," the chronicler of suffering and oppression. Nevertheless, the chronicler did not entirely destroy the poet in him. In his *Shevet Yehudah,* in the vessel of pain and sorrow, *Dichtung* and *Wahrheit* are artistically woven together.

The author indicates in the introduction to his work that he found some information concerning "the forced apostasies and decrees" directed against Jews in various lands in the writings of his grandfather, Jehudah Ibn Verga, who died as a martyr in Lisbon.[20] He drew information about other expulsions and persecutions, as he points out, from historical chronicles, both Jewish and Christian.[21] But even purely historical material is adorned by Ibn Verga with legends and poetic tales. He recounts many of these with the remark "I heard this from the mouth of an emissary," or "from the mouth of a Kabbalist," or "from the mouth of a pious and wise man." He relates, for example (No. 61):

18. *Shevet Yehudah,* 108 (Wiener's edition).
19. Ibn Verga notes (*ibid.,* 89) that he composed another work called *Shevet Evrato,* but it has not been preserved.
20. *Shevet Yehudah,* 94.
21. Fritz (Yitzḥak) Baer, in his thorough work *Untersuchungen über die Quellen und Komposition des Shevet Yehudah,* showed that Solomon Ibn Verga employed Jewish sources only and that the "Latin chronicles" to which the author quite frequently refers never existed. Baer also notes how diligently Ibn Verga utilized *Josippon* and Isaac Abravanel's works (pp. 52–56).

I heard that a Christian boy who had been killed was once found in Spain in the house of a Jew. A libel was given out against the Jews to the effect that they had stabbed him for religious purposes. In this city lived a great Kabbalist, Don Solomon Ha-Levi, and he put a slip of paper with the Ineffable Name written on it under the tongue of the slain boy. The boy at once opened his eyes and pointed to the real murderers, who were the men who had libeled the Jews.[22]

Nevertheless, all the descriptions given in *Shevet Yehudah*, even those whose historicity is extremely doubtful, have a significant cultural value. The author, who himself lived through the terrors of the Inquisition and the great sufferings of the expulsion, reports the most tragic, heart-rending events in an altogether calm, epic tone. It is precisely the sedate calmness of the narrator that most clearly renders the deathly terror of that dark age. It was enough for some low fellow, some half-mad or vile criminal, to devise a slander for a whole Jewish community to be in the greatest jeopardy and for hundreds of people to perish, burned at the stake or slaughtered like sheep.

"Why," King Alfonso asks with astonishment of the Jewish representatives, "do you teach your children music and song when you spend all your years in sorrow and lamentation?"[23] And when the king tries to show what a sinful people the Jews are and enumerates all their defects, the Jewish *parnassim* or officials reply: "Of all of our diseases which you have just listed, you have forgotten the greatest and most grievous, namely, that we have not a single protector to take up our cause and speak a good word for us without hatred and fanaticism."

As in a kaleidoscope, scene after scene of deep affliction and sorrow follow in *Shevet Yehudah*. Now the Jewish "emissaries" stand before the pope, and over against them is a venomous prosecutor, an apostate, who denounces them before the pope and devises the most horrible slanders against them. The Jews listen to the apostate's denunciations and to the pope's angry speech and weep with bitter tears. "Not at my angry words should you weep," says the pope, "but at your evil deeds!" "To weep," the emissaries reply, "is the only thing left to us, for tears are the sole consolation of such miserable men as we. Look now [they point at the apostate denouncing them], he is of our flesh and blood and he, too, perse-

22. The same story is also given in the *Maaseh Buch*, but there the miracle with the Ineffable Name is performed by the renowned Kabbalist Jehudah Ḥasid. This motif was very popular among the eastern peoples and is already encountered in Apuleius' *Golden Ass*.
23. *Shevet Yehudah*, 26.

cutes us and has no mercy. We are like a bird whom wild beasts have hunted down, trampled with their feet, ripped with their nails and bitten with their teeth."[24] "Adopt our faith," calls out the apostate, "and you will be changed from the oppressed into the oppressors." "You are certain," the Jews answer, "that by accepting the new faith you have a place prepared for you in heaven. We would rather go to hell than be with you in heaven."

Some of the descriptions create a tremendous effect with their tragic pathos. Ibn Verga relates the terrible fate that befell a group of Spanish exiles. The captain on whose ship these miserable wanderers found themselves abandoned them in the midst of the sea on a desolate island and sailed away. Most of the exiles soon died of hunger. Those who survived summoned up their last energies and set out for the interior of the island, hoping that they would perhaps come to some settlement. Among them was a family consisting of a husband and wife and two children. The wife fell dead on the way. The father and the two children went on until they, too, collapsed in a faint. When the father came to himself he saw that both his sons had died. Beside himself with grief, the miserable man sprang up and cried out: "Master of all worlds, You have done everything to make me lose the faith of my fathers! But know that, against the will of all the heavenly inhabitants, I am a Jew and shall remain a Jew, despite all the afflictions You will visit on me!" And he gathered sand and earth and grasses, covered his children with them, and set out further to seek a settlement.[25]

Very characteristic of the author of *Shevet Yehudah* is his fervent longing for his motherland, despite the fact that she was the cruelest of stepmothers to him. When he describes the expulsion of the Jews from France, he relates movingly how those who had been driven out, as soon as it was proposed to them that they return to France, at once decided to accept the proposal, despite the fact that they were very apprehensive that new persecutions would soon be initiated there. They said, "Let us return to the land where we were born; it is, after all, our mother!"[26]

From the purely literary point of view the most interesting thing in *Shevet Yehudah*, however, is not the descriptions of the persecutions and expulsions but of the religious disputations. These take up almost half the entire book. Of all of the disputations described in *Shevet Yehudah*, only one, that in Tortosa, has any historical foundation. But even in the description of this disputation numer-

24. *Ibid.*, 82
25. *Ibid.*, 9.
26. *Ibid.*, 46.

ous details of significant historical value are interwoven with fantastic legends. All the other disputations, however, are things that never were; they are purely legendary in character. Despite this, there is in Ibn Verga's *Dichtung* a great deal of *Wahrheit*. All the long debates between kings and popes on the one side, and Christian and Jewish scholars on the other, present very clearly and in vivid color the contemporary way of life, the mood and spirit of that age. And not without reason have many scholars noted the great significance of *Shevet Yehudah* for Jewish folklore.[27] In Ibn Verga's disputations everything is typical and interesting—the allegorical comments he makes on certain verses of the Bible,[28] his view of various natural phenomena,[29] the polemic attacks, parables, and legends which the debaters employ.[30] Over everything the author's ironic smile, his half-hidden sarcasm, hovers.

Ibn Verga frequently feigns ignorance and puts into the mouths of the Christian disputants words in which the fullest denial of the foundations of Christian doctrine is implied. The wise King Alfonso, for example, calls out astonished, "Has it ever been heard that a king should offer his beloved son as a sacrifice to atone for the sins of his rebellious servants?"[31] And the pope, when he becomes convinced that the slander devised against the Jews is untrue and that they are innocent, says to his associates: "I must now believe that the story to the effect that the Jews killed Christ is also only a false libel."[32] "Whenever we fall into doubts," declares the Christian scholar Thomas, "we turn to the Jews, the faithful keepers of the Biblical word, and they enlighten us."[33] The previously mentioned King Alfonso allows himself to express such a highly heretical idea as that religions exist only because of imagination. "The Jew imagines," the king declares,

that there is only one true faith in the world and that is the Jewish, and whoever believes in another religion is likened by him to a beast. The Christian, for his part, imagines that the Jew is merely an animal

27. See the interesting work of Loeb, *Le Folklore juif dans la chronique d'Ibn Verga* (*REJ*, XXXIV).
28. See, e.g., *Shevet Yehudah*, 64.
29. *Ibid.*, 58–59.
30. See, e.g., the clever story about the rooster which the Jew relates in the debate in order to mock the Christian theologians who endeavor to show from Biblical verses that the Hebrew prophets long ago uttered prophecies about Jesus and the Christian church (*ibid.*, 61).
31. *Ibid.*, 24.
32. *Ibid.*, 126.
33. *Ibid.*, 117.

in the form of man and his soul will be banished to the lowest division of hell. And if you ask the Moslem, he will at once tell you that hell is prepared both for Jews and Christians.[34]

"Which belief, then, is the one true one?" asks the old king Don Pedro of the Jewish sage Ephraim ben Shango and demands a clear answer from him.[35] The Jewish sage requests three days for reflection, after which he will give a reply. Three days later the Jew answers the king with the parable which Nathan the Wise relates to Saladin in Gotthold Lessing's play.[36] Here, however, there is no talk of rings but of precious stones. "I cannot," concludes the Jewish sage, "appraise these diamonds. Turn to our Creator, the marvelous jeweler who bestowed these precious stones on His children, and let Him determine which is the best."[37]

"Why are the Jews always persecuted and oppressed?" King Alfonso asks the wise Thomas.[38] This question, however, is not posed by King Alfonso alone but by Solomon Ibn Verga as well. It is in fact the leitmotif, the life-nerve, of all of *Shevet Yehudah*. There is no doubt that it was the desire to throw light on this painful question from every side that was one of the major factors that induced Ibn Verga to write his chronicle.

"Jewishness is one of those diseases for which there is no cure." These sad words with which the wise Virshorish replies to the king burst with a deep sob out of the embittered heart of the author himself. Ibn Verga is convinced that the Jewish people is the "chosen" people, that Judaism is the connecting link "which unites heaven and earth." And yet the chosen people is so hated and persecuted, and its path in life so terribly difficult.

"Why is the divine wrath against Israel so great?" asks the author of *Shevet Yehudah*. "Why are Jews punished more than other peoples?" Ibn Verga remembers the statement of Proverbs that "him whom God loveth, He reproveth." He also has not forgotten the harsh words of the prophet: "Thus saith the Lord to the children of Israel, 'You only have I known of all the people of the earth; therefore I will visit upon you all your iniquities.'"[39] And yet the author cannot be satisfied with this. He endeavors not only to cast light on this difficult problem from the purely religious

34. *Ibid.*, 16.
35. *Ibid.*, 54.
36. We have found the oldest version of this parable in the Kabbalist Abraham Abulafia.
37. *Shevet Yehudah*, 54.
38. *Ibid.*, 16–17.
39. Amos 3:2.

standpoint but also to uncover its social and psychological foundations. Typical in this respect is the attention he gives to the blood libel. With fine irony he stresses how astonished the Moslem is that Christians can believe in such wild, fabricated stories.[40] But the author realizes very well that the blood libel cannot be overcome by logical arguments, because it is nourished not merely by ignorance and superstition but, above all, by poisonous hatred. And he has the courage to confess that for this hatred the Jews themselves are, to a certain extent, responsible.

"Why is hatred of the Jews so intense among the peoples of the earth?" This question is the central point not only of the long disputation, Number Seven, which is extremely interesting from a cultural-historical point of view, but of all of *Shevet Yehudah*. The author knows quite well the large part played in this hatred by the fanatical Catholic priests, with their venomous preachments that Jews must be persecuted because "they crucified Christ." But he also knows of many other causes and, above all, of the following: First, there is the puffed-up pride of the Jews. Though they are repeatedly persecuted and degraded, as soon as they come to themselves and begin to succeed again they start throwing themselves in everyone's eyes and wish to overwhelm everyone with their brilliance and wealth. This naturally arouses great jealousy in the mob. In former times, says the author, the Jews behaved very modestly, for they remembered that they were aliens and strangers in the land. Their dress was poor and simple. Hence, they did not stand out and did not arouse envy or hatred of themselves. For this reason the blood libel was unknown at that time. The second factor is the large fortunes that certain segments of the Jewish populace have accumulated. Through loans and usurious rates of interest they have seized almost three-fourths of all of the landed estates in the country. The third cause is the separateness of the Jews and their customs in eating and drinking.

Ibn Verga does not cover up the failings that he sees among Jews. He notes the greed of some Jews for money, and in this connection remarks wrathfully that "these Jews entirely forget about their religion as soon as there is some expectation of profit." But, along with this, he speaks with intense emotion of the Jewish community which sacrifices itself for the sanctification of God's name with such enthusiasm. He stresses the power of the spiritual bond between the patriarch Abraham and the generation of the

40. The author, incidentally, several times stresses (*Shevet Yehudah*, 27, 40, 49) that one ought not to place any value on the fact that those charged acknowledged their guilt under terrible tortures. These miserable tortured persons confessed sins that they never committed.

great expulsion, whose children proudly go to the stake and offer up their lives for the sake of God's name. "The Jews," we read in *Shevet Yehudah*, "are like a burning torch; while it is consumed in its own flame, it lights up the way for others."[41]

Granted that the suffering Jews have to endure may be punishment for their sins against God and man. But these sufferings are so unbearable and last so terribly long! "When will an end come to the troubles?" the author of *Shevet Yehudah* sorrowfully asks. And the younger Ibn Verga, Joseph ben Solomon, concludes his father's chronicle with the moving prayer:

O holy God, Thou seest that we are consumed by the fire of incessant troubles and sufferings. Our enemies wish to root out the last remnant of Jacob. It is pitch-black about us; the last spark is snuffed out. We are come to the extreme boundary; our last powers expire. Our soul is at its final throb . . . O God in heaven, Thou hast sent upon us one expulsion after another. We have always said: This is a punishment for our sins; soon now God will accept us and our day will brighten. But lo, new troubles have come over us. We hoped for the dawn, and we grope in the darkness while beasts surround us, wolves and leopards pursue us. . . . Almighty God, see how everything around is risen against us. Even the stars in heaven fight against us. The earth shakes under our step. There is no stone in the wall that does not fall upon us. Every twig, every little grass and grain of sand on the way, even children in their cradles who still cannot bring the word "mama" or "papa" to their lips—even they are among our enemies . . . O Thou merciful and gracious God, how canst Thou look upon Thy people in such sufferings? Look down from Thy holy habitation on our great destruction! Quickly spread over us the cloak of Thy grace! Help us, for Thy name's sake, to see the day of redemption! Fulfill as quickly as possible what Thou hast proclaimed to Thy prophet!

An altogether unique place among the Jewish historical chronicles of the sixteenth century is occupied by the work of the Portuguese Marrano Samuel Usque, *Consolaçam as Tribulaçoens de Israel* (Consolation for the Sorrows of Israel). This work is distinguished not only by its language (it is written in Portuguese) but by its form. It is really not a chronicle but a poem, rich in lyric images, written in an exaltedly emotive style.[42]

41. *Ibid.*, 117.
42. We have utilized not the original (for we are not familiar with its language), but merely the fragments of the German translation which Steinschneider, Griff, and Kayserling published (*Festschrift zur zehnten Stiftungsfest des akademische Vereins für jüdische Geschichte und Literatur*, pp. 38–77). Steinschneider declared (*ibid.*) that he had completed

We have very little information about the life of its author. It is known only that Usque, together with many other Marranos, found protection in Ferrara, where the enlightened Duke d'Este ruled. At the end of the 1550's he went to Safed, where he became a member of the Kabbalist circle. A man of high culture and with a poetic, sensitive soul, Usque wished to aid his brethren, to "strengthen the hearts of the fallen so that they might courageously endure all their trials for the sake of the faith of their fathers," as he expresses it in the introduction to his work. To this end he wrote his poem in which he portrays in vivid imagery the suffering of his people and endeavors to discover the causes of their endless persecutions and oppressions.

The poem is divided into three conversations carried on among three shepherds, Jacobo (Jacob), Numeo (Nahum), and Zicareo (Zechariah). The first shepherd is the symbol of the Jewish people, and through him the author himself speaks. Jacob laments the agonies which the "Jewish sheep" have had to endure among the peoples, who are like wolves, throughout so many generations, since the days of Rome up to the Germans and Spaniards of the Middle Ages. Jacob's two friends seek to comfort him. They point out that the sufferings of the Jews are the test which purifies and refines them. Jews are innocent victims who suffer for others. But the redemption will come, and great and boundless will be the joy; what the prophets promised will be fulfilled. In the first two conversations there is an account of the sorrowful way of the Jews in the Biblical age up to the destruction of the Second Temple. In the third conversation the terrible persecutions which the Jews had to suffer in the Middle Ages up to the expulsion from Spain and Portugal are related.

As sources for his historical overview, Usque employs the works of Flavius Josephus, the apocryphal Books of First and Second Maccabees, as well as Latin, French, and Spanish historians, and especially the Spaniard Alfonso de Spina, the author of *Fortalitium fidei* (The Fortress of Faith). These dry reports collected from various sources are transformed by our author into poetic images, forged together through his tragic feeling, permeated with pain and wrath. "Where shall I turn," the shepherd Jacob who sorrows over his scattered flocks cries out,

where can I find healing for my wounds, salve for my sufferings, and consolation for my wearied soul? O Europe, Europe, my hell

---

and ready for the press a complete German translation of Usque's poem with a historical-critical introduction and many notes. The translation, apparently, was not published.

on earth, with what words can I greet you, seeing that you have beautified all your victories with my dead and mortally wounded? How can I love you, O fierce and corrupt Italy? You have devoured my sheep like a hungry lioness. O accursed fields of France, my little lambs have fed on your poisoned grasses. O proud Germany, with your wild mountains, you have hurled my children from the peaks of the rocky Alps. O sweet and cold waters of England, a bitter and salty drink did my flock find in you. O hypocritical, cruel, and wolf-like Spain, your rapacious wolves have swallowed and still swallow my curly lambs.

The Marrano Usque, who fled from the fangs of the Inquisition, speaks with burning hatred of this terrible institution steeped in blood and inhuman cruelty:

This monster, with its diabolical countenance and terrible looks that have cast a deathly terror over all of Europe, stems from Rome. It is fashioned out of iron and stone, infused with poison and snake venom, and coated with armor of the strongest steel. It has covered the earth with its thousands of wings heavy as lead. . . . This monster is like the dragon of the African deserts. . . . Rivers of sulphur and fire flow from its mouth. It feeds on thousands of human victims. With its black shadow it casts darkness in all corners, wherever its foot treads. No matter how brightly the sun may shine, the monster makes things as dark as the darkness which fell upon Egypt. Wherever it turns, everything dies and becomes waste, all the grasses are withered, all the blossoms on the trees are dried up, and the most fruitful land is changed into a desolate, arid wilderness!

Usque's poem, which appeared in Ferrara in 1552, had a definite influence on the previously mentioned historian Joseph Ha-Kohen. Autobiographical details are provided by Joseph in his works.[43] He was descended from a Sephardic family which lived in the Spanish city of Chuete. After the expulsion, Joseph's father, Joshua ben Meir, settled in Avignon, where Joseph was born in 1496. Five years later the whole family moved to Genoa, where the young Joseph received the finest education. His major study was medicine, and in time he acquired such a reputation as a doctor that he was invited to become court physician to the famous doge Andrea Doria. When the Jews were expelled from Genoa in 1516, Joseph Ha-Kohen was occupied with his medical practice, but also devoted himself considerably to communal matters. At that time

43. *Emek Ha-Bacha*, Introduction, 91, 93, 94, 102, 103, 106–7, and 109. See also Isadore Loeb in *REJ*, XVI, 41–44.

Andrea Doria, together with the emperor Charles V, was waging war against Turkey, and the Genoese warships frequently made piratical raids on the shores of Greece and Africa, capturing many of the inhabitants, among them a substantial number of Jews. Joseph then dispatched numerous letters to all the dispersed Jewish communities, requesting them to fulfill the commandment of ransoming captives as quickly as possible.[44] In 1538, when the Jews were driven out of the little town of Novi, Joseph once more settled in Genoa, and in 1550, when again an order was issued expelling the Jews from the city, the inhabitants of the small town of Voltaggio invited him, as an expert physician, to settle in their midst. But Joseph did not remain there permanently. In 1567, a decree was issued expelling all the Jews from the entire republic of Genoa. The inhabitants of Voltaggio prevailed on the government to exempt the aged and meritorious physician from the decree, but Joseph declined to be an exception and to live on sufferance. He again took the wanderer's staff in hand and settled in Costoletto, where he was warmly received by the populace.[45] Only in 1571 did he again settle in Genoa, where he spent his last years, dying in 1575.

Joseph Ha-Kohen's extensive medical practice did not diminish his strong interest in history and literature. While still a youth, he devoted himself considerably to poetry, and numerous poems which the young man composed have been preserved.[46] Especially characteristic is one in which the youthful poet, a child of the Renaissance era, celebrates thirty-three principles of feminine beauty. Aside from his previously mentioned translations, *Sefer Ha-India Ha-Hadashah* and *Sefer Hernando Cortez*, Joseph wrote a work on Biblical names (*Sefer Peles Ha-Shemot*, an alphabetical listing of all the nouns in the Bible) and one on Hebrew style.[47] But he acquired his fame with his historical chronicles, and it is because of these that his name has survived in the history of Hebrew literature.

While Joseph was living in Voltaggio he completed in the fall

---

44. For a more extended discussion of this, see Loeb, *Le Folklore juif*, pp. 46–49.
45. See *Emek Ha-Bacha*, 131.
46. *Shirim She-Hibbarti Ani Yosef Ha-Kohen Be-Baharuti* (Poems That I, Joseph Ha-Kohen, Composed in My Youth). This collection of poems and many other manuscripts of Joseph's are in the library of the Alliance Israélite and are described in Loeb's article. Another manuscript of Joseph's poems is in Baron Günzburg's collection (No. 212: *Shirim Ve-Haruzim Ve-Toarei Shevahim Mi-Rabbi Yosef Ha-Kohen*).
47. See Loeb, *op. cit.*, 31.

of 1553[48] his work *Sefer Divrei Ha-Yamim.*[49] It is known to every-one, he proudly declares in the introduction to his history, that from the time Josephus the Priest (Flavius Josephus) wrote the history of the war between Rome and Jerusalem, no historians appeared among the Jews until he, Joseph Ha-Kohen the historical investigator, came and wrote down as a memorial for his brethren what took place in earlier times.[50] It must be conceded that Joseph compared himself to the celebrated contemporary of Titus and Yohanan ben Zaccai with a certain justification. Since the time of the author of *The Jewish War* the Jews, in fact, had not had as brilliant a historian as the author of *Divrei Ha-Yamim.*

A man of comprehensive education, and a talented and witty narrator, Joseph was also endowed with a genuine historical sense, thanks to which his descriptions and conclusions are quite objective and well grounded. Proficient in Latin and European languages, he was able to utilize the most varied sources and to illuminate critically all the historical material he employs in his work. He begins his historical overview with the destruction of the Roman empire, but dwells mainly on the period of the Crusades and later generations. He himself witnessed the obdurate battle waged by the Christian nations against the powerful empire of the Ottomans who set Mohammed's flag on the ruins of the Byzantine empire and with their military might triumphantly invaded the heart of Europe. In the course of the last period he saw a historic struggle between two great powers, Asia and Europe, Islam and Chris-tianity.[51] Between these two contending powers the third world, the house of Israel, the "persecuted sheep," the faithful bearer of God's word and proclaimer of redemption, was pressed.

Thus our author interweaves general history with Jewish his-tory, with the melancholy description of the Jewish exile, of Jewish sufferings and troubles. The persecutions and massacres which his brethren had to suffer in the bloody days of the Crusaders elicit cries of pain and anger from our historian. The account of the horrible events that took place in the Jewish communities of the Rhineland at the time of the First Crusade is concluded with the following lines expressing his thirst for vengeance:

48. At the end of his work Joseph Ha-Kohen notes: "I completed this at the end of the month of Ḥeshvan 1553."
49. The complete title of the work is *Sefer Divrei Ha-Yamim Le-Malchei Tzarefat Ule-Malchei Bet Otoman Ha-Togar.* The first edition ap-peared in Sabionetta in 1554. It has been translated into Latin, French, and English.
50. We cite from the first edition.
51. Joseph Ha-Kohen regarded France as the most powerful kingdom, leading the Christian world.

Thus says Joseph Ha-Kohen: Now I will relate what happened to the bands of Crusaders who set out for Jerusalem, all the troubles they had to suffer on the way, so that Jews may know that our God is the God of vengeance. Grievously did He punish them and take revenge on them for His people Israel. Therefore I praise His name among all peoples.[52]

In 1558 Joseph Ha-Kohen first became familiar with Samuel Usque's *Consolaçam*. The beautiful poem of "the Portuguese" (as he calls Usque) had a tremendous effect on him. He at once determined to recount in a special work, following Usque's pattern, all the troubles and expulsions which Jews had endured from the Crusades to his own day. Two years later, in the summer of 1560,[53] he had already completed the first draft of his *Emek Ha-Bacha*. Later he continued to add further supplements and in this way brought his chronicle down to 1575.[54]

Joseph Ha-Kohen placed before his work an introduction in the form of a poem in which he addresses the reader:

My work is called *Emek Ha-Bacha* [The Valley of Weeping] and the title fits the content. . . . Where is anyone to be found, of any people whatever, so cruel that he can read my book and not sob, not weep with bitter tears? Every Jew should read it on the anniversary of the sorrowful night when the Temple was destroyed. Let him weep and lament over the bitter fate of his people Israel. Let him raise his eyes, two wells of tears, on high and ask: How long will the oppressor oppress? Awake, my God, my redeemer, my consolation! Speedily redeem Thy people from shame and distress. Speedily send them the redeemer of Jesse's stock.

In one respect Joseph Ha-Kohen's wish was fulfilled: in many Italian communities it became the custom to read *Emek Ha-Bacha* on the Ninth of Av, the anniversary of the destruction of the Temple, together with the *kinot*, the laments and elegies prescribed for the day.

In this work we see harmoniously combined the careful scholar and keen observer with the fervent, temperamental patriot who mourns the bitter fate of his own miserable people. Joseph

52. *Divrei Ha-Yamim*, 45b.
53. In the manuscript which Loeb utilized the author's supplement reads as follows: "And it was completed the first day of the month of Elul in 1560."
54. See *Emek Ha-Bacha* in Letteris' edition, pp. 126–35. Some anonymous later proofreader or corrector brought Joseph Ha-Kohen's chronicle up to 1605. *Emek Ha-Bacha* was translated into German by Wiener (1858) and into French by Julian Set (*La Valée pleurs* [1881]).

Ha-Kohen made use in his *Emek Ha-Bacha* not only of Jewish sources[55] but also of German, French, and Latin historical chronicles, Sebastian Muenster's *Cosmographia*, and numerous other sources and documents from which he introduces at times fascinating and little-known information. Interesting, for example, is Joseph's report that after the great victory scored by the Arabs over the Persians in 690, many Jews fled from Persia and settled in the land of the Russians, as well as in Germany and Sweden, where they found numerous co-religionists who had lived there for a long time.[56]

Joseph is very cautious in reporting various details which cannot be corroborated and which may be suspected to be not altogether free of legendary elements.[57] But he rarely maintains the sedate and calm tone of the detached historian when he reports the terrible persecutions which transformed the life of the Jews in the Middle Ages into a veritable valley of weeping. The accounts of the troubles and massacres which the Jews suffered at the time of the Crusades are, in his work, frequently interrupted by passionate cries of woe and wrathful exclamations:

Dost Thou see all this, O God, and remain silent? Who besides Thee will come to our aid?
O God, Creator of all that lives and breathes, take vengeance for the blood of the innocently perished martyrs and let their pure souls rest under Thy footstool.
Over such a great misfortune I must weep and pour out my tears. Ye daughters of the people of Israel, weep also. Clothe yourselves no longer in silk and bright garments; adorn yourselves no more in splendid garments, because for our sins the splendor of our people is trodden down. Everywhere, on all sides, Israel is persecuted. He is surrounded and given no rest. Fallen is Israel, terrible his distress.[58]

The account of the blood libel in "Bloyes" (Blois) is preceded by the following lines: "Says Joseph Ha-Kohen: Woe to my mother who gave birth to me! I must tell of a great misfortune in France, of a terrible destruction in Bloyes, where the robber

55. Usque's poem (Letteris' edition, pp. 62, 64, 67, etc.); the chronicles of Eliezer ben Nathan and Ephraim ben Jacob of Bonn (*ibid.*, pp. 24, 29, and 31); Kalonymos ben Kalonymos, *Even Bohan* (*ibid.*, pp. 44, 48); and many others.
56. *Ibid.*, p. 9. Also interesting are the details related by Joseph Ha-Kohen about the Hussite movement.
57. See, e.g., *ibid.*, p. 100, where Solomon Molcho's tragic death is related.
58. *Ibid.*, pp. 23, 46, 75, 85, etc.

carried through his bloody work unhindered."[59] Elsewhere we read: "Says Joseph Ha-Kohen: The expulsion from France and the exile from Spain aroused in me the decision to write this work. Let the children of Israel know what our enemies have done to us in their lands, in their castles and palaces. For the day will come . . ."[60] In this unfinished sentence of Joseph's the monitory voice of yet unstilled revenge and wrath is felt: "Vengeance is Mine, and recompense" (Deuteronomy 32:35).

But the author of *Emek Ha-Bacha* has occasion to write not only of past terrors and former troubles. He saw in his own lifetime the intensification of reaction in Italy and witnessed the terrible deeds of the venomous Jew-hater Pope Paul IV and his associates. He describes in his chronicle all the melancholy events which began in the middle of the sixteenth century and were the warning signals that the lovely Renaissance era was coming to an end and the shadows of night spreading. With this the sorrowful chronicle of our talented historian concludes.

Similar in many respects to Joseph Ha-Kohen as a writer is his contemporary, Elijah ben Elkanah Capsali (1489–c. 1555). Born on the island of Crete, which was then under the rule of Venice, Elijah ben Elkanah at the age of nineteen (1508) went to Padua, where he carried on Talmudic studies with the celebrated rabbi of that era, Meir Katzenellenbogen (Maharam of Padua). In 1524 he returned to his birthplace and was there appointed head of the community and shortly afterwards chief rabbi. A man of strong character and independent thought, Capsali had a very critical attitude not only toward recognized authorities but toward firmly accepted customs as well, and his decisions and rulings not infrequently brought him into controversy with the contemporary rabbis and scholars.[61] Not, however, as a rabbi and legal decisor did he obtain renown but as a talented historian, as the author of a brilliantly written history of the Turkish empire, *De-Vei Eliahu*, which is a valuable source for both general and Jewish history.

The external factors which induced Capsali to undertake his historical work are extremely interesting. He himself tells of them at length, and when one reads his account one is forcibly reminded of Boccaccio's description of the circumstances under which his *Decameron* was produced. Shortly after Capsali returned to Crete the plague broke out there and wrought fearful havoc. Like Boccaccio in his day, Capsali gives a masterly portrait of the terrible

59. *Emek Ha-Bacha*, p. 37; *Divrei Ha-Yamim*, 57.
60. *Emek Ha-Bacha*, p. 87.
61. On his controversy with Rabbi Jehudah Delmedigo, see the *Responsa* of Rabbi Moses Alashkar, 179.

visitor and his deeds.[62] It was in these dark days of death and terror that he began to write his work. "Frozen with dread," Capsali relates in his conclusion,

with the horrible visitor, who ruthlessly performed his destructive work both under the cloak of night and by the light of the sun, before our eyes, none of us was able to occupy his thoughts with any serious matter. Surrounded by thousands of fresh victims, each of us expected that soon the lot would fall on him, too, and that death was already lying in wait for him. Then I decided to write this work and to read it in circles of my acquaintances to drive away their sorrow and terror. This was my purpose in those horrible days of cruel judgment, aside from the other goals of which I have written in my introduction.[63]

In the introduction Capsali emphasizes how instructive the history of the people is, how many moral lessons can be derived from it. In the course of human history, he insists, the marvelous wisdom of the Creator in whose hands lies the fate of all the nations is most clearly disclosed. He is the judge who regards all human beings and judges every people according to its deserts. Capsali witnessed the remarkable victories of the Ottoman armies under the sultans Selim and Suleiman the Magnificent and, like many other Jewish writers of that generation,[64] saw in these the revelation of God's will and considered the *Togar*, the great Ottoman power, as God's rod of punishment stretched out over a Europe that was steeped in blood and sin. "Read my book attentively," Capsali exclaims with feeling,

pay attention to what is related there. Then you will see and understand that God, in His wisdom, has made the Turkish people great, strengthened and increased its power, brought it from distant lands and made it successful and blessed. The *Togar* is the punishing rod of His anger. Through it God judges and recompenses all the many-tongued nations and states, the measure of whose sin has overflowed.[65]

It is beyond doubt that all the necessary historical material was ready-made for Capsali. Only so is the fact that he was able to complete his work in three-and-a-half months explicable.[66]

62. *Likkutim Shonim* (Padua, 1869), 18–21. The editor utilized the manuscript in the library of Venice.
63. *Ibid.*, 28.
64. We shall deal with this at greater length in a later part of our work.
65. *Likkutim Shonim*, 26.
66. The author himself reports: "I began this work on the fourteenth of Sivan 5283 (1523 C.E.) and I completed it on the 25th of Elul the same year. Praise and laudation to God."

When Capsali relates the history of the Ottomans (to 1523), he provides, incidentally, extremely valuable information about the history of the Jews in Turkey during the period 1453–1523. In the second book of his work he presents an overview of the Jewish community in Spain and describes the great expulsion from Spain and Portugal. Especially interesting are the chapters in which Capsali portrays the role the court Jews played in all the intrigues that were carried on to bring about the ascension of Ferdinand and Isabella to the Spanish throne.[67]

Capsali's work also has a significant literary value. This rabbi, educated in Italy, was endowed with genuine literary talent. His language is clear and pictorial, without the rhetorical flourishes which were so favored in those days. It is truly deplorable that this interesting and talent-filled work has never to the present day been completely printed and is known to the reading public only in the fragments which Moses Lattes published in 1869.[68]

Capsali's other historical work, the history of his metropolis, the Venetian republic (*Divrei Ha-Yamim Le-Malchut Vinitziah*), was also published only in fragments (in 1924).[69] In this work the author is not content to deal with Venice alone. He also, incidentally, provides information about other cities in Italy and, in a separate chapter, describes the persecutions and libels which Jews suffered in Germany.

"I proclaim beforehand," Capsali declares in *De-Vei Eliahu*, "that I shall relate only events that actually occurred; I shall not mention any fabricated stories, for the truth is more precious than everything."[70] Capsali fulfilled his promise. Like many in his day, he was mystically minded. The Kabbalah for him was the "wondrous wisdom" (*hochmah niflaah*), and the *Zohar* "the divine and holy book."[71] Nevertheless, thanks to his genuine sense of history, Capsali's historical work is sober and clear, without any trace of mysticism and fantasy. Only at the end of *De-Vei Eliahu*, in a special section under a separate heading, "Koaḥ Adonai" (The Power of God), do we see in the foreground not Capsali the historian but Capsali the pietist and Kabbalist. Here he speaks at

---

67. *Likkutim Shonim,* 48–66.
68. *Likkutim Shonim.*
69. By N. Porges in *REJ*, LXXIX, 28–60. A collection of Capsali's *responsa* and letters, in which interesting details about the rabbis of his age are to be found, has also remained in manuscript. One of these letters is published in *Likkutim Shonim*, pp. 13–18, and by Graetz, *Geschichte der Juden*, VII, 443.
70. *Likkutim Shonim,* 37.
71. "*Sefer ha-Zohar ha-gadol veha-norah, sefer ha-Zohar ha-muflag.*"

length of reward and punishment and of the "views of the sages of the Kabbalah concerning the secret of transmigration."[72]

Of an altogether different type is the historical work of Elijah Capsali's younger contemporary, Gedaliah Ibn Yaḥya, the well-known book *Shalshelet Ha-Kabbalah.*

Gedaliah Ibn Yaḥya was born in 1515 in the Italian city of Imola, where his father, Joseph ben David, already known to us as the author of *Torah Or,* had settled several years previously. Gedaliah spent his student years in the Talmudic academy of Ferrara. In 1549 he settled in Ravigo and from there went to Codiniol. Later he spent three years in Salonika, and in 1568 returned to his native city. He did not remain there long, however, because all the Jews were driven out of Imola by order of Pope Pius V. From that time on Gedaliah led a wanderer's life, travelling throughout Italy from one city to another and giving addresses on religious-scientific themes. He died in Alexandria in 1587. Despite the fact that Gedaliah led an itinerant life, he devoted himself greatly to literary activity. He himself lists[73] twenty-one works that he wrote, but he acquired fame with only one, *Shalshelet Ha-Kabbalah,* which he composed in his old age[74] and dedicated to his oldest son, Joseph.

Modern scholars generally regard *Shalshelet Ha-Kabbalah* with great contempt and declare that in it "truth and falsehood, recognized facts and incredible legends, are interwoven."[75] In so doing they really repeat the indignant words of the learned Joseph Delmedigo of Crete, who judged in his day that "Gedaliah Ibn Yaḥya ought to be flogged with iron whips because he filled his work with falsehoods and old wives' tales."[76] But the writer of *Shalshelet Ha-Kabbalah* certainly does not deserve such a harsh verdict. The pious author declares in his introduction that he set himself the goal of "strengthening hearts," in order that faith in the greatness of the lovingkindness of God, the protector of the house of Israel, should be firmly implanted in them. "When one king issues a decree against us and drives us out of his land, we obtain grace in the eyes of another and find protection and support with him." He sets himself the task of "awakening desire for the Creator of

---

72. *Likkutim Shonim,* 29.
73. At the end of the first part of *Shalshelet Ha-Kabbalah.* Since he there indicates the city in which every work was written, one obtains a clear picture of the wanderings which the itinerant author experienced.
74. Gedaliah Ibn Yaḥya began his *Shalshelet Ha-Kabbalah* in Ravenna in 1580.
75. See Graetz, Vol. VIII; Dubnow, *Weltgeschichte des jüdisches Volkes,* VI, 128.
76. *Matzref Le-Ḥochmah,* 7a. We quote according to the first edition of 1629.

the world," of sustaining "the flame of self-sacrifice for the sake of Heaven, that man should be prepared to offer himself up, suffer the most grievous sorrows, and go into exile for the sake of God's holy name." To be sure, Ibn Yaḥya immediately adds that he undertakes to relate only true and confirmed events. "Know, my son," he writes in the introduction,

> that I shall attempt, as far as possible, to write down in my book only firmly established facts and events; I swear to you that I shall not mention a single name, either of Jewish sages or those of foreign nations, nor a single legend or story that I have not read about either in a printed book or in a manuscript or heard orally from an honorable and trustworthy man. But if you observe that here and there in my book important matters are omitted, you must remember the difficult times in which we now live, when the lack of books is so great, since the source of our knowledge, the Talmud, has been burned in heaps along with other works.[77]

Gedaliah Ibn Yaḥya in fact diligently utilized all the Jewish sources, printed and unprinted,[78] available to him, as well as numerous Latin chronicles and historical works of Christian scholars.[79] It must be conceded that the author of *Shalshelet Ha-Kabbalah* does not rely blindly on his sources. For example, he manifests critical sensitivity to such a high degree that he doubts the historicity of the well-known legend of the "ten martyrs" of Talmudic times. Gedaliah had also heard of a legend to the effect that a law of the famous proselyte Avtalyon, the president of the Sanhedrin in Jerusalem, is quoted in the ancient Roman law code. He therefore searched carefully through the old Roman chronicles and finally came to the conclusion that this legend is nothing more than an old wives' tale.

It must not be forgotten, however, that Gedaliah Ibn Yaḥya did not set himself the task of writing a strictly historical work. His intention, as he himself insists, was to present the "chain of tradition" from Moses "to the present day." It is therefore quite

77. On the persecutions of the Talmud in Italy see the chapters that follow.
78. The author of *Shalshelet Ha-Kabbalah* frequently declares: "and I saw this in an old notebook," or "and I labored over books on traditions that are oral and notebooks that are handwritten." One of the notebooks which Gedaliah Ibn Yaḥya utilized was published by D. Kaufmann in *REJ*, IV, 208–25.
79. In *Shalshelet Ha-Kabbalah* we encounter very frequently indications such as: "I saw this in their chronicles," or "according to what I found in their chronicles." The most reliable of all of the chroniclers, in Ibn Yaḥya's view, is Fra Giacomo Felima of Bergamo. Hence, he uses his work more frequently than all others.

understandable that he deemed it essential to include in the "chain" all the traditionally hallowed legends and tales which popular imagination braided around its beloved heroes. The author suggests to his son that he "should believe fully in the oral tradition of the sages of the present day." Hence, *Shalshelet Ha-Kabbalah* includes not only legends from the ancient Midrashim but also many direct from the mouth of the people in which the living breath of popular creativity is still felt. Thanks to this, Gedaliah's work is of great value for Judaic folklore. It preserved precious treasuries of legends about the heroes of the Jewish spirit: Solomon Ibn Gabirol and Rabbi Amram, Jehudah Halevi and Abraham Ibn Ezra, Maimonides and Rashi, Rabbenu Tam and Rabbi Samuel Hasid, Rabbi Amnon the author of the "Unetaneh Tokef" and Rabbi Yehiel of Paris.

Gedaliah Ibn Yahya, however, is not content with reporting the "chain of tradition." In order "to recognize the greatness of God and His deeds," he deems it necessary to touch upon many important questions about the spheres and planets, about the mystery of transmigration and the nature of the destroying angels, about the angels and the human soul, about devils, magic, and possession by demonic powers. All these are discussed in the second part of *Shalshelet Ha-Kabbalah*, in which information is also provided about coins, weights, and measures. A historical overview of the peoples among whom the Jews lived and a description of the troubles and persecutions they had to endure are presented.[80] An especially significant historical value pertains to the details about the persecutions which occurred in Ibn Yahya's own time— the burning of the Talmud in Italy and the restrictive laws which Pope Paul IV issued regarding the Jews. The second part of *Shalshelet Ha-Kabbalah* is also interesting inasmuch as in it the whole era, with its credulity and superstition, is clearly reflected. A fervent admirer of the "holy *Zohar*," Ibn Yahya follows it faithfully in describing the nature of the human soul and the transmigrations it is compelled to undergo after a person's death. He believes totally in magic and demons, destroying angels, and possession by demonic powers. In connection with this, he relates at length how he himself had occasion to carry on a conversation with a *dybbuk*, a demon who had entered the body of a young woman. The most interesting and characteristic point in this connection, however, is the fact that when our author discusses magic and destroyers and evil spirits, he takes his evidence chiefly from Christian authorities: "And foreign sages say that this spirit entered

80. As sources Ibn Yahya utilizes *Shevet Yehudah* and Joseph Ha-Kohen's works.

that body—it was a demon and not another creature." "The peoples of the world relate," Ibn Yaḥya further reports, "that all the evil ones were brought into being in this manner: on the day the angels were created, among them an angel called Lucifer was also created."

The famous scholar Jacob Burckhardt presents in his *Die Kultur der Renaissance in Italien* many interesting details about "the superstitions of the humanists." Even the most radical among them, those "who fought for the abolition of the nobility and for human equality," believed not only in destroying angels and the webs of magic that the Middle Ages produced but also in the miracles and wonders of the ancient world—in all kinds of sea-satyrs, in tritons with beards and horns and the fins of a fish, etc. It is therefore not surprising that Gedaliah, relying in this matter on Christian sources, speaks of all manner of wild creatures "who are called 'monsters' among the peoples of the world," about a double-natured creature with the body of a horse and the head of a goat, or with the body of a lion and the head of a man, about people with three rows of teeth and one foot, about satyrs with horselike hooves, about transmigrated souls who run around all summer in the form of a wolf and when winter comes again assume the form of a man. All this information Ibn Yaḥya derived from Christian, even from humanist, sources. It should therefore occasion no surprise that in Jewish circles, even educated ones, men also believed in magic and evil spirits. Abraham Ibn Migas, court physician of the sultan Suleiman II and author of an interesting book, *Kevod Elohim*, wrote a special work entitled *Emek Ha-Siddim* in which demons, with all their actions and way of life, are portrayed.[81] A special work about spirits and evil ones was also written by the well-known Menaḥem Kohen Porto.[82] And when, at the beginning of the seventeenth century (in 1608), a freethinking rabbi in Italy publicly declared that he did not believe in demons and spirits, the Inquisition at once intervened and threatened the rabbi with the direst punishment if he would not recant such "heresy."[83]

A further point is worth noting in *Shalshelet Ha-Kabbalah*, a point characteristic not only of this work but of all the historical chronicles with which we have dealt in this chapter. No matter how greatly these differ from each other in style and character, they are all united by one feature: over them hover, like black clouds, the memories of the terrible events which the exiles from Spain and Portugal lived through. Under the influence of these

81. *Kevod Elohim*, 67a.
82. *Minḥah Belulah*, 201a.
83. D. Kaufmann, *Minḥat Kenaot*, 50.

memories, the hope for the speedy redemption that the Messiah would bring becomes ever stronger. The cultured physician Bonet de Lattes proclaims the tidings that the redeemer will come in the year 1505.[84] The mathematician Abraham Zacuto takes pains, in one of his astronomical works, to calculate the year when the Messiah will doubtless arrive and concludes that this will occur in 1530.[85] But the learned Zacuto was mistaken, and Gedaliah Ibn Yahya shows with great acumen in his *Shalshelet Ha-Kabbalah* wherein Zacuto's error lay and declares that it is now quite clear that the "end" will come in the year 1598.

Another feature in all these historical chronicles is to be noted. Their authors probe very lovingly into Biblical archaeology and do not tire of describing the splendor and beauty of the national sanctuary, the Temple in Jerusalem. In *Shalshelet Ha-Kabbalah* the description of the Temple takes up several pages. Solomon Ibn Verga introduces into his *Shevet Yehudah* a translation of a Latin account of the magnificence of the Temple,[86] and Gedaliah Ibn Yahya's contemporary, the court physician of the princes Gonzaga of Mantua and the author of numerous Latin medical works,[87] Abraham ben David Portaleone (Shaar Aryeh), wrote a special work entitled *Shiltei Ha-Gibborim*, in which the structure of the Temple, all its vessels, and the order of the religious ceremonies conducted in it are described in full.

In the "conclusion"[88] of the book, in which Portaleone presents numerous autobiographical details, he also relates the circumstances under which he decided to undertake his Hebrew work. Busy with his medical practice and scientific investigations, he came to "neglect of the Torah" and completely abandoned Judaic studies. In his old age,[89] in the year 1605, he was stricken with illness; the left side of his body became paralyzed. Portaleone regarded this as a punishment for the fact that he had "shamed the Torah." Thereupon he became a penitent and, though sick, took to studying Torah with great diligence and, as a sacrifice to atone for his "sin," completed his *Shiltei Ha-Gibborim*, one of the most valuable books in the field of Hebrew archaeology, in two years.[90]

84. See Vogelstein and Rieger, *Geschichte der Juden in Rom*, II, 415.
85. Azariah dei Rossi, *Imrei Binah*, Chapter 43.
86. *Shevet Yehudah*, 95–108.
87. In one of his medical works, *Dialogi tres de auro*, Abraham ben David notes that the Jews were the first who employed gold in healing.
88. The work consists of ninety chapters and after them come, as supplements, three *meginim* on the Jewish cult.
89. Abraham Portaleone was born in 1542.
90. Published in Mantua in 1612.

Portaleone indicates that, in writing his work, he made use of ten languages—both the ancient ones, Latin and Greek, as well as modern ones, French, Italian, etc. Well versed in the literature of antiquity, the author emphasizes the fact that the sages of the Talmud utilized Greek words and expressions extensively. He therefore considers it necessary to present, at the beginning of his work, some principles regarding the Greek language and style. The following point is also noticeable in Portaleone. As a true citizen of Mantua and an intimate of the Gonzagas' court, to which, as we shall later see, Jewish artists and musicians repaired from all parts of Italy, he was also a lover and connoisseur of music. When he has to describe how the Levites served in the Temple, he first devotes a special chapter to the theory of music.[91] Then he takes pains to show that in the Biblical era the art of music was cultivated at an even higher level among the Jews than among the Greeks. Portaleone lists thirty-four musical instruments which the Levites employed in their orchestra. When designating each instrument by its Hebrew name, he adds an explanation of its meaning in Greek, Latin, or Italian.[92]

But this scholar of versatile culture, like so many others of that era, lacked historical-critical sense and consequently arrived on occasion at conjectures that smack of absurdity. For example, on the basis of a verse in the Book of Job in which the expression "Oh that my words . . . were inscribed in a book" (19:23) appears, Portaleone comes to the firm conviction that the printing press was already known among Jews in the time of Job.[93]

91. *Shiltei Ha-Gibborim,* Chapter 4. The author utilizes many old Greek and Latin sources and also more modern ones. Some time later Portaleone's work was translated into Latin.
92. *Ibid.,* I, Chapters 5–11; II, 108–9.
93. *Ibid.,* 183–84. Incidentally the author provides some interesting information about the material from which type fonts were forged at that time (*ibid.,* 183, 8) and provides recipes for making good ink (181, 4).

CHAPTER FOUR

The Belated Battle Against Philosophy; AZARIAH DEI ROSSI

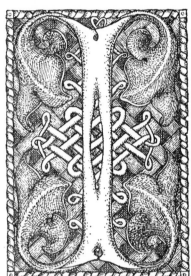

WENT to Pavia," Abraham Portaleone relates in the conclusion (*ḥatimat ha-sefer*) to his *Shiltei Ha-Gibborim,* "and there under the medical faculty studied the philosophy of Aristotle and the medicinal knowledge of the Greeks, Hippocrates and Galen, and of the later Arabic physicians." In that era, however, Aristotle's philosophy no longer occupied the most prominent place among the scientific disciplines, as had been the case earlier in the heyday of medieval scholasticism. It is true that in the age of the Renaissance Aristotle's logic was still studied assiduously, and the Greek thinker continued to be regarded as one of the highest authorities in the realm of the natural sciences. But he was no longer the recognized guide, the pointer of the way and the teacher of life, either among Christians or among Jews. Hence, the orthodox, the guardians of tradition and piety, no longer deemed it necessary to wage war against the Stagirite and his heretical doctrine. They saw no danger in him; his system, with its weakened influence, could no longer arouse any fear of him as "one who sins and causes many to sin." The honored place of Aristotle's system was already taken over by other ideas and currents. It is therefore not at all surprising that in the course of the sixteenth century only a single book was composed which still battles against the Jewish Aristotelians in the militant and irate tone reminiscent of the controversies in the days of Rabbi Solomon ben Adret and Yedaiah Ha-Penini. This book is entitled *Minḥat Kenaot* and was written by Yeḥiel ben Samuel of Pisa, a grandson of the famous Yeḥiel of Pisa who carried on an interesting correspondence with Isaac Abravanel[1] and whose death in 1490 was mourned in lengthy poems (running to one hundred tercet stanzas each) by the astronomer Abba Mari Ḥalfon and by Eleazar Ezra de Volterra.[2]

Yeḥiel ben Samuel[3] was orphaned early in life when his father died, but his cultured mother[4] gave him an excellent education. A recognized authority in the field of Talmud, Yeḥiel studied medieval philosophy thoroughly and was also versed in the philosophical literature of the Renaissance era.[5] Most loved by him, however, were the mystics and Kabbalists, such as Menaḥem Recanati and the like. His supreme authority was Naḥmanides. "We have no need of the Greeks," declares Yeḥiel;

whoever has a heart that yearns after the light of truth, let him read the great Naḥmanides' introduction to his commentary on the Torah. Whoever wishes no longer to grope in the dark and desires that his eyes be enlightened, let him listen to Naḥmanides' words which open to us the source of life.[6]

A deeply believing spirit and ardent follower of the Kabbalah, Yeḥiel of Pisa not surprisingly was enraged by the rationalist idea frequently expressed in the Maimonidean literature to the effect that the Torah requires the support of philosophy, that it must be confirmed by the logical arguments of speculative thought. Yeḥiel was convinced that religion and philosophy are two separate and distinct realms in competition with one another; they are not two sisters of the same lineage; one is from heaven, revealed by

1. See *Otzar Neḥmad*, II, where Abravanel's letter to Yeḥiel of Pisa is printed, and D. Kaufmann in *REJ*, XVI, 100–106.
2. Published in *REJ*, XVI, 106–10, 227–31.
3. Born around 1492. The year of his death has been established only in modern times. David Kaufmann published (in *REJ*, XXXIII, 84) a document dated 1574 with Yeḥiel ben Samuel's signature. It was in that year that he died, for Azariah dei Rossi speaks of him in 1575 as of someone deceased (*Imrei Binah*, Chapter 3).
4. Interesting details of Yeḥiel's family are given in David Reubeni's memoirs (see Neubauer's *Seder Ha-Ḥachamim Ve-Korot Ha-Yamim*, II, 166 ff.).
5. He relies with special frequency on the works of his contemporary Agostino de Sessa.
6. *Minḥat Kenaot*, 13, 16, 26, 73, 106: "He whose heart impels him to look upon the light of truth should study the introduction to the commentary on the Torah of the great Rabbi Moses ben Naḥman . . . and he who wishes to remove the veil of blindness from his face should study the words of Rabbi Naḥmani . . . from whose words we live."

God, and the other a product of man's limited mind. Hence he considered it necessary to declare war against the Jewish Aristotelians, and as the target of his attack chose the well-known *Ketav Ha-Hitnatzlut* of Yedaiah Ha-Penini, which we discussed at some length in the third volume of this work.

First of all, Yeḥiel believes it essential to assure us that he is not at all opposed to the sciences; on the contrary, he considers them useful and important. He only fights against their pretension to usurp all power and their claim that the Torah from heaven requires their assent. In fact, however, when the author of *Minḥat Kenaot* attempts to define the boundaries to which, in his view, the sciences have the right to extend their rule, one perceives immediately how restricted and petty this extent is. According to Yeḥiel ben Samuel, the Torah from heaven is not only the pointer of the way, the divine guide which leads to the source of bliss and immortality, but also the source and root of all the sciences.[7] He is persuaded that the most certain knowledge about the creation of the world, about the nature of the universe and the origin of the cosmos, is given not by the natural sciences or by philosophy but only by the Torah of Moses. It is impossible clearly and definitively to demonstrate that the world is created *ex nihilo* through any kind of philosophical argumentation, he insists, but this is the foundation of the Jewish faith.[8] "With purely philosophical speculation," Yeḥiel asserts, "one cannot demonstrate either God's unity and complete spirituality or His nature and the nature of the angels."[9] All this man can grasp only with the aid of the light of the sacred Torah, in whose every letter, vowel point, and crownlet the profoundest mysteries are hidden.[10] And man is able to uncover these not with the aid of philosophical speculation but only through the "thirty-two divine ways" of the "true wisdom" which is transmitted by tradition throughout the generations from the time of Abraham to the present.[11] In connection with this,

---

7. *Minḥat Kenaot*, No. 10.
8. "He who does not believe in the creation of the world out of nothing in time," the author of *Minḥat Kenaot* declares, "has no part in the Torah of Moses and is a denier of the root principle."
9. *Minḥat Kenaot*, 36.
10. *Ibid.*, 11–12, 108, etc.
11. Yeḥiel, incidentally, considers the *middot* merely divine vessels, not independent entities (*ibid.*, 23–25). It is interesting that the same ideas are expressed by another Italian, Yeḥiel's contemporary, David Messer Leon, the son of the well-known author of *Nofet Tzufim*. In his *Tehillah Le-David* Messer Leon endeavors to show that "in the profound question of the nature of divinity the philosophers cannot in any way be compared with the Kabbalists," for "in these matters the

Yehiel, an authentic Kabbalist, at once enters into the mysteries of emanation (*atzilut*), in order to explain how the divine attributes (*sefirot*) flow out of the primordial power, the source of all being.

Almost a third of the entire work is taken up by the question of the nature of man's soul and the problems of immortality and divine providence.[12] Here again the author attempts to show that not Aristotle and his commentators but the Torah alone gives a definitive solution to these difficult questions. The Torah teaches us, Yehiel insists, that eternal life is not dependent on philosophical speculation and abstract concepts but on study and performance of the commandments; and just as light is not to be compared with darkness, so religion, with its teaching about immortality and reward and punishment, is remote from philosophy.[13] As with Hillel of Verona and the Kabbalists, so also in Yehiel's world outlook the most important place is held by the human personality. He, too, insists that man, in the person of his finest exemplar, the righteous man (*tzaddik*), is higher than the ministering angels and the heavenly spheres, for he is the major link connecting the earthly with the heavenly.[14] And the human personality fulfills its great role not with the aid of the natural sciences, philosophical speculation, and mental ingenuity, not through thought, but through deeds, through doing and fulfilling the precepts and commandments, each of which is an incarnate divine symbol, a source of exalted spiritual revelations.[15] The mystery of the divine commandments cannot be grasped in a rational way. This, even such a great scholar and thinker as Maimonides was not able to do; all his attempts to explain intellectually the "reasons for the commandments" were, in Yehiel's view, "weak and vain." Only one person managed to lift the curtain covering the marvelous secrets hidden in every commandment, Yehiel was convinced, and this was the "great giant" Rabbi Simeon ben Yohai, the creator of the holy *Zohar*.[16]

The author of *Minhat Kenaot* insists that the universal role of the Jewish people, which is the bearer of God's word and faithfully fulfills all the divine commandments and precepts, is vast. Like

---

Kabbalists have much clearer concepts than the philosophers. The Kabbalists penetrate into the profoundest depths of the problem of divinity, while the philosophers are like blind men who only hear but do not see" (*Tehillah Le-David*, Part Three, Chapter 1).

12. *Minhat Kenaot*, 52–90.
13. *Ibid.*, 72, 81.
14. *Ibid.*, 73, 84–85.
15. *Ibid.*, 11, 85 ff.
16. *Ibid.*, 109.

Joseph Ibn Yaḥya, to whom he refers, Yeḥiel ben Samuel assures us that the chosen people is a unique species of the human genus. Israel, Yeḥiel repeats the words of Jehudah Halevi, is "the heart of mankind,"[17] the supreme goal of creation.[18] Jewish souls come directly from under the Throne of Glory, from the infinite source of light. They sojourn in the world under a special divine providence,[19] and extraordinarily beautiful will be the reward and marvelously great the joy that await the children of the chosen people for the sufferings which they endure in exile and for the sacrificial devotion with which they fulfill God's precepts and commandments.[20] Only the Jewish people is endowed with the wondrous gift of the holy spirit of prophecy, the living source of faith.[21] And how greatly mistaken, the author of *Minḥat Kenaot* adds, are Yedaiah Ha-Penini and other philosophizers (*mitpalsefim*) who believe that one can explain the nature of prophecy in a purely speculative, philosophical manner. The direction of philosophical speculation is from below to above, from the effect to the cause. It wishes to grasp and explain all phenomena only through logical argumentation and mechanical regularity, and it therefore frequently arrives at altogether false conclusions and falls into a tangle of contradictions. Quite different is the way of prophecy. Its way is the way of intuitive revelation. Before it the great mystery of God's nature lights up as brightly as lightning, and the eye illuminated by the divine radiance penetrates into the substance of all causes and phenomena which are, all of them together, a reflection of the one thought, the source of all causes and everything that is.[22]

We noted that the battle against the Jewish Aristotelians was, in Yeḥiel's generation, somewhat anachronistic. Apparently it is this that brought it about that his *Minḥat Kenaot* remained in manuscript and was published only in modern times.[23] On the other

17. *Ibid.*, 85.
18. *Ibid.*, 89.
19. This idea is reiterated by David Messer Leon in his *Tehillah Le-David* (14, 35, 85, etc.). Even if a Jew desecrates the Sabbath and is led astray by an alien faith, Messer Leon indicates, he still does not become like the native adherents of that faith, for "the Israelite faith is so strongly and firmly interwoven with the Jewish soul that they can never be separated."
20. *Minḥat Kenaot*, 81: "For the good and the joy of Israel, it is fitting that they receive manifold on account of the fact that they suffered the yoke of the exile and endless commandments."
21. *Ibid.*, 40.
22. *Ibid.*, 117–18.
23. By David Kaufmann in 1898.

hand, it was precisely in Yeḥiel's time that the idea so strongly emphasized in *Minḥat Kenaot*—that not only questions of morality but even purely scientific problems, e.g., those about matter, motion, or the creation of the world, obtain their solution in the sacred books of the Bible in a much clearer and more definitive way than in Aristotle and his disciples—gained ever greater recognition. Indeed, at the same time as *Minḥat Kenaot* a work appeared which was devoted especially to this theme. This was *Or Ammim* by Obadiah Sforno, who himself translated his work into Latin and sent it in 1548 as a gift to the king of France, Henry II.

Obadiah Sforno was an example of the type of universal man (*l'uomo universale*) in whom the Renaissance era in Italy was so rich. Born in the town of Cesena in 1475, he studied medicine in Rome and soon acquired renown as a physician. In the Hebrew literature of that period he is mentioned as "the great doctor" (*abir ha-rofeim*). Sforno was also proficient in Talmudic literature, mathematics, and philosophy. In Bologna he established a Talmudic academy, and he himself served as the head of an academy all his life until his death in 1550. He composed a commentary on Euclid's mathematics, *Biur La-Sefer Uklid*, but obtained his fame chiefly through his commentaries on Scripture. Sforno wrote a commentary to the whole Pentateuch, the Book of Psalms, the Song of Songs, Ecclesiastes, Job, and other books, and also to *Pirkei Avot*.[24] His world outlook, however, is systematically disclosed only in his philosophical work *Or Ammim*.

This versatile and cultured man battles with extreme determination against the widely accepted notion that the Torah is based merely on belief and not on knowledge.[25] It is for this reason, Sforno laments, that all who will not and can not be content merely with blind faith, who wish to understand God's commandments and prohibitions with their minds, have turned to philosophy, chiefly Aristotle's philosophy, in which many among us, e.g., Maimonides, saw the supreme level of human wisdom and knowledge. But precisely Aristotle's philosophy, Sforno emphasizes, denies some extremely important sources on which the sacred Torah is based.

Sforno endeavors to show that both the Torah and the prophets teach that one must not be content with belief but must also search and know.[26] And the holy writings present scientific truths in a much clearer and more persuasive form than does philosophy. In

24. This commentary was printed in *Maḥzor Romi* (in 1540).
25. *Or Ammim*, 8b (we quote according to the first edition of 1537).
26. *Ibid.*

this connection Sforno dwells on the well-known twenty-seven Aristotelian propositions which are supposed to demonstrate scientifically that the First Cause is one alone and free of all matter whatsoever. He then passes on to the problems of motion, of the nature of matter, of free will and necessity, of divine knowledge and providence, and of immortality. Sforno is firmly persuaded that only the Bible provides a definitive solution to all these questions, while Aristotle's philosophy becomes entangled in contradictions. Only from the Bible, Sforno further asserts, do we learn of the central role of man in the structure of the universe. Only from it do we become aware that the whole extent of the universe, all the spheres and planets, were created for the sake of man who bears God's image and is endowed with free will so that he can strive to become like his Creator. "That is why the righteous man who fulfills God's will is more precious to the Creator than the whole universe and all the heavens."[27] Only the divine Torah, Sforno declares in conclusion, illuminates our eyes with true knowledge based on the most assured arguments and assuages all our doubts; and this way in which it leads us is very far from the confused paths that philosophers show us.[28]

It must be conceded that the work of Yeḥiel ben Samuel and Obadiah Sforno bears witness to the definite decline in philosophic thought in their age. These philosophically schooled theologians complain strongly of philosophy because it wishes to overstep its boundaries and spread its hegemony over foreign realms. But, in point of fact, they themselves had a very slight understanding of the barrier separating religion from philosophical speculation and confused the realm of faith with the realm of knowledge and free inquiry. The intellectual currents which then dominated both Jewish and Christian circles in Italy contributed in definite measure to this result. In the Christian world there was a powerful enthusiasm for neo-Platonic ideas colored with mystical-theosophical notions, as well as great interest in the world of antiquity, with its mythology, and in Latin rhetoric and Greek art. At the same time, under the influence of the nearby Orient and the old Jewish cultural centers, mystical and Kabbalistic currents became ever stronger in the Jewish community of Italy. All this brought it about that the talented representatives of Italian Jewry revealed their finest intellectual powers not in the realm of speculative-philosophical investigation but in other areas that were much more congenial to them. In this respect the prominent Jewish cultural

27. *Ibid.*, 53–57.
28. *Ibid.*, 59b.

center in Mantua, the capital of the cultured ducal family of the Gonzagas, is especially interesting.

In the Renaissance era (the fifteenth and sixteenth centuries) Mantua was one of the major centers of civilization in Italy. Despite the fact that the ducal court of Mantua was not particularly wealthy and its treasury was not infrequently empty, Mantua was the place where the most brilliant representatives of Italian Renaissance culture assembled. There, at the court of the enlightened Gonzagas, such figures as Ludovico Ariosto, Torquato Tasso, Pietro Bembo, Matteo Bandello, and others used to read their works aloud.[29] The condition of the prominent Jewish community in Mantua was quite favorable.[30] "We desire," reads the ducal decree of 1545, "that the Jews in our city shall engage in their commerce and crafts freely and without hindrance, on terms of equality with the Christians." That this decree was actually carried through is testified by the French traveller of the sixteenth century, de Villamont. In his memoirs he notes with astonishment: "The Jews in Mantua enjoy the greatest freedom and can be distinguished from Christians only by the little yellow or orange stripe they wear on the left shoulder of their cloaks."[31]

The Jewish community of Mantua was at the summit of contemporary Italian civilization and took a considerable part in the humanist movement. The Jews of Mantua devoted themselves greatly to art, and in the first quarter of the sixteenth century Jewish artists attained such a reputation on the Italian stage that the duke Gonzaga requested the local community to organize a troupe for his court theater from its artistic crafts. The community splendidly fulfilled the duke's request. The theatrical troupe it organized existed for about a hundred years and holds an honored place in the history of the Italian theater.[32] Thanks to this troupe, Mantua became a center that attracted Jewish musicians and artists from all corners of Italy.[33] At the head of the Jewish court troupe

29. See Burckhardt, *Die Kultur der Renaissance in Italien.*
30. In the middle of the sixteenth century the number of Jewish residents in Mantua reached 1,844; in 1596 four hundred forty-five Jewish families (about twenty-two hundred persons) lived there.
31. "Les juifs de Mantoue ont une liberté trop grande, parce quils ne sont recognues entre tous les chretiens sinvu à un petit de passements jaune ou orange quils portent au coste gauche de lor manteau." We quote according to Alessandro d'Ancona, *Origino del teatro italiano,* II, 409.
32. See *ibid,* II, 398–429, and our work in *Yeyreyskaya Lyetopis,* No. IV, "Jewish Theater in the Renaissance Era."
33. See our "Jewish Theater in the Renaissance Era," and also S. Birnbaum, *Jüdische Musiker am Hofe von Mantua.*

for some decades was an extremely clever and talented director, Jehudah Leone ben Isaac Sommo.[34]

Jehudah Sommo (died after 1591) was well versed in rabbinic literature[35] and, as a good Hebrew stylist, participated in the unique debate which the "enemies of women" and the "defenders of women" carried on with intense heat at that time. We noted in the first volume that as soon as the romance of "the enemy of women," Shabbetai, appeared, the "friend of women," Isaac, immediately came forward with a response, and that some time later the young poet Yedaiah Bedersi also replied. In the Italy of the Renaissance era the old debate was renewed. Under the influence of contemporary Italian *belles-lettres,* a special "women's literature" sprang up among the Jews. Quite unique tournaments were conducted, with tercets, stanzas, sonnets, and epigrams as weapons. The enemy of women, Abraham of Sarteano, issued forth with a lampoon of fifty tercets in which he endeavors to show that woman deserves no name other than Lilith.[36] This greatly annoyed the friend of women, Avigdor of Fano, who answered with a long poem, also written in tercets, in which he very enthusiastically celebrates a well-known lady of Pisa, Hannah Volterra.[37] The Kabbalist Elijah Ish Genazzano then came to the aid of Abraham. In his lampoon this bitter misogynist does not spare even the matriarchs, Sarah, Rebecca, and Rachel, in order to show that Ecclesiastes was quite correct in his melancholy conclusion that "among all these I found no woman," i.e., that no decent woman is to be discovered.[38]

Against this crude lampoon David Messer Leon, already known to us as the author of *Tehillah Le-David,* came forward with a "praise of women." This orthodox and extremely prolific writer,[39] who declared that Gersonides' *Milhamot Adonai* deserves burning because of its heretical ideas, was a very gallant cavalier and admirer of women. His dithyramb *Shevah Ha-Nashim* so delighted a prominent Jewish lady named Sarah that she begged him to de-

34. In Christian sources he is called da Sommi and also Leone Ebreo. In Hebrew he used to sign himself Yehudah Yitzhak Sommo Mi-Shaar Aryeh. For more about him, see our "Jewish Theater in the Renaissance Era." In recent times a Hebrew comedy, *Tzahut Bedihuta De-Kiddushin,* of which we shall speak in a later volume of our work, was found and precisely described (*MGWJ,* 1931, pp. 97–117).
35. Sommo wrote a Hebrew work *Imrei Noam* (see Azariah dei Rossi, *Imrei Binah,* Chapter 18) which was lost.
36. The tract was published by Neubauer in *Letterbode,* X, 98–101.
37. *Ibid.,* pp. 101–3.
38. *Ibid.,* pp. 104–5.
39. For a list of Messer Leon's numerous compositions see *Letterbode,* X, 106–11; *Tehillah Le-David,* 97a; *Kevod Hachamim,* Introduction.

vote a larger work to the same theme. Messer Leon fulfilled her request in an extremely unusual way. He composed the desired work in the form of a commentary to the last chapter of Proverbs, where the virtues of the "woman of valor" are so enthusiastically praised. This "commentary" is very characteristic of the period in question. David Messer Leon, the pious rabbi[40] and ardent Kabbalist, was a great lover of music and poetry, studied the Latin and Italian poets with much enthusiasm, and himself frequently wrote Hebrew and Italian poems.[41] In order to demonstrate the great virtues of the female sex, he lists in his commentary to the chapter on the "woman of valor" the beautiful deeds and the devotion manifested by famous women in various ages. As sources, Messer Leon employs not only the Talmud and Midrashim but also the old Roman and the newer Italian literature. Verses from the Song of Songs and the Psalms are set beside quotations from Ovid and Catullus and arguments from Dante and Beatrice, and Petrarch and Laura. To the heroine of Petrarch's poem Messer Leon devoted a special work in which he endeavors to prove that those who think that the beautiful Laura is merely a poetic invention of the author's imagination are mistaken. He adduces arguments showing that the heroine of the world-famous sonnets is a real person named Lavretta, who resided in the vicinity of Avignon.[42]

With no less enthusiasm than Messer Leon did Gedaliah Ibn Yaḥya, the author of *Shalshelet Ha-Kabbalah*, issue forth as a defender of the female sex. Like the medieval knights in their day, so the pious Jewish historian attempts to show that woman is endowed with all the virtues and adorned with all the gifts of the Muses. That woman is of greater worth than man is to be seen, in Ibn Yaḥya's view, from the fact that man was created out of the dust but woman out of man's rib. His apologetic work ends

40. David Messer Leon was ordained a rabbi at the age of eighteen. The last part of his collection of *responsa* was in the Harkavy Collection of the library in Leningrad of the Society for the Dissemination of Enlightenment Among Jews. Messer Leon's verdict on the controversy between the Portuguese and Spanish communities in Valona was published by S. Bernfeld (*Kevod Ḥachamim* [1898]).

41. In his address to the above-mentioned lady, Sarah, Messer Leon relates: "A sea of troubles would have lain in wait for my head had not the Lord been for me; for in His mercy He bestowed on me of the abundance of His wisdom and the spirit of His generosity and supported and aided me to write numerous compositions . . . and I carried on extensive inquiries in Torah, in *piskot*, and in philosophy, *and also wrote many verses in Hebrew and in the Christian language* in my leisure time." See *Letterbode*, X, 108; *Tehillah Le-David*, 97; *Hebräische Bibliographie*, XII, 33.

42. See *REJ*, X, 94–97.

with a *laudi della donne* (praise of woman), and he enumerates many famous women of former times who acquired renown in various realms.[43]

The theater director of Mantua, Jehudah Sommo, also came forward as a defender of women. In reply to the hostile lampoons, he wrote his *Magen Nashim*. His opponents could not forgive him for this, and one of the enemies of women, Jacob Fano, wrote an indignant tract, *Shiltei Ha-Gibborim*, in which he settles accounts with Jehudah Sommo, "the man of Mantua."[44]

It was not only in the realm of art but in various fields of science as well that the Jewish community in Mantua had gifted representatives. We have noted that already in the fifteenth century the cultured physician Abraham Conat established one of the first Hebrew presses in Mantua (in 1476). There also Jehudah Messer Leon produced his scientific works, and there in the sixteenth century the first attempt to found a special Jewish university was made. This attempt is associated with the names of two members of the cultured Provinciali family, David and his son Abraham.

David Provinciali was very learned not only in the Talmud but in various scientific fields. The commentaries and philosophical works that he wrote have not come down to us and only about one of them, his *Dor Ha-Haflagah*, does Azariah dei Rossi provide some interesting details.[45] We noted in one of the earlier sections that not merely among Jews, but in the Christian scholarly world as well, the notion that Hebrew is the oldest language and that all the nations of the world spoke Hebrew until the "generation of the dispersion," after the building of the tower of Babel, was widely believed. David Provinciali attempts to establish this scientifically by showing that in all later languages there are numerous elements of the ancient tongue of the Bible. He enumerates, incidentally, all of two thousand Greek and Latin words which, in his view, are derived etymologically from Hebrew.[46]

In the spring of 1564 David Provinciali and his son Abraham, a prominent physician in Mantua, circulated to the most important representatives of the communities a "proclamation"[47] in which

43. *Letterbode*, X, 139–47.
44. *Ibid.*, X, 124–33.
45. *Meor Enayim*, Chapter 57.
46. From the examples given in *Meor Enayim* it is easy to realize that Provinciali's arguments have, from a present-day standpoint, no scientific value. They merely testify to the relatively low level of comparative philology at that time.
47. The "summons" was first published by Halberstam in *Ha-Levanon*, V, Nos. 27–29. Güdemann reprinted it with a German translation in the Berliner Festschrift, pp. 164–75.

they announced their project of establishing a "place of gathering for the wise," for Jewish young people who might there study, along with Jewish subjects, such general sciences as medicine, philosophy, cosmography, rhetoric, etc. In this Jewish academy, we read in the proclamation, the ancient languages Latin and Greek, as well as philosophy and the art of writing, are to be taught.

Close friends of the Provinciali family were the foremost leaders of the Jewish community in Mantua: the most brilliant preacher in Italian Jewry in the sixteenth century, Jehudah Aryeh ben Joseph Moscato,[48] and the great Jewish scholar of the Renaissance era, Azariah dei Rossi.

Very few details of Moscato's biography have come down to us. We know only that he was born in the middle of the 1540's in the little town of Osimo near Ancona. Because of the persecutions which the Jews of Ancona suffered at the hands of Pope Paul IV in 1554–58, the young Moscato was compelled to leave his home, and settled in Mantua, where he received a very cordial welcome from the cultured family Minzi Beretaro.[49] Thanks to this family, he had the opportunity to obtain a well-rounded education under the supervision of Abraham Provinciali's elder son, the expert mathematician Moses Provinciali.[50]

Jehudah Moscato is undoubtedly one of the most interesting personalities of Italian Jewry in the Renaissance era. Nature endowed him richly with her gifts. He was an excellent stylist with the spark of the true poet, a splendid preacher who with his oratorical artistry charmed the celebrated thinker Giordano Bruno,[51] and along with this was filled with all the contradictions that are so characteristic of his remarkable age: great enthusiasm for the ancient world with its classical art together with a strong feeling for mystical tendencies; an impetuous drive for free investigation and knowledge combined with a childishly naive faith in all kinds of old wives' tales and in destroying angels; intense interest in the history of antiquity without the least critical sense regarding the historical past.

48. There are various theories regarding the origin of the family name Moscato. Abba Apfelbaum attempts to show in his *Toledot Yehudah Moscato* that this word derives from the word *Mi-Zacuto*, since Jehudah ben Joseph was, on his mother's side, a great-grandson of the well-known Abraham Zacuto.
49. See Moscato's letter at the beginning of *Nefutzot Yehudah* (first edition).
50. Born in 1504. After his death (in 1576) his pupil Moscato wrote a long eulogy about him (published in *Nefutzot Yehudah*, Sermon 33).
51. See *ZHB*, VII, 29.

Moscato, the rabbi, preacher, and revered head of a Talmudie
academy, was also a connoisseur of music.[52] He composed tender
prayers and religious poems,[53] eulogized in lovely stanzas the death
of the famed codifier and author of the *Shulḥan Aruch* and *Bet
Yosef*, Joseph Karo,[54] and also wrote elegies after the death of
the young duchess of Savoy, Margaret.[55] In Moscato's work
verses from the Bible stand in close proximity to Greek myths,
and among the words of the Talmudic sages he weaves quotations
from Cicero, Quintilian, Ovid, Pico della Mirandola, Aristotle,
Heraclitus, and, more frequently than from all others, the "divine
Plato."[56] The Greek philosopher's teachings about the Ideas, the
soul of the world, and divine emanation, interwoven with statements from Jewish mystics, serve as the major themes of many
of Moscato's sermons.[57] The intellectual affinity between Plato's
doctrine and the conceptions which play such a prominent role
in Jewish mysticism was considered by Moscato quite natural,[58] for
he firmly believed in the old legend that the philosopher, during
his sojourn in Egypt, came to know the prophet Jeremiah and
became his faithful disciple and admirer.[59]

Like many other scholars, both Jewish and Christian, Moscato
was persuaded that all wisdoms and sciences stem from the Jews,
and, indeed, it is with this conviction that he defends himself for
quoting the sages of foreign nations and relying on their views
so frequently. All this derives, after all, he insists, "from our own
sources; I merely return our own treasures."[60] Furthermore, he
had no doubt whatever that the task of all the sciences is to "serve"
faith and religion, the Torah revealed from heaven. In this also
the conflict of his era, which was still at the parting of the ways,

52. See *Nefutzot Yehudah*, Sermon 1. Menaḥem Porto testifies in his
    Minḥah Belulah: "Rabbi Jehudah Muscato was one of the great scholars
    of our generation in the science of music."
53. Especially lovely is his prayer "Ka-Ayyal Taarog El Afikei Mayyim,"
    composed in 1590 at the time of the great drought when everyone
    was longing and praying for rain (the prayer is published in the collec-
    tion of penitential prayers *Ayelet Ha-Shaḥar* which the society *Shom-
    rim La-Boker* issued in Mantua [1612], pp. 161–62).
54. See *Otzar Neḥmad*, III, 167.
55. Apfelbaum, *op. cit.*, pp. 57–59.
56. *Nefutzot Yehudah*, 35, 37–38, 40, 41, 60, 76, 133, 138, 200, and 222.
    We quote according to the first edition (Venice, 1589).
57. In his collection of sermons *Nefutzot Yehudah*.
58. *Nefutzot Yehudah*, 37–38. Before Moscato, Yeḥiel of Pisa (*Minḥat
    Kenaot*, 32, 84) already noted the affinity between the Platonic system
    and certain views of the sages of the Talmud.
59. See *Kol Yehudah*, Chapter 4, No. 3.
60. *Nefutzot Yehudah*, 30b.

is clearly manifest. Moscato preaches with great enthusiasm that man's investigative thought must be free and that scientific speculation can admit no restraints and prohibitions. "We must not be frightened," he explains,

by the stern words of Ecclesiastes: "For God is in the heavens and thou art on earth; therefore let thy words be few" (Ecclesiastes 5:2). For those who come to the realm of speculation in God's name the gates are not closed; on the contrary, every enlightened person is obliged to penetrate with his searching thought as far as he can.[61]

But, along with this, Moscato is convinced that of the two "lights," religion and science, only the first shines with its own radiance, while science is lit up by reflected rays, those that it enjoys from the divine Torah.[62] For this reason, he asserts, it is inconceivable that true science should ever come into contradiction with the Torah. In all cases in which one encounters in scientific investigators such thoughts as are inconsistent with the divine Torah, those responsible are the "philosophizers" alone, who have falsified the scientific knowledge which they drew from Jewish sources.[63]

Everyone, however, must bear in mind—Moscato repeats—that eternal bliss cannot be obtained through the sciences created with the aid of the human understanding. "The acquired intellect, the understanding developed by scientific investigation, is the proud banner, the highest symbol of human progress in the realm of culture; but it is not the true flag of love, which alone endows our soul with eternal life."[64]

A man with richly developed sensitivities and a poetic spark, Moscato devoted himself with great enthusiasm to the "esoteric wisdom," wrapped in Platonic dress. The great men of the generation, the highest authorities and guardians of the profoundest mysteries—these, for him, are the "true sages," the Kabbalists, and foremost among them is the author of the holy *Zohar*, the "divine" Rabbi Simeon ben Yoḥai, "whose words will live for all time." The spirit of the Kabbalists is, in fact, clearly discernible in the poetic imagery with which Moscato portrays *maaseh bereshit*, the origin of the infinite universe out of the *nekudah rishonah* (first point), the primordial source of being and becoming.[65]

Through quotations from the *Zohar* Moscato underscores the

61. *Ibid.*, 20a.
62. *Ibid.*, 63, 72, and 174.
63. *Ibid.*, 68.
64. *Ibid.*, 63.
65. *Ibid.*, Sermons 4, 8, and 31.

vast significance of the human word and speaks with great emotion about the universal role of prayer and petition.[66] Basing himself on the "true sages," he further attempts to show that the chief thing is the deed, the action accomplished by the human will. The commandments, he insists, are indeed merely symbols, but only through the fulfillment of the commandment, through its embodiment in action by the exertion of the will, is it revealed as a living link in the infinite chain of being and becoming in which the divine mystery of world creation is disclosed.[67] Moscato therefore especially stresses the universal role of the person who observes the commandments and incorporates them in action. The famous dictum of Hillel the Elder, "If I am here, everything is here," is interpreted by the Italian scholar in his own unique manner: "Man, this microcosm, is in reality the focal point of the whole world; he is the measure of all values, he is all that is [*ha-kol*]." For this reason, Moscato notes, it is said in the Torah that only after God brought man into being did He see how good and beautiful the world He had created was.[68]

The ideas of the Kabbalists and the views of the humanists on the indispensable role of the human personality are forged by our skillful preacher into an integral whole and incorporated in lovely imagery. An ancient Talmudic legend relates that over King David's head there hung a wondrous lyre, and that each midnight a breeze would touch its strings and the most magnificent tones would resound. This marvelous lyre, Moscato declares in his first sermon, which deals especially with music, was King David's soul. Every living creature that feels and thinks, he explains, is a separate chord in the marvelously ingenious melody of the world which is sung as a paean to its Creator. Every man is a musical instrument; the primordial source and essence of every soul is a melody, a harmonious chord. The *Shechinah* (divine Presence) does not rest in sadness and sorrow but in joy, in the song and jubilation of heaven and earth, in the praise and paean which the whole wide world sings. The entire divine Torah is also a single harmonious song.[69] That is why man's soul yearns so greatly for music from

66. *Ibid.*, Sermons 43 and 44. At times the Kabbalist triumphs over the orator in Moscato and he delves into "combinations of letters" and ingenious *notarikon* and *gematriot* (see *Nefutzot Yehudah*, 54, 55, and 208 ff.; *Kol Yehudah*, IV, Chapter 3).
67. *Nefutzot Yehudah*, 36. Cf. *ibid.*, 17, 83–84, and 87 ff.
68. *Ibid.*, 38–40.
69. "And the divine Torah is called a song . . . 'And this is the Torah which Moses placed before the children of Israel': he placed it in their mouths in order that this song might be among the children of Israel forever."

his earliest childhood to old age; it thereby yearns for the divine song, for the melody of the world, with which it desires to be united as with its primal source. For this reason, Moscato explains further, every individual person is considered a microcosm. His soul is a musical instrument on whose strings all the heavenly and earthly chords tremble. Every soul experiences and renders in its own way the marvelous melody, the great praise and song of thanksgiving that all the worlds sing to the Creator; and every chord sounding on the strings of the human soul obtains an echo in the divine symphony. Indeed in this, Moscato adds,[70] lies the profound secret of the *Zohar*'s statement that every word, every intention born in the human heart, finds a response in the upper worlds.[71]

The Holy One, blessed be He, said to Moses: Go tell Israel that my name is *ehyeh asher ehyeh*. This means, I shall be with you as you with Me. I will be your reflection, your shadow. To your laughter, I will reply with My laughter; to your weeping, I will respond with weeping; and to your anger, My anger will be the reply. The Holy One says to man: My light is in your hand, and your light in My hand. If you kindle My light, your light also flares up at once.[72]

This means, Moscato explains, that as soon as man strives toward the heights, the light of his soul shines brightly and sweet chords tremble over its strings; at once the marvelous divine light, which illuminates the whole world with the rays of "God's eyes," as it were, lights up over against it.

Moscato preached his sermons in Italian, and the Hebrew translation of the fifty-two addresses collected in his *Nefutzot Yehudah* can naturally provide no more than a very slight notion of the fiery oratorical power of the highly gifted preacher. On the other hand, however, this work serves as the best evidence of how much Moscato accomplished in the field of homiletics. He managed to breathe the air of fresh, palpitating life into the dry, old-fashioned forms, refreshing them with bright, gleaming colors and renewing them with the elixir of youth of the life-loving Renaissance tones. Jehudah Messer Leon in his day had attempted to arouse among his contemporaries love for beautiful style and classical oratorical artistry. That for which Messer Leon strove, Moscato magnificently accomplished. *Nefutzot Yehudah* is the loveliest monument produced by Italian Jewry in the realm of homiletics, and some of

70. Sermon 46.
71. *Nefutzot Yehudah*, 212.
72. *Ibid.*, 211.

its sermons are reminiscent of the masterpieces of ancient oratorical art. Even those that deal with philosophical-theological problems—creation, God's attributes, and the like—are remarkable by reason of their ingenious structure and magnificently polished style.

Nefutzot Yehudah is, however, not the only work in Hebrew literature left by Jehudah Moscato. He also acquired fame with another book which is closely associated with Jehudah Halevi's *Sefer Ha-Kuzari.* We noted in the third volume of our history how the battlers against rationalist currents—not only such zealots as Shemtov ben Shemtov, the author of *Sefer Ha-Emunot,* but also Profiat Duran and Hasdai Crescas—regarded the *Kuzari* as the highest authority and faithful guide. It is therefore not surprising that in the Renaissance era, when Aristotelian tendencies were replaced by neo-Platonic ones, in which the inclination toward mysticism was more or less discernible, the slogan "Back to Jehudah Halevi!" was heard ever more frequently in Italian Jewish circles.

Typical in this respect is the paean placed by Meir ben Joseph Ibn Yaḥya before the first printed edition of the *Kuzari,* which appeared in 1506. The poem is written in the same unique "echo" meter in which Meir's great-great-grandfather Joseph ben Solomon Ibn Yaḥya composed his well-known elegy after the death of Rabbi Solomon ben Adret. Meir ben Joseph indignantly asks,

Why do you follow all the magicians and false priests who wander confused over dark and crooked ways? Depart from those who have forgotten the tradition of the fathers and in their pursuit of alien doctrines have obtained wooden idols and lifeless images. They bestow the best incense on inanimate idols, and the divine word is trampled underfoot by them. Cast off the serpentine net of philosophical theories and logical speculations that suffocate the feelings and hold all tender claims in captivity. Come hither, all of you, old and young, men and women and gray-haired elders, take of the spiced wine that we carry toward you. . . . Here is the book about the sage, the *Kuzari.* This book will rejoice all human hearts. The sweetness of its words and its marvelous beauty will satisfy all who yearn for truth and knowledge. Like a light cloud its rays drive the darkness away; set against it, other works are like glowworms compared to the radiance of the planets. Its sacred fire destroys heretical doctrines. . . .[73]

Even such a sober and clear-minded scholar as Azariah dei Rossi declares that "every pious Jew should thoroughly study the *Kuzari*

73. This song of praise was published by David Kaufmann with a German translation in *ZHB,* I, 116–17.

and inscribe in the hearts of his children and disciples the message: Take care not to forsake Halevi."[74]

Moscato was also an ardent admirer of the great Castilian poet and philosopher. Because the text of the *Kuzari* in Jehudah Ibn Tibbon's cumbersome translation was, in places, quite obscure and incomprehensible, many of Halevi's admirers requested Moscato in 1573 to write a commentary to the *Kuzari* and thereby make the famous work accessible to broader segments of readers.[75] Moscato very eagerly undertook the task. In executing it he made use not only of various handwritten versions of Ibn Tibbon's translation but also of the little-known translation of Jehudah ben Isaac Kardinal. Until his death he was constantly working on his commentary to this work that was so precious to him, and only in 1594 did his children publish it under the title *Kol Yehudah.*[76] It was later reprinted several times.

Contemporaneously with Moscato, Azariah ben Moses dei Rossi, the most important investigator and scholar that Italian Jewry produced in the Renaissance era, lived in Mantua. Azariah was born in that city around 1511[77] into one of the oldest Jewish families in Italy. According to an ancient legend, his was one of the noble Jewish families driven out of Jerusalem and settled in Rome by Titus.[78] Despite the fact that dei Rossi was sickly from childhood on, he received a very careful and comprehensive education. Besides Jewish and general subjects, he studied medicine, which served him as the source of his livelihood. To be sure, he enjoyed prosperity only in small measure. A sick and weary man, he had to wander from city to city.[79] Living in poverty and want, he

74. *Meor Enayim*, Chapter 36: "Since the book [*Kuzari*] is full of the blessing of the Lord and of true opinions, it is proper for every Jew faithful to his covenant to study it himself and to endeavor that it be written on the tablets of the heart of every one of his sons and pupils with the command and admonition: Take heed that you do not forsake Halevi." The author of the *Kuzari* is called by dei Rossi "the godly sage."
75. See the introduction to *Kol Yehudah*. The commentary to the *Kuzari* that Nathaniel Kaspi completed in 1387 had no success and remained completely unknown (see *Literaturblatt des Orients*, 1848, p. 571).
76. Moscato mentions (*Nefutzot Yehudah*, Sermon 3; *Kol Yehudah*, III, Chapter 17) a third work of his, a commentary to the Song of Songs. However, it has not been preserved.
77. In the first chapter of *Imrei Binah* Azariah dei Rossi remarks: "And I am now sixty years old." He began the work in 1571.
78. *Imrei Binah*, Chapter 60.
79. In 1543 dei Rossi went from Mantua to Ferrara. Later he lived in Ancona, Bologna, and Sabonietta. In 1569, after Pope Pius V expelled all the Jews from his domain, dei Rossi returned to Ferrara. From

nevertheless devoted all his days "to Torah and worship" and did not abandon his beloved books.

Azariah dei Rossi was a great scholar not only in Hebrew but in ancient European literature as well. A true son of the Renaissance era, he thoroughly explored the life of ancient Greece and Rome. He was also quite familiar with the theological literature of the medieval church and applied himself assiduously to history and the natural sciences. His immense scholarship is manifested in the numerous quotations which he introduces from the works of Plato, Xenophon, Homer, Horace, Plutarch, Herodotus, Pliny, Quintilian, Augustine, Eusebius, Justinian, Isadore, Dante, Pico della Mirandola, and many other older and later writers.[80] Remarkable learning and an extraordinary capacity for work were happily combined in this scholar with such virtues as a profound, clear intellect, a stupendous memory, and a genuine sense of history. In addition, he was blessed with significant literary talent. Dei Rossi wrote quite successful poems[81] and was a remarkable stylist, as may easily be seen from his masterly description of the earthquake in Ferrara. Yet this richly endowed scholar was a retiring man and up to the age of sixty published nothing. It is not difficult to find the reasons for this remarkable phenomenon. This free investigator and founder of scientific historical criticism was too far in advance of his generation. He was one of those whose fate made him live before his time, and only in the nineteenth century did it become possible properly to appreciate his value and significance. Dei Rossi himself apparently apprehended this. He understood that he had arrived too early, and he was not a fighter by nature. Weak and sickly, he desired rest and solitude above all else. Hence he believed that it would be much better for him if he concealed his scientific investigations and conclusions and did not publish them. So he sat quietly hidden in his little room. But suddenly a catastrophe occurred which compelled the solitary scholar to abandon his hiding place and appear before the public. In the fall of 1570 in Ferrara, where dei Rossi was then living, a tremendous earthquake took place. Over two hundred people perished in one

---

there apparently he went to his native city, Mantua, where he died (*REJ*, XXXII, 81–87).

80. See, e.g. *Meor Enayim* (Vilna edition, 1865), I, 5, 9, 10, 78, 84, 85, 90, 106, 117, 122, 123, 150, 154, 212, and 226; II, 55; *Matzref La-Kesef*, 100, 116, etc.

81. Like Moscato, Azariah dei Rossi lamented in several elegies the premature death of the young duchess of Savoy (see *Meor Enayim* in David Cassel's edition). In the last chapter of his major work dei Rossi presents an interesting discussion of Hebrew poetry.

terrible night, and dei Rossi and his family saved their lives only, as it were, miraculously. Seeing death face to face, dei Rossi, as he himself relates,[82] undertook an "inventory of the soul." He began to think of a memorial for future generations, so that his name would not be forgotten and the scientific treasures collected by him not be lost. He then decided to create a memorial stronger than stone and iron. After the catastrophe, in which most of the houses in Ferrara were destroyed, dei Rossi settled in one of the neighboring villages and there became acquainted with a Christian scholar who was well versed in the Apocryphal and Hellenistic Jewish literature produced in the generations of the Hasmoneans and the Tannaim.[83]

The Christian scholar inquired of dei Rossi whether the Hebrew translation of the well-known Letter of Aristeas had been preserved. Dei Rossi was forced to admit that the Jews know nothing of this work, and thereupon determined to acquaint his brethren who were unfamiliar with the classical languages, Latin and Greek, not only with Aristeas but with Hellenistic Jewish literature in general and with the entire period in question. In one-and-a-half years[84] he managed to write and edit his monumental *Meor Enayim*, which consists of three parts: (1) *Kol Elohim*, the description of the earthquake in Ferrara; (2) *Hadrat Zekenim*, a translation of the Letter of Aristeas;[85] and (3) *Imrei Binah*, a collection of studies in Jewish history and archaeology. The last part, consisting of sixty chapters, is the most important segment of dei Rossi's work.

We have already noted the factors which produced the burgeoning of historiographical literature among the Jews in the sixteenth century. Azariah dei Rossi was the first important Jewish scholar who devoted himself not to purely philosophical problems, to the criticism of systems and ideas, but to *historical* criticism, to investigating and illuminating historical sources. A child of the Renaissance age, which was so infatuated with the ancient world, dei Rossi was the first to introduce the works of the Judeo-Hellenistic era into Hebrew literature and to acquaint the Jewish reader with Philo of Alexandria[86] and the Septuagint.[87] Not without justification did he entitle his work *Meor Enayim* (Enlightenment of the

---

82. *Imrei Binah*, Chapter 1.
83. See the end of *Kol Elohim*.
84. From spring 1571 to fall 1572.
85. On a Yiddish translation of *Hadrat Zekenim*, see B. Wachstein's article in *Filologishe Shriften*, III, 267–74.
86. *Imrei Binah*, Chapters 3–6.
87. *Hadrat Zekenim; Imrei Binah*, Chapters 7–9.

Eyes). He was truly a man with bright and open eyes. In that age, when both the Christian and Jewish worlds still believed blindly in the tradition of the fathers and the authority of the ancients, he had the courage critically to inquire, in a rigorously scientific manner, how far one can rely in historical questions on the ancients, on the sources hallowed by tradition. To accustom the reader to the idea that he must not blindly trust the ancient sources and that not everything they relate is historical truth, dei Rossi dwelt especially on *Josippon*.[88] This work was at that time still not enveloped in the garment of sanctity, and to criticize its text did not smack of heresy. The author of *Meor Enayim* therefore showed with great acuity how strongly corrupted *Josippon* had become in the course of time and how clumsily and crudely the later copiers and compilers had distorted and altered the ancient text. Dei Rossi was also the first who critically explored and illuminated the most obscure period of Jewish history, the Persian period from Cyrus the Great to Alexander of Macedon.

The sages of the Talmud were generally not at all punctilious about matters of chronology. Stories of events that occurred in the days of the destruction of the First Temple are in the Talmud not infrequently mingled with tragic details from the time of Titus. The whole Persian period, which embraces more than two centuries, is concentrated in the Talmud into one generation of some thirty years. It was due to dei Rossi that this forgotten but extremely important era for the history of the development of Judaism was revived.[89] He compared with great keenness the Jewish sources from the Talmud and the Midrashim with the information provided in the Judeo-Hellenistic and classical Roman literature. In this way he managed to revive for the Jewish reader the forgotten generations from the time of Ezra the Scribe to the Seleucid Era, i.e., till after the death of Alexander the Great. When dei Rossi takes up the question of how long the period of the Second Temple lasted, he gradually uncovers for the reader the obvious truth (which, however, at that time appeared to be the greatest heresy) that the traditional Jewish mode of reckoning time from the creation of the world has no real foundation, for no mortal can properly and without error calculate the whole chain of generations from Adam on. In this connection, dei Rossi incidentally presents a sharp criticism of the "calculators of the end" who believe that, with the aid of combinations of letters and *gematriot*,

---

88. *Imrei Binah*, pp. 114, 118, 224–25, and 229 (we quote according to the Vilna edition of 1865).
89. *Imrei Binah*, Chapters 29–41.

they can predict when the Messiah will come. "This is pure folly and blindman's buff," he cries out indignantly.[90]

Many other very important questions are critically illuminated with the aid of the most varied sources by dei Rossi, who frequently arrives at conclusions and results that are totally inconsistent with tradition. To be sure, he realizes quite well that this smacks strongly of heresy, and so he does it extremely cautiously, taking pains to veil his scientific truths in a pious garment of reverence. He even considers it necessary to apologize to the reader for employing foreign sources.[91] Very gradually, step by step, he seeks to bring the reader to the conviction that the sages of the Talmud, who are truly great authorities in religious questions and laws, in other areas express views that are completely inconsistent with scientific assumptions.[92] One must also, dei Rossi insists, regard many of their homilies, legends, and dicta as poetic similes and purely rhetorical ornamentations; no one is obliged to take them seriously or believe in their literal meaning.[93]

Besides great scientific value, Azariah dei Rossi's work also has a tremendous literary significance. After Maimonides, dei Rossi is the foremost master of scientific style in the old Hebrew literature. Educated on the classical prose of ancient Rome, he introduced into Hebrew scientific literature the lucid, exact Latin style, exalted and enlivened with the rhythm of the narrative prose of the Bible.[94]

As we have observed, dei Rossi was extremely cautious. He took pains to wrap himself in a pious dress so that his heresy should not strike people in the eyes. But all of this was to no avail. His ideas and conceptions were too liberal and extraordinary not to elicit protest in the orthodox circles. It was dei Rossi's fate to have his masterwork appear in a time of twilight and spiritual and intellectual decline, when the rays of humanism and the Renaissance had just been covered by the dark clouds of militant reaction. His *Meor Enayim* provoked a violent storm even before it left the press.[95] In rabbinic circles intense excitement was generated by the report that dei Rossi denied the Jewish mode of reckoning time, which was hallowed through the tradition of the fathers,

---

90. *Ibid.*, II, 104: "The reckoning of words or letters through combination and *gematria* is all vanity and a striving after wind."
91. *Ibid.*, Chapter 2.
92. *Ibid.*, Chapter 11.
93. *Imrei Binah*, Chapters 15–16.
94. Moritz Güdemann especially noted the great importance of Azariah dei Rossi as a stylist in *Ha-Safah* (1912), I, 25–26.
95. *Meor Enayim* was printed in the period 1573–75 in Mantua.

and had the presumption to explain certain miracles naturalistically and to consider the story given in the Gemara (*Gittin*, 56b) about the death of the Roman emperor Titus—that a little flea penetrated his brain with its iron beak—simply a poetic legend. The sickly and quiet dei Rossi, who by nature was a man of peace, wrote commentaries and explanations to many of his expressed views while they were still being printed, and here and there eliminated passages already printed which, with their sharp expressions and critical conclusions, were overly offensive.[96] While his work was still on the press he included in the text his replies to many of the attacks made by the orthodox rabbis. All this, however, could not allay the clamor or quiet the tempest which his free criticism called forth in Jewish learned circles. Finally the calm dei Rossi lost his patience. "I have written my work," he declared, "only for the understanding who yearn for knowledge. To them it will bring great joy and pleasure, but fools and hypocrites who bite like snakes—let them not touch my book."[97]

But the expected consolation that all who yearn for knowledge would be rejoiced by his book also disappointed the solitary thinker. Against his work, the "memorial" which he wished to create for future generations, others besides "fools and hypocrites" came forth. His old friend, the previously mentioned mathematician Moses Provinciali, whom dei Rossi acquainted with his work before it came off the press, attacked *Meor Enayim* with indignant critical notes (*hassagot*), because the author had ventured to express doubts regarding the accuracy of the Jewish system of chronology, despite the fact that it was hallowed by tradition.[98] Soon after Provinciali, Isaac Finzi of Pesaro also came out against dei Rossi.[99] The report of dei Rossi's heretical work agitated all the Italian rabbis and Talmudic scholars. Even before *Meor Enayim* appeared, the rabbis of Venice, led by Samuel Jehudah Katzenellenbogen, the son of Maharam of Padua, circulated a proclamation[100] among all the Italian communities (on the fourth

---

96. *Imrei Binah*, Chapters 28 and 42.
97. *Ibid.*, Chapter 2.
98. Provinciali's *hassagot* were published by dei Rossi himself at the end of his work, along with his reply.
99. See *Matzref Le-Hochmah*, 1.
100. We present here the text of the interesting proclamation: "Let the fear of God be upon you! Word has been heard of the book that Rabbi Azariah dei Rossi wrote and published recently, entitled *Meor Enayim* with the parts *Kol Elohim, Hadrat Zekenim*, and *Imrei Binah*. Some of the chapters of Part Three were prepared long ago. And lo, since all of it is full of new explanations and interpretations some of which our holy ancestors never imagined in their lives,

of Nissan 1574) in which they declared that no pious Jew may dare possess, without special permission from the local rabbi, Azariah dei Rossi's heretical *Meor Enayim*, in which thoughts such as our holy ancestors had neither heard nor known are uttered.

Immediately after the Venetian rabbis, those of other cities (Rome, Ferrara, Padua, Pesaro, Verona, Ancona, and others)[101] also came out against *Meor Enayim*. The rabbi of Cremona, Abraham Menaḥem Porto, the author of the well-known work *Minḥah Belulah*, notwithstanding the fact that he himself had not actually seen *Meor Enayim*,[102] was not content with presenting the proclamation of the rabbis of Venice to his congregation on the Sabbath day after the reading of the Torah, but also preached a sermon in which he admonished the congregation not to allow itself to be led astray by the heretical book which bears the name "Enlightenment of the Eyes" but in fact darkens sight and undermines the foundations of Judaism.[103]

Dei Rossi's work created a sensation not only in Italy. The report of the dangerous book that had the arrogance to enter the realm of sacred tradition with the weapon of scientific criticism reached the distant community of Safed in Palestine. The renowned author of *Bet Yosef* and the *Shulḥan Aruch*, the eighty-six-year-old Joseph Karo, who already stood with one foot in the grave, requested the rabbinic judge Elisha Gallico to prepare the text of the ban with which the rabbis of Safed would issue forth against dei Rossi's work.[104] But Joseph Karo died shortly thereafter,

---

the undersigned scholars of every city in the holy community of Italy have agreed that no person of any congregation and court nor all others who tremble at their words may have this composition in their possession, either in whole or in part, or study it, unless they shall first have obtained permission in writing from the sages of their city. It will go hard with those who violate the words of the sages, but well will it be with those who obey them and blessing will come upon them." The proclamation was published by D. Kaufmann in his article "Contribut à l'histoire des luttes d'Asarja de Rossi" (*REJ*, XXXIII [1896], 77–87), in which several other extremely interesting documents regarding the battle which then erupted over *Meor Enayim* are also published.

101. See Kaufmann, "Contribut," pp. 84–85.
102. Menaḥem Porto indicates in his letter to the Kabbalist Menaḥem da Fano that he has not yet seen *Meor Enayim* but knows from personal conversation with dei Rossi that the latter rejects the Jewish mode of reckoning time.
103. See Porto's letter, published by Halberstam in *Tehillah Le-Mosheh*, 1–3.
104. Dei Rossi himself speaks with great respect in his work of the great Torah scholar Joseph Karo.

and the proclamation of the rabbis of Safed went out without his signature. The rabbi of Prague, Jehudah Loew (Maharal), the hero of numerous popular legends, was so enraged by *Meor Enayim* that he declared, "I am certain that the memory of this book will be erased among the Jewish people and it will be considered among the heretical books which have been adjudged forbidden to be read."[105]

In Mantua, where *Meor Enayim* was published and where such a prominent role was played by dei Rossi's old and intimate friends Jehudah Moscato and Moses Provinciali, the rabbis forbade anyone who was not yet twenty-five to read the work without special permission.

Against all these attacks and excommunications dei Rossi came forth with a *ketav hitnatzlut* (apology) under the title *Matzref La-Kesef*. In calm, sedate tones he endeavors to show the indignant rabbis that the traditional Jewish mode of reckoning time is not at all a "law of Moses from Sinai."[106] In ancient days a different chronology was accepted among the Jews, and only in a later period did they come to calculate time from the creation of the world. He hoped that his arguments would also persuade the "sages of Safed" and therefore dispatched a copy of *Matzref La-Kesef* to the rabbis of Safed.[107]

Matzref La-Kesef, which is written in classic style, was dei Rossi's swan song. The harsh attacks on his work completely shattered his weak physical energies, and he died shortly thereafter (not later than 1578). Long after dei Rossi's passing his *Meor Enayim* continued under the strict ban. A document published by David Kaufmann testifies that forty years after the scholar's death (1619) one of the members of the dei Rossi family requested authorization from the rabbi of Ferrara to study *Meor Enayim*, and the well-known rabbi of the end of the seventeenth century, Leon Briel, when quoting *Meor Enayim*, deems it necessary to indicate that he has received special permission from a great Talmudic scholar to read the proscribed work.

Yet, dei Rossi was not really mistaken, and his hope was finally vindicated. His lifework did remain a monument that withstood the ravages of time better than stone and iron. The prophecy of the aged Maharal was not fulfilled, and the memory of *Meor Enayim* was not erased, either among Jews or in the Christian world. To be sure, appreciation of its great scientific value came

105. *Be'er Ha-Golah* (1589), pp. 388, 424.
106. *Matzref La-Kesef*, 109. Cf. *Imrei Binah*, Chapter 35 and the end of Chapter 39.
107. *Matzref La-Kesef*, 116–35.

only in modern times, but even in those periods when the rabbinic ban hung over dei Rossi's work, *Meor Enayim* elicited great respect. Its author was, indeed, considered a dangerous freethinker, and the fanatical Jacob Emden in the eighteenth century still declared that Azariah dei Rossi's work should not be called The Enlightenment of the Eyes but rather The Blinding of the Eyes. Nevertheless, it was diligently studied and no less diligently quoted—to be sure, mainly anonymously and without calling it by name, in order not to give it fame.[108] For this reason also *Meor Enayim* was not reprinted until the end of the eighteenth century, when the "enlighteners" of Berlin, the Meassefim, became its saviors and published a new edition in 1794. The attitude of the Christian Hebraists of the seventeenth and eighteenth centuries toward *Meor Enayim* was far friendlier. Such scholars as Buxtorf, Bartolocci, Buckhardt, and others not only mentioned dei Rossi with reverence in their works but also translated entire chapters of *Imrei Binah*, the third part of *Meor Enayim*, into Latin.

108. See Zunz, *op. cit.;* M. Strashun, Supplements to *Kiryah Ne'emanah,* 307–10.

CHAPTER FIVE

The Decline of the Renaissance Era; LEO DE MODENA

OT only the orthodox rabbis of Italy and the Kabbalists of Safed participated in the battle against Azariah dei Rossi's free-thinking but also men of comprehensive European education such as Moses Provinciali and Jehudah Moscato.[1] In this fact clear signs of the great change which occurred in the intellectual environment of Italian Jewry in the second half of the sixteenth century may be seen. The sharp alteration in the mood of Jewish intellectual circles is intimately associated with the extremely unfavorable external conditions which, as time progressed, pressed ever more heavily on the economic and cultural life of Italy. On the one side, foreign armies overran the land and, on the other, the Catholic reaction (the Counter-Reformation) bared its claws ever more ruthlessly. The Spanish military power, which ruled Naples and Milan and as a

1. See Moscato's letter to dei Rossi which Kaufmann published in his "Contribut à l'histoire des luttes d'Asarja de Rossi" (*REJ*, XXXXIII [1896]), 81. Moscato's anger at dei Rossi for the latter's having cast doubt on the accuracy of the numbers and dates given in the Talmud in regard to the question of how long the first and second Temples lasted is very clearly discernible in the letter.

by-product extended its hegemony over all of Italy, stifled the spirit of humanism with its oppressive breath and trampled the tender flowers of the Renaissance with its spurred boots. Along with the despotic Spanish oppression, the dark wings of the Catholic reaction spread over Italy.

The emperor Charles V (1500–1558), who wore the Spanish crown as well as the imperial crown of all Germany, declared fiercest war against the Reformation movement. He wished to suffocate in blood, with an iron hand, the fresh shoots of free, "heretical" thought. In this struggle Charles found the most powerful support in the Catholic Church. It, too, rushed impetuously on the way of destruction and annihilation. In 1540 two priests, the Spaniard Ignatius of Loyola and the Italian Gian Pietro Carafa, founded the Jesuit and the Theatine orders respectively, whose goal was again to shore up, through rigorous discipline and ruthless warfare against heresy and liberal thought, the Catholic fortress which had been severely battered by the storm of the Reformation. Thanks to the stubborn fanatic Carafa, whose influence grew ever greater in clerical circles, a new institution was introduced into the papal provinces—the Inquisition, whose task was to search through the land for the "plague" of heresy. It was also Carafa who, with his burning hatred for free investigation, declared war against the noblest instrument of culture, the printing press. He was the first to introduce censorship of books, in order to stifle thought and enchain the free word. Even such an innocuous book as the famous work of Raphael's friend Baldassare Castiglione, *Il Libro del Cortegiano* (The Book of the Courtier) left the hand of the censor toothless and eyeless; the censor's pencil, for example, removed the word *fortuna*, and wherever a joke was made about a priest, the cleric was immediately transformed into an ordinary citizen. Boccaccio's *Decameron* suffered the same fate, as did numerous other works. But the lot of Hebrew books was even more bitter. Simply because humanism and the Reformation manifested considerable interest in Hebrew literature, the Catholic censors, the executioners of thought, deemed it necessary to regard the Hebrew book with special hostility.

To illustrate the situation succinctly, a generation earlier, at the wish of the head of the Catholic church, the cultured Pope Leo X, a Christian publisher printed the entire Talmud in twelve volumes for the first time, and thirty years later, at the command of another pope and through the efforts of Christian printers, the Talmud was burned on pyres.

Operating a Hebrew press was at that time an excellent business. Two wealthy merchants of Venice, Giustiniani and Bragudini, opened large Hebrew printing houses. These men were intense competitors, and a controversy broke out between them so strong that it ended in outright libel. One of them bribed two apostates, Joseph Morro and Ḥananel de Folinia, and these, together with Elijah Levita's grandson Solomon Romano (also an apostate), presented a denunciation before a session of the Inquisition to the effect that the Talmud and some other Jewish books are filled with attacks on Christianity.[2] The inquisitors were delighted, but for the sake of propriety formally appointed a commission of cardinals to determine how justified the denunciation was. "Thus," bitterly remarks the cultured Hebraist A. Matthias, "the blind were requested to give their view of the quality of colors."[3] The commission soon issued its verdict and, on its authority, a request was promptly submitted to Pope Julius III that the dangerous and extremely pernicious Hebrew books be rooted out as quickly as possible. The pope agreed, and on August 12, 1553 issued a special edict. The Inquisition at once dispatched its officers, who made house-to-house searches among the Jews in Rome and seized all the copies of the Talmud they could find. On the second day of Rosh Ha-Shanah, a Sabbath day, thousands of volumes of the Talmud were burned in a public square in Rome. The same thing happened in Bologna, Ferrara, Mantua, Venice, and other centers of Italian Jewish culture.[4] "This great sin," the afore-mentioned Matthias cries out indignantly, "will cover the throne of the Roman pontiff with eternal shame."[5]

But St. Peter's throne was decked with even greater shame after it was occupied by the fanatical Gian Pietro Carafa (the "Theatine," as he is called in Hebrew literature), who assumed the name Paul IV.[6] This zealot, whose hatred for Jews reached pathological proportions,[7] was no longer willing to content himself with pyres for Jewish books; he also desired human victims. In the course of the several decades, from the tolerant Pope Leo X

---

2. For a discussion of this, see the interesting letter of André Matthias, published by Perles in his *Beiträge*, pp. 221–31.
3. *Ibid.*, p. 225.
4. See Joseph Ha-Kohen, *Emek Ha-Bacha*, 111; Vogelstein and Rieger, *Geschichte der Juden in Rom*, II, 146.
5. *Ibid.*, pp. 223, 229.
6. *Emek Ha-Bacha*, 116 ff.; Abraham Graziano in *REJ*, IV, 96–97. In a number of Hebrew sources it is even noted that Teatino is equivalent in *gematria* to Haman, the arch-enemy of the Jews.
7. Joseph Ha-Kohen reports the following fact (*op. cit.*, 116–17): Pope Paul once ordered his nephew to set fire to the ghetto in Rome secretly under the cover of night, but thanks to Cardinal Farnese, who accidentally learned of it, the barbaric order was not executed.

to Pope Julius III, papal territory had served as a place of refuge for Marranos fleeing from Portugal who, with the tacit consent of the popes, openly returned to the religion of their fathers. The number of Marranos who reverted to Judaism was especially large in the city of Ancona. Paul IV could not bear this. He saw in it a "desecration" of the Christian faith and issued an edict ordering these "breakers down of the fence" seized and handed over to the judgment of the Inquisition. Many of the Marranos in Ancona managed to escape, among them the pride and ornament of the contemporary medical world and the author of the famous medicinal compendium *Centuriae,* Amatus Lusitanus. Some of those who were arrested, being Turkish subjects, had to be released by the Inquisition at the strict command of the powerful sultan Suleiman the Magnificent, but twenty-four Marranos died at the stake on May 24, 1556.[8]

Pope Paul, however, was not satisfied merely to persecute Marranos. Shortly after he ascended the throne of St. Peter, he issued his famous decree *Cum nimis absurdum,* with its explicit goal of bringing about a complete destruction of the economic condition of the Jews and degrading them morally to the lowest possible level. Among other prohibitions and restrictions,[9] the decree forbade Jewish physicians to treat Christian patients. We have noted the prominent role Jewish doctors played in Italy. This prohibition therefore created a great sensation and, to defend the honor of the Jewish medical fraternity, two of its honored representatives came forward. These were David d'Ascoli[10] and David ben Isaac de Pomis,[11] the well-known author of the lexicographical work

---

8. See *Emek Ha-Bacha,* 117–18; *REJ,* XVI, 66–68; and *Shalshelet Ha-Kabbalah* (end), where the names of martyrs who died at Ancona are given.

9. The decree, which consists of eighteen points, prohibits Jews from employing Christian servants. Furthermore, they may not engage in trade, with the exception of dealing in old clothes. Jews may not own any real estate. They may reside only in a separate, isolated quarter and are permitted to have no more than one synagogue. Every Jew is obliged to wear a yellow hat and every Jewess a special veil so that they may easily be distinguished from the Christian populace. Christains may not associate or celebrate with Jews. They may also not address a Jew with the honorific title *domini* (see *Shalshelet Ha-Kabbalah,* end; Vogelstein and Rieger, *op. cit.,* II, 152–53).

10. See Vogelstein and Rieger, *op. cit.,* II, 193; L. Fürst, *Beiträge zur Geschichte der jüdischen Ärzte,* Jahrbuch für die Geschichte der Juden, 11, 358.

11. For a discussion of this interesting personality, see L. Fürst, *op. cit.,* II, 358–69, and the introduction to *Tzemaḥ David.*

Tzemaḥ David[12] and of numerous medical works which won him a vast reputation among the scholars of his day. But no influence could be exerted by apologetic works on fanatics such as Paul and his associates. David d'Ascoli was imprisoned for his courageous act,[13] and in the last days of the pope's reign thousands of Hebrew books again flared up on the pyres.

The large-scale burning of the Talmud which took place in the fall of 1553 necessitated the closing of all the Talmudic academies in the papal provinces. Hence, a new center of Torah was established in the city of Cremona, which belonged to the duchy of Milan. Cremona became the "city of refuge." To it the books saved from the executioner's hand were transferred. Talmudic academies as well as a large Hebrew press, which provided Italian Jewry with new books, were founded. But this did not last long. The Dominicans, the zealous servants of the Catholic reaction, became aware of the situation and promptly raised a great clamor. Since the duchy of Milan was at that time under the rule of Spain, the Dominicans applied to the envoy of the Spanish government in Milan, obtaining from him an order to destroy the noxious and "heretical" books of the Jews at once. Twelve thousand volumes were seized in 1559 from the Jews of Cremona and burned in the middle of the city. Along with Hebrew books, Protestant works and the recently published Italian translation of the Bible were also consigned to the flames.[14] In the same year the *Index*, the first register of proscribed books, among which were included the Talmud and all of its commentaries and supplements, was published in the name of the pope.

To save a "remnant" and to prevent the prohibition from being applied to all their religious books, the Italian Jews struck on an original scheme. Shortly after the burning of the Talmud in 1553, a rabbinical conference was held in Ferrara, and the decision was there taken that henceforth no Hebrew manuscript might be printed without the approval of three rabbis who would first thoroughly familiarize themselves with the content of the work.[15] The press opened in Cremona in 1556 instituted a kind of censorship for itself. It would first submit every work which it wished to print to the examination of the apostate Vittorio Eliano, the

12. A Hebrew-Aramaic-Italian-Latin dictionary, in which de Pomis utilized the works of David Kimḥi, Nathan ben Yeḥiel, Elijah Levita, and others.
13. Vogelstein and Rieger, *op. cit.*, II, 153.
14. See *Emek Ha-Bacha*, 120–22; L. Fürst, *op. cit.*, II, 340.
15. Vogelstein and Rieger, *op. cit.*, II, 148; *Hebräische Bibliographie*, V, 74.

brother of Solomon Romano, while it was still in manuscript. With much trouble and at great expense the Jews managed to save books already printed on condition that all these would be examined and properly "expurgated"[16] by special censors, for whose labors the Jews themselves had to pay.[17] To simplify the work of the official censors, several respected rabbis (e.g., Abraham Provinciali) compiled a list of suspect passages which ought to be removed. A special handbook, *Canon purificationis* (in Hebrew it was called *Sefer Ha-Zikkuk*), which the censors were to use in "expurgating" the Hebrew works, was produced.[18] The authors of that period, taking account of the rigorous censors of the Inquisition, themselves "purified" their works so that they would not be trapped when they fell into the hands of the "expurgators." The following case is an interesting example. Azariah dei Rossi quotes the well-known Christian Hebraist Sebastian Muenster quite frequently in his work. This erstwhile monk, however, became a sceptic and one of the chief leaders of the Reformation movement. The Catholic Church therefore declared him a heretic and blasphemer, and dei Rossi was afraid to mention his name. He therefore refers to him anonymously as "so and so" or simply as "a Christian scholar."[19]

Given such a strict censorship and the atmosphere of the ruthless warfare which the Inquisition waged against heretical books, it is not surprising that the rabbis themselves began to look more suspiciously on every new idea and saw in dei Rossi's free critical inquiries the most dangerous heresy.

Here, however, we must pause on an extremely interesting point. Precisely at this time of growing reaction, when the Talmud was persecuted and burned, the Catholic Church itself contributed not a little to disseminating Kabbalist books more widely and to bringing it about that they occupied the foremost place in Jewish cultural life. The same Jewish apostates who raved so much about the great "harmfulness" of the Talmud took pains to persuade the Catholic priests that the *Zohar* is not alien to the basic idea of the Trinity and that in general a very friendly attitude toward Christianity prevails in it. It is therefore not surprising that Pope Paul IV's associates, who persecuted the Talmud so ferociously, were extremely tolerant of Kabbalist books and, at the time when in most of the cultural centers of Italy the agents of the Inquisition

---

16. A special term, *zikkuk*, was created for this in Hebrew.
17. See *Hebräische Bibliographie*, V, 73.
18. On *Sefer Ha-Zikkuk* and in general on the censorship of Hebrew books in Italy in the sixteenth century, see *Hebräische Bibliographie*, V, 72–77, 96–101, and 125–28; *ibid.*, VI, 68–70; *ZHB*, VII, 166.
19. On this see Perles, *Beiträge*, p. 40.

burned the Talmud and its commentaries on the pyres, one Kabbalist work after another began to appear in print—first *Sefer Ha-Emunot* of Shemtov ben Shemtov (1555), then *Marot Elohim* (1556), *Livyat Ḥen* (1557), *Maarechet Ha-Elohut* (1558), etc.[20]

In 1559, the year when twelve thousand Jewish books were burned in Cremona, the *Zohar* was published for the first time, and this in two editions at once—in Cremona itself and simultaneously in Mantua. Paul IV himself and the tribunal of the Inquisition gave their approval to this publication, and in the Cremona edition a large part was taken by the same Vittorio Eliano[21] (a grandson of Elijah Levita), as a result of whose denunciation the Dominicans managed to obtain from the Spanish envoy an order to burn the "Christian-hating" Talmud.

The appearance of the *Zohar* in print—and this in such a time of trouble—agitated the entire rabbinate of Italy. Some of the rabbis, led by Maharam of Padua, believed that it was by no means desirable that the "hidden wisdom" of the *Zohar* should become accessible to all. But there were also those who saw a danger precisely in the tendencies and ideas in the *Zohar* which so pleased such bitter enemies of the Talmud as Paul IV and his associates. The view was even publicly expressed that "study of the *Zohar* may lead to denial of God."[22] On the other hand, the idea of publishing the *Zohar* had such ardent proponents as Moses Provinciali, the Kabbalist Moses Basula, and Isaac de Lattes, thanks to whom the entire undertaking was not abortive. The argument set forth by de Lattes against the view that studying the *Zohar* may lead to atheism is interesting:

20. The naive comment of a well-known rabbi of that time, Menaḥem Porto, in the closing word of his *Minḥah Belulah* is interesting: "And I know that many will mock and deride me, especially since after the Gemara was taken away from us the land was filled with the doctrine of the Kabbalists, the men of the divine wisdom who dwell amidst the supernal secret and look through a bright mirror. But as for me, in my poverty and foolishness, these things are great and exalted in my sight; hence in my work only a smattering of such things will be found" (we quote according to the first edition published in Verona in 1544).

21. At the end of the Cremona edition is the following remark: "And the holy work of all that we labored and found in the *Zohar* was completed . . . today, the sixth day of the month of Kislev of the year 5319 from the creation of the world [1559 C.E.], and was supervised by . . . the young . . . Vittorio Eliano, the grandson of the chief of the grammarians, Rabbi Elijah . . . may his memory be for blessing."

22. This view is quoted in de Lattes' *haskamah* or approval to the first edition of the *Zohar* in Mantua.

That the hand of the government which rules over us with great wisdom has not touched us [the Kabbalists] is to be explained only by the fact that the government has the good intention of removing the thorns and harsh expressions that provoke enmity between Christian and Jew. But those rabbis [i.e., the opponents of the *Zohar*] who wish to uproot everything are the true destroyers of the world.[23]

These caustic words remind one forcefully of Abraham Abulafia and his wrathful onslaughts against the rabbis and the Talmud.

Precisely at that time Jewish mysticism arrived at a new stage in its development. In the new Jewish center of culture that was formed in the Ottoman empire[24] the Kabbalah was enriched with novel elements. Safed became the center of the new Kabbalist doctrine whose founders were the renowned Rabbi Moses Cordovero and Rabbi Isaac Luria (Ari). Soon a special emissary came from Safed to Italy. This was Israel Saruk (Sarug),[25] an energetic propagandist who very successfully disseminated the teaching of the Kabbalists of Safed. In Mantua, Saruk managed to obtain a devoted follower of the Lurianic system of Kabbalah in the person of the rich and highly respected Menaḥem Azariah (Immanuel) da Fano.[26] Born into an extremely wealthy and distinguished family,[27] da Fano received a well-rounded education but from his youth on was strongly attracted by the magic of the "esoteric wisdom." He was acquainted with Moses Cordovero, frequently wrote letters to him,[28] and after his death purchased from his widow for a large sum of money all the writings he had left. After da Fano was familiarized with Isaac Luria's system by Saruk, he became a fervent advocate of it. With great enthusiasm he propagandized Luria's ideas in the numerous works he wrote[29] and also in his large academy, which had an outstanding reputation and which attracted young people not only from all of Italy but from Ger-

23. See de Lattes' *haskamah* to the Mantua edition of the *Zohar* (de Lattes, *Responsa* [Vienna edition, 1860], p. 124).
24. On this, see Volume V.
25. Israel Saruk himself left no works except a commentary, *Neim Zemirot Yisrael*, on the hymns sung at the Sabbath table.
26. Born in 1548, died in 1620.
27. For a discussion of the da Fano family, see Kaufmann's work in *REJ*, XXXV, 84-91.
28. Moses Cordovero's son, Gedaliah, writes in the introduction to the first edition of *Or Ne'erav:* "The perfect sage, Rabbi Menaḥem Azariah of Fano, the light of Israel, was most faithful among all the household of my father; he loved to write to him about many of his teachings and adhered strongly to them in love."
29. The complete list of da Fano's work is given by Y. Vidaslavsky in his *Toledot Rabbi Menaḥem Azariah da Fano* (1904), pp. 47-56.

many and Poland as well. This Kabbalist and *yeshivah* head, to whom Joseph Solomon Delmedigo of Crete gave the title "master of the Kabbalists of the lands of the West,"[30] was not content to regard the *Zohar* as the recognized source of the hidden wisdom; he also saw in it one of the major authorities in the realm of *halachah* (religious law) and therefore established the principle that "the Babylonian Talmud, the Jerusalem Talmud, and the *Zohar* all say the same thing."

Even such a free investigator as Azariah dei Rossi acknowledged the great authority of the "true sages"[31] and believed that the *Zohar* was written by the "godly" Rabbi Simeon ben Yoḥai.[32] To be sure, it did not escape his keen critical eye that several parts of the *Zohar* could certainly not have been written in the days of Simeon ben Yoḥai, but he ventured merely to note that the parts in question were edited in later generations.[33] Dei Rossi rejects Elijah Levita's view that the musical notations and accent marks of the Biblical text were introduced among Jews centuries after the destruction of the Second Temple[34] merely on the grounds that the *Zohar* frequently mentions the vowel points and musical notations.[35] Dei Rossi's contemporary, the Italian Rabbi Jacob ben Isaac Luzzatto, who later settled in the Kabbalist center of Safed, declares definitely that only he who fathoms the mystical secrets concealed in the text of the holy books can be called "a man of Torah in truth," and in his *Kaftor Va-Feraḥ*, which he published at the end of 1580 in Basel, he endeavors to point out "by way of the Midrash of Rabbi Simeon ben Yoḥai" (i.e., the *Zohar*) "the true meanings of the *aggadot*," the profound mystical allusions concealed not only in the Torah but also in the fantastic legends of the Babylonian Talmud, the Jerusalem Talmud, and the Midrashim.[36] He also complains strongly of those who wish "to set the Gemara naked and bare" and to interpret the Talmudic text merely by way of reason. "Woe to this shame, woe to this disgrace!" Luzzatto indignantly cries out.

Thus gradually, under the frosty breath of the reaction, the living spirit of humanism died both in the Christian milieu and in

---

30. In *Matzref Le-Ḥochmah*, 14a.
31. See *Meor Enayim*, I, 86; II, 28, etc.
32. *Ibid.*, I, 99; II, 186.
33. *Ibid.*, 223: "It is also possible that the entire *Midrash Ha-Ne'elam* as well as *Raaya Mehemna* were composed mainly by the Amoraim, most of whose words—to be sure—came from ancient sages."
34. See *supra*, Chapter 2.
35. *Meor Enayim*, Chapter 59.
36. See Luzzatto's statement in the introduction to his *Kaftor Va-Feraḥ*.

the Jewish ghetto of Italy. The influence of the Lurianic Kabbalah
of distant Safed and of the strict, melancholy rabbinism of neighboring Germany grew ever greater. In this connection, one must
take account of the fact that even in the heyday of the Renaissance
the major role in the Jewish communities of Italy was played by
rabbis who came from Germany. The reason for this lies in the
unique way of life of the Italian Jews. With the significant freedom
they enjoyed, the Jewish young people of Italy devoted themselves
relatively little to the Talmud and religious codes. We have noted
that the Italian universities were open to Jews on equal terms with
Christians. Jewish youths studied the natural sciences, astronomy,
and especially medicine with great eagerness. The result was that
there were few who volunteered to attend the Talmudic academies
and to devote themselves especially to rabbinic studies. In addition,
studying at the university cost considerably less than in the Talmudic academies. Evidence of this is provided by a very interesting
document of that period, a letter of Jacob Provinciali to David
Messer Leon written in 1490,[37] in which the reply made by the
Jewish youth to the reproach that they devote themselves so
slightly to the Talmud and rabbinic literature is frankly given.
"It is, after all, much better for us," they argue, "to listen to lectures by Christian scholars who study with us for a very small
fee because they receive extensive support from the government
or the city administration; furthermore, they make no distinction
between Jews and Christians."[38] Hence, it is not surprising that
Italy at that time was no center of Torah, and that when a large
and wealthy community required a rabbi it sought him in
Germany.[39]

Of the two foremost rabbis who then lived in Italy, Jehudah
Minz (c. 1409–1509) and Joseph ben Solomon Colon (c.
1420–80), the first came from Germany and the second was of
the Jews exiled from France. Colon, however, drew knowledge
of Torah from Germany through his father, who was a pupil of
the Maharil. And it was Colon who, with his great authority, contributed much to the fact that the influence of the German rabbis,

37. *Divrei Ḥachamim* (1849), 65.
38. *Ibid.*, 73. The author of *Minḥat Kenaot*, Yeḥiel of Pisa, also considers
    it necessary to note: "And it is not as some of our contemporaries
    have said: 'Why should we dream all our days about the textual variants
    of the Talmud and the controversies of the Amoraim? It suffices for
    us to know the decision concerning the substance of the command-
    ments, and we do not need the views and discussions of the Amoraim.' "
39. For an extended discussion of this see Weiss, *Dor Dor Ve-Doreshav*,
    V, Chapter 27.

with their customs and world outlook, became ever more powerful in northern Italy.

Joseph Colon was one of the outstanding Talmudic scholars of his generation,[40] but he had not received any European, non-Talmudic, education and therefore carried on an intense controversy with a convinced opponent of the Kabbalah, Jehudah Messer Leon, who did have such an education.[41] An obdurate battle with another antagonist of Kabbalah, the philosophically educated Elijah Delmedigo, was waged by the other great rabbi of the generation, Jehudah Minz. Minz had more general education than Colon;[42] nevertheless, he also saw pure heresy in the free thoughts to which the author of *Beḥinat Ha-Dat* gave utterance.

The fact that the customs of the German rabbis were soon accepted in Italy was aided not inconsiderably by a contemporary of Minz and Colon, the well-known and recognized legal decisor Jacob Baruch Landau, who, together with his father Jehudah Liva, moved from Germany to Padua and later settled in Naples. His wealthy pupil Ezra Abraham ben David Obadiah occupied himself to such an extent with philosophy and natural sciences that he could not devote much time to Talmudic studies. In order that his pupil might nevertheless be versed in all the religious laws and regulations, Jacob Landau composed his work entitled *Agur*, which went through numerous editions.[43] In this collection of approximately 1,500 decisions and customs, Landau appears as a strict constructionist of the law and a devoted follower of the rabbis of Germany.[44] He was also practically the first who, as a decisor, took account of the *Zohar* and other Kabbalist works even in questions of what is permitted and forbidden.[45] It is therefore not surprising that Landau's work was widely accepted not only in Italy but in Germany as well and was regarded by the German Jews as one of the major legal codes.

In the Talmudic academy founded by Jehudah Minz in Padua many young people who had fled from Germany were educated, and it was from this academy that the greatest rabbi in Italy in

40. On the significance of Joseph Colon as a Talmudist, see Weiss, *op. cit.*, V, 269–74.
41. The end of the controversy was that, at the command of the duke, both rabbis had to leave Mantua.
42. Ghirondi, in his *Toledot Gedolei Yisrael*, p. 122, relates that he himself saw in a hall of the University of Padua a portrait of Jehudah Minz with an inscription to the effect that Minz in his day lectured at the university.
43. See the introduction to *Agur*.
44. *Agur*, 51a ff.
45. *Ibid.*, 5a; we cite from the Offenbach edition of 1718.

the sixteenth century, Meir ben Isaac Katzenellenbogen (better known by the name "Maharam of Padua"), came.[46]

The rabbis who migrated from Germany to Italy could not, with their rigorously orthodox outlook, be at all pleased with the free way of life of the Italian Jews in which, in the Renaissance era, the strong assimilationist influence of the external environment was discernible. They wished to restrain the overly swift and rushing life stream as much as possible with severe rulings and hedges, to extinguish the joy and love for laughing, palpitating life with their melancholy and strict prohibitions. In this, the general reaction which became so powerful in Italy in the second half of the sixteenth century with the Catholic Counter-Reformation aided them greatly.

Nevertheless, in the Italian Jewish community the echoes of the Renaissance era were still loudly heard. It was not so easy to choke the drive for the pleasures of the present world and the thirst for the joys of life. It suffices to mention that even at the end of the sixteenth century the sport of hunting in forests was still widespread among the Jews of Italy.[47] The German rabbis wished to introduce the ascetic and strictly orthodox way of life of the German communities as quickly as possible into the Jewish communities of Italy. This necessarily produced controversy and dissatisfaction. The most brilliant representatives of the mood of protest in that era were two fascinating personalities, Jehudah Aryeh (Leo) de Modena and Joseph Solomon Delmedigo.

Jehudah ben Isaac de Modena's life is known to us in all its details, thanks to his autobiography, completed several days before his death.[48] This document and the packet of letters that have come down to us[49] have a significant cultural-historical interest, for they acquaint us not only with the life of Leo de Modena and his family but also with the life style of the contemporary Jewish community in Italy, especially in Venice.

46. He married Jehudah Minz' granddaughter and after Minz' death took his place as rabbi in Padua. His son Samuel was the first to give his signature to the proclamation of the rabbis against Azariah dei Rossi.

47. In Abraham Jagel's *Ge Ḥizzayon*, 14 (written in 1578) it is related: "And it happened on a certain day that we rode together in a forest where we went to walk and to hunt animals, for this was our custom two or three times a week."

48. *Ḥayyei Yehudah*. Extracts of this work were published by Luzzatto and Abraham Geiger in their day. Abraham Kahana first published *Ḥayyei Yehudah* in full in 1912.

49. L. Blau, *Leo Modenas Briefe und Schriftstücke (Kitvei Ha-Rav Yehudah Aryeh Mi-Modena)* (1906).

Despite the Counter-Reformation and its attendant persecutions, the wealthy Jewish populace in Venice fully enjoyed the foaming cup of life. It must be remembered that Venice in the sixteenth century was one of the most beautiful and life-loving cities of the world. Its social life was highly developed. More than all else the Venetians loved exciting gatherings of thousands of persons, parades, processions, and presentations with dazzling, splendid garments and ornaments. They were intoxicated by the colorful, festal radiance of laughing, joy-loving life. "In no other city," writes such a connoisseur of Italy as M. Muratov,

were ever assembled such wealth, such colorful, splendid tapestries as in sixteenth-century Venice. On holidays, festivals, and days of solemn processions and presentations, the palazzos, the churches, the front walls of the houses, the gondolas, even the marketplaces—everything was bedecked with silk, brocade, and the rarest carpets. In the processions over the great canal of Venice the hundreds of gondolas were ornamented with bright red silks. But we can have no conception of this splendor, we are incapable of imagining it. We have lost the feeling for properly appreciating the extraordinary beauty of colorful precious stones covering whole buildings or descending in dazzling cascades from high roofs. Life today does not provide our sight with such celebrations. . . . For this reason we can have merely a pallid notion of the festival decorations in Venice, just as a man who throughout his life has seen only small rivers can have no idea of the size of the ocean.[50]

Their environment had a great influence on the Jewish populace of Venice. Only when the carefree and life-loving Venetian milieu is taken into consideration can we explain how such a serious and sober scholar as Elijah Levita would permit himself to write so frivolous a tract, filled with so much lascivious talk, as *Ha-Mavdil*.[51] The influence of contemporary life in Venice is also strongly discernible in the talented son of the Venetian ghetto Leo de Modena. In his childhood, he relates, he was taught singing and dancing. When he was already a rabbi and preacher, de Modena devoted himself a great deal to the theater and music, himself wrote pastorals, rehearsed plays for the theater, and served as choirmaster and director of a musical school in which he gave two concerts a week.[52] His brother-in-law Moses wrote plays in couplets,

50. M. Muratov, *Obrazii Italii*, I, 26 (Russian).
51. First published by N. Shtiff in *Tzeitshrift*, I, 150–58, and in *Shriften*, I, 148–79.
52. For more on this subject, see our work in *Yevreyskaya Lyetopis*, VI, on the Jewish theater in the Renaissance era.

and would himself sing these couplets. De Modena's son-in-law Jacob Halevi, a fervent mystic and the author of a Kabbalist book,[53] earned his living from being a professional singer and dancing teacher.[54] How greatly de Modena's family was devoted to the theater is attested by a letter of his fourteen-year-old son Mordecai. In the winter of 1605 he writes from Ferrara to his uncle Moses, the singer and playwright: "I know that the time is approaching when your comedy is to be presented. Keep me in mind then and let me know, I beg you, which of the boys plays the role that was designated for me." A short time later, he again touches on the same matter in a letter to his uncle and points out, incidentally, that he writes briefly "and hastens to finish the letter, for he knows that uncle is extremely busy with his comedy." Characteristic is the phrase with which this young son of a rabbi ends his letter. Because it was the week of *Shabbat Shirah* (the Sabbath of Song, on which the pericope from the Book of Exodus beginning "Then sang Moses" is read in the synagogue) he parodies the text of the Torah and dates the letter with the following words: "The week of the pericope 'Then sang Moses' in the *intermedia*"[55] (i.e., the week that his uncle Moses was to sing in the interludes). De Modena's other son, Zebulon, a singer, playboy, and fierce duelist, died tragically in a sword fight with a company of young drunkards.

How strongly the influence of the Christian environment was felt in the Venetian Jewish community and how little this influence harmonized with the ideals of the orthodox German rabbis is clearly visible from the conduct of de Modena's family. This will have to be taken into consideration when we have occasion later to speak of the bitter struggle that de Modena, himself a rabbi, waged with the rabbis and their outlook on the world.

Leo de Modena was born April 23, 1571, in Venice into a wealthy, privileged family.[56] As a child he displayed brilliant capacities; at the age of two and a half he read the lection from the Prophets in the synagogue on the Sabbath. At the age of three,

53. *Naḥalat Yaakov.*
54. *Ḥayyei Yehudah*, 33.
55. Blau, *op. cit.,* p. 115. Mordecai de Modena's end was a tragic one. He passed away as a young man because of his experiments with alchemy. The extremely noxious gases of lead and arsenic poisoned him and he died very prematurely.
56. De Modena's family came from France. Leo de Modena's grandfather Mordecai acquired fame as a physician and philanthropist, and the emperor Charles V raised him to knighthood and designated him a member of the order of Knights of the Golden Fleece (see *Ḥayyei Yehudah*, 10–11).

he went through the weekly Scriptural pericope and fluently interpreted verse after verse.[57] As a five-year-old he was already filled
with doubts and questionings, reflected on immortality, dreamed
of literary fame, and frightened himself with the thought that perhaps he would not manage to become famous and would depart
from the world unknown.[58] The boy's father gave his *Wunderkind*
a well-rounded education. Leo studied Hebrew language and literature with Samuel Archevolti, the leading Hebrew philologist
of that period. He himself later noted a number of times the great
influence exercised on his entire literary activity by the time he
spent with Archevolti.

Samuel Archevolti (1515–1611) was endowed with a spark of
the poet and with an excellent philological sense. This is attested
by his liturgical poems[59] and his well-known grammatical work
Arugat Ha-Bosem (Venice, 1603).[60] To be sure, as a child of his
time, Archevolti was quite certain that fearful mysteries and tremendous powers are hidden in the letters of the Torah.[61] For the
idea that the cantillation, the vowel points, and the musical notations of the Biblical text were already accepted among Jews in
ancient times, he saw the best proof in the fact that the *Zohar*
testifies that "the accents were given at Sinai."[62] On the other hand,
Archevolti presents in his work, in very clear and original form,
all the unique qualities of the Hebrew language. Particularly interesting are the chapters in which the author passes from the elementary poetic forms (Chapter 24) and oratorical style (Chapters

57. *Hayyei Yehudah*, 15: "And when I was three years old . . . I would
interpret the weekly *parashah* and understand it."
58. See de Modena's introduction to his *Midbar Yehudah*: "I must confess
that I was zealous for such praises. All my days, from the time I
was a five-year-old studying the Bible, I was troubled and said: 'When
will I accomplish something? Woe to me for I shall die, I shall depart
and be an empty wind. . . . I shall go from my place without leaving
any recognizable impress'" (we quote according to the edition of
1602).
59. Many of Archevolti's liturgical poems found their way into the Festival
Prayer Book of the Italian Jewish communities (*Minhag Romanya*).
Especially popular were his "Arzei Ha-Levanon" and the Zion ode
"Tziyyon Tzevi U-Pe'er Le-Rosh Banecha." On Archevolti's other
works, see M. Ghirondi, *Toledot Gedolei Yisrael*, 354–55. His collection
of letters *Mayyan Gannim* was in Baron Günzburg's manuscript collection, No. 247.
60. Joseph Solomon Delmedigo, when listing in his *Iggeret Aḥoz* the major
Hebrew philologists from Hayyuj to Elijah Levita, adds that
Archevolti's *Arugat Ha-Bosem* is better than all their works."
61. *Arugat Ha-Bosem*, 4b.
62. *Ibid.*, 91b.

28–29) to neo-Hebrew poetry and, along with this, provides original examples of Hebrew meter (Chapters 31–32). The last chapter so delighted the Christian scholar Buxtorf the Younger that he translated it into Latin and published it as a supplement to his Latin translation of Jehudah Halevi's *Kuzari* (1660). An altogether new phenomenon in Hebrew literature is the thirtieth chapter, in which Archevolti speaks of shorthand and cipher writing.

Leo de Modena was Archevolti's favorite pupil and all his life carried on a friendly correspondence with him. He himself admits that he was greatly indebted to his teacher. "To him," he writes, "I owe my literary style, and from him I learned the art of writing poetry."[63]

At the age of twelve, de Modena translated the first canto of Ariosto's poem *Orlando Furioso* into Hebrew. A year later he composed his polemic on games of chance, *Sur Me-Ra*, which appeared in numerous editions and was translated into Yiddish, Latin, French, and German.[64] This work of the thirteen-year-old boy testifies to his distinctive literary talent and has, incidentally, characteristics to be found also in his later creativity. In *Sur Me-Ra* a heated debate is carried on by the ardent devotee of card playing, Medad, and the no less convinced opponent of this pastime, Eldad. It is clear that it is not the battle against the harmful play that is the intention of the young author. He is interested above all in the wager itself, the excitement of the debate, the art of dialectical argumentation. De Modena himself relates how from the age of ten on he loved to carry on debates on religious themes with both Jews and Christians. In connection with this, he proudly adds that there is not a single apologetic work in which the Jewish faith is touched upon, whether in Latin or in Italian, Spanish, or Hebrew, with which he is not familiar.[65] This strong attraction to religious-polemic literature, however, does not arise with de Modena out of the imperative desire to attain the truth or defend the faith of the fathers. He delighted in the polemical process for its own sake and loved the atmosphere of battle, the triumphant disclosure of logical fallacies and inept arguments on the part of his opponent.

De Modena was a man of rounded culture, had a substantial knowledge of classical literature, mathematics, philosophy, and the

63. *Ḥayyei Yehudah*, 17–18.
64. According to Steinschneider, de Modena is also the author of the well-known poem about chess playing "Ma'adenei Melech," which until modern times was considered a work of Abraham Ibn Ezra (see *Hebräische Bibliographie*, XII, 60–63).
65. See *Ari Nohem*, Chapter 3; *Beḥinat Ha-Kabbalah*, XIV.

natural sciences and, along with this, constantly endeavored to broaden and increase his learning.[66] Nevertheless, he was very little like those "seekers" (*mevakkeshim*) of whom we spoke in the previous volume. With de Modena the thirst for knowledge was not the product of a searching soul yearning to find the right way leading to the ideal of truth and justice. He merely sought suitable intellectual nourishment for his considerable capacities. His was a restless and excitable, but not a profound, nature. De Modena merely hovers over the surface; he mainly touches only the outer garment of the matter in question, despite all his great knowledge, brilliant capacities, and definite literary talent. For him the greatest authority is man's common sense; this is the only recognized criterion by which one ought to measure all spiritual treasures, all cultural and historical values.

In his logical consistency, in his unwillingness to know of contradictions and of forked and tortuous ways, lies de Modena's power but also his weakness. To a limited extent de Modena's only recognized guide and criterion, common sense, may be extremely useful, by reason of the fact that it makes everything clear and comprehensible and does not allow the plain and obvious to be obscured. But it becomes helpless, as well as inhibitive, when it attempts to go beyond these definite boundaries and presumes to become the only judge and the only measuring rod of all cultural values, of all human demands and desires. To be sure, at times de Modena himself rebels and refuses to acknowledge the power of this sole judge and criterion. But he does not do this because he has become convinced that one cannot always rely on common sense, but out of altogether different motives. With his restless and excitable nature, de Modena did not have a firm character; his will was weak and inconstant, and his actions and moral conduct were therefore inconsistent and full of contradictions. He made his debut in literature, as we have observed, with a tract against card playing, but was himself all his life a compulsive card player. He admits[67] that this "accursed" addiction of his brought him much trouble and shame. In one of his poems he relates with bitter laughter how he cannot sleep at nights because of the debts that he is unable to pay.[68] Yet his will was too weak for him to be able to renounce

66. Typical in this respect are the following words of de Modena (*Ari Nohem*, 5): "Would that I could praise, exalt, and glorify God, that He might help me to know everything in the world."
67. *Hayyei Yehudah*, 26, 28, 29, 30, 33, 34, 39, 46, 51, 62, and 63.
68. Half the night I worry about my debts;
The day of payment has come and there is no one from whom to borrow.
On the morrow I shall say to my creditors:

the "accursed game." He did not even have sufficient character to recognize his own fault, to accept personal responsibility for his addiction. He sought to persuade himself that he was not guilty. It was a decree from heaven; the planets and the fearful astrological powers had brought it about that he must be a gambler all his life. "How am I guilty and what can I do," he laments in a letter,[69] "if the stars in the heavens persecute me mercilessly?" "The celestial luminaries," he writes elsewhere, "rule the fate of men and no one can deflect their severe decree."[70] "The planets," he writes in his autobiography, "have again cheated me, and in the course of two months I have lost two hundred ducats."[71] This fervent battler for common sense believed in chiromancy[72] and dreams,[73] and devoted himself much to alchemy.[74] A convinced rationalist and fierce opponent of mysticism and the Kabbalah, de Modena himself dealt in amulets and nostrums, and composed all kinds of incantations.[75] He tells of this in his autobiography in which he lists no less than twenty-six occupations and professions with which he busied himself, though all of them could not save him from extreme want since his entire earnings were swallowed up by his passion for gambling.

It is worth while to list the occupations in which this unique Italian rabbi of the seventeenth century was involved. He 1) studied with Jewish pupils and 2) with Christian pupils; 3) taught letter writing; 4) was a preacher; 5) composed sermons for others and received payment therefor; 6) was a cantor in a synagogue, 7) secretary of various societies, and 8) rabbi; 9) wrote legal decisions; 10) served as a rabbinic judge; 11) was a teacher in a Talmudic academy; 12) wrote official documents and 13) letters; 14) occupied himself with music; 15) composed poems for weddings and inscriptions for tombstones; 16) wrote Italian sonnets and 17) comedies; 18) rehearsed theatrical presentations; 19) drew up contracts; 20) was a translator; 21) earned royalties from his own works; 22) was a proofreader; 23) taught the art of writing pre-

---

The second half of night I shall let *you* worry.
You think about my debts until the white dawn,
And I — I will forget all cares in sweet slumber,
Recalling the sage counsel, "Worry not about the concerns of tomorrow."

69. *Kitvei Aryeh de Modena*, No. 45.
70. *Ḥayyei Yehudah*, 50.
71. *Ibid.*, 52.
72. *Ibid.*, 35.
73. *Ibid.*, 37 ff.
74. *Ibid.*, 30, 34 ff.
75. De Modena's incantations are collected in *Sod Yesharim* (1595).

scriptions and amulets; 24) sold books of prescriptions; 25) was a middleman and 26) a marriage broker.[76]

Whatever de Modena earned he immediately lost in card playing. The following point is interesting. Card playing at that time was a universal plague and extremely widespread among the Italian Jews. The previously mentioned Abraham Jagel tells us in his *Ge Hizzayon* of an interesting type of ardent card player who endeavored to prove that card playing is a very profound matter and that in the pictures on the cards fearful secrets and philosophical ideas of very great compass are hidden.[77] To fight against gambling, the Italian rabbis decided in 1638 to issue a monition that whoever engages in card playing and other forms of gambling will be thrown under the ban. Leo de Modena immediately issued forth against this proposal and composed a brilliant counterargument,[78] and nothing came of the ban. One of the arguments that he set forth has a certain cultural-historical interest. We have noted that card playing was universal; in Italy, the birthplace of all kinds of lotteries, the passion for gambling was very widespread already in the Renaissance era. Hence, de Modena points out that the Jews who carry on business with the urban merchants must frequent the playing houses and clubs, because only there can they find their clients, and the latter often compel them to take part in the games.

De Modena, the gambler who was so unlucky in cards all his life and had even less luck in his family life,[79] regarded all of human life as a melancholy game, a cruel jest on the part of the Creator. The idea, so widely accepted in Judaism, that man is the major purpose and the focus of the whole universe received in de Modena an altogether strange form. Yes, he declares with bitter irony, God created man, the midpoint of the world, for the sake of His own pleasure. Man is for Him a joke, a plaything like a trained little dog or a monkey among earthly princes. The movements of the spheres and planets are strictly determined and regular, but this is tedious and uninteresting. The same boring regularity prevails here below, in the world of animals and plants. Only man with

---

76. *Ḥayyei Yehudah*, 64–65.
77. *Ge Ḥizzayon*, 7–8.
78. De Modena's response was published by Isaac Lampronti in his *Paḥad Yitzḥak* under the heading *Ḥerem*.
79. Of de Modena's three sons, one died at the age of twenty-six, the second was killed in a fight, and the third, a profligate young man, emigrated to Brazil where he disappeared and his father never heard from him again. Both his sons-in-law and one of his daughters died while quite young, and his wife lost her mind.

his free choice is an exception. Now he rises to the heavens and presumes to become like the angels, and now he falls deep into the swamp and scrabbles like a worm in the dust of the earth. This constant sequence of risings and fallings, this indefatigable, painful climbing to the heights is, after all, extremely interesting to observe. And just as an earthly king makes sport not of princes or of servants but of trained dogs, apes, talking birds, and horses that can perform tricks, so God makes His sport of man. For this reason do all creatures serve man, just as in a royal palace both the princes and the common servants gladly serve the king's favorite—the monkey.[80]

It is therefore no surprise that de Modena, when noting that the Talmud emphasizes that one of the most important among the 613 commandments is the commandment to procreate, cries out angrily:

Ah, how greatly they blinded our eyes and darkened our souls with this commandment! They destroyed our body and our material existence, saddened and embittered our whole life with it. How many sins, how many wicked deeds, does a man commit to support his wife and children. A heavy millstone have they hung about our necks so that we should not be able to raise our heads. . . . Large volumes would not suffice to describe how all our troubles and crimes, all our poverty and distress, derive from this commandment.[81]

But this was not the only commandment which aroused Leo de Modena against the old-fashioned rabbinic Judaism. It must be remembered that this rationalistically-minded rabbi had, from his youth on, intimate relationships with the Christian society of Venice, in which he was a highly respected and popular figure.[82] His brilliant oratorical talent attracted numerous Christian auditors to his sermons. Catholic priests and many of the nobility would frequently come to hear him. Clever, witty, and entertaining, de Modena was welcome in the most prominent social circles of Venice. Among his pupils were courtiers and archbishops. He also made acquaintances at the card table. De Modeno proudly relates how he had frequent occasion to carry on religious debates with well-known Christians and with apostates as well, and how easy

80. *Kol Sachal* (Göritz, 1852), pp. 8–9.
81. *Ibid.,* p. 62.
82. De Modena's grandson, Isaac ben Jacob, writes in the introduction to *Magen Va-Herev:* "He was better known among the Christians than among us, beloved and admired for his wisdom and his modesty in the eyes of the cardinals, dukes, priests, emissaries of kings and princes of every people and language."

it was for him to refute and annihilate all their arguments and attacks. But there is also no doubt that the constant tournaments and religious disputations, whether he willed this or not, weakened the religious sentiment in the depths of his heart and made him indifferent to those questions that create boundaries between various faiths and are not entirely suited to sober "common sense." And the flabbier the foundations of de Modena's religious outlook became, the greater grew his ire at orthodox rabbinic Judaism, which precisely at that time, in the period of intensified reaction in the Italy of the Counter-Reformation, sought to obtain complete power over Jewish life. The rationalist de Modena could not observe with apathy the mystical and strictly orthodox rabbinic tendencies becoming constantly stronger and spreading their influence ever more widely. But since he was not at all a fighter by nature, with a firmly established character, his battle against rabbinism took on altogether unique forms.

In 1616 the representatives of the Sephardic community in Hamburg applied to de Modena, as a great expert in polemical literature, with the request that he write a decisive reply to eleven questions with which a local rationalist apostate had attacked the Oral Torah and the tradition of the fathers. From modern scholarly investigations[83] there is no longer any doubt that this anonymous heretic who so disturbed the leaders of the Sephardic community in Hamburg was none other than the well-known Uriel Acosta, who was then temporarily living in Hamburg[84] and from there personally sent to Venice a copy of his work in which his eleven arguments against the Talmud are set forth. De Modena did not hesitate long and soon responded to the heretic of Hamburg with a brilliant polemic document entitled *Magen Ve-Tzinnah*.[85] In his letter to the representatives of the Hamburg community,[86] de Modena speaks very indignantly of this "heretic and Sadducee" who has so arrogantly slandered the Oral Law. But this "heretic" and "Sad-

---

83. See N. Porges in *ZHB*, 1911, pp. 80–82.
84. *Ibid.*, p. 41. De Modena also notes in his *Magen Ve-Tzinnah* that this heretic resided in Hamburg only temporarily: "His name was Ish Kesil and he *then* lived in Hamburg." We believe that the words "his name was Ish Kesil" actually confirm that Acosta is here meant, for Ish Kesil in *gematria* is equivalent to Uriel D'Acosta or Gabriel D'Acosta.
85. First published by Geiger in 1856. Geiger, however, is mistaken in thinking (*Leo de Modena*, pp. 25–27) that this heretic against whom de Modena polemicizes never existed. De Modena himself translated his *Magen Ve-Tzinnah* into Italian (see *Hebräische Bibliographie*, VI, 23–24).
86. See Blau, *op. cit.*, p. 146.

ducee" fought with rationalist weapons; in his attack on the Talmud he appealed to the very authority so revered by de Modena—sober common sense. This necessarily made a definite impression on the author of *Magen Ve-Tzinnah*. We must therefore not be greatly surprised that the very theses of the heretic of Hamburg against which de Modena polemicizes so cleverly in his *Magen Ve-Tzinnah* are afterwards recognized as persuasive arguments by de Modena himself. An excellent polemicist and practiced dialectician, he refutes his opponent's arguments while deep in his heart agreeing with them.

The same thing occurs in de Modena when he fights against the ideas of another "heretic," the apostate Abner of Burgos, of whom we spoke in Chapter Seven of the previous volume. De Modena himself tells of the great impression made on him by Abner's tract against the Talmud.[87] "Such a work," he writes with feeling,

> could have been written only by a man with immense knowledge. A pupil of Naḥmanides, Abner drew wine from the best cellars, but with him the good wine was eventually spoiled. All my days I have had much intercourse with Christian scholars and from childhood on have had occasion to carry on religious debates . . . I can say with pride that I have never bypassed a single polemic work in Latin, Italian, Spanish, or Hebrew which criticizes the foundations of the Christian and the Jewish faiths. In none of these, however, are all the appropriate verses of the Bible and the explanations of the Talmud used so cleverly and with such scholarship for a definite goal as by the author of this work. One sees at every step that he has to do with a profound thinker and an extraordinary student of the Talmud.[88]

De Modena adds that he decided to reply to Abner's arguments in a special work. The promised work, however, was never written and later, when he himself declared war against the Talmud and the rabbis, he in fact relied on the arguments of "Rabbi Abner."[89]

Unfortunately we lack the essential information which might disclose to us in all details the psychologically very interesting process whereby such a prominent rabbi and preacher was transformed into a bitter enemy of the Talmud and rabbinic Judaism. In his autobiography he is completely silent on this very important matter—out of what motives, we shall later see. The hatred of a religious teacher for the cult whose official representative he is

87. De Modena does not mention the title of the polemic work but there is no doubt that Abner's *Minḥat Kenaot* is here meant.
88. *Beḥinat Ha-Dat*, xiii–xiv.
89. *Kol Sachal*, 51.

that we observe here reminds one forcefully of another religious teacher, also a child of the seventeenth century, the French priest Jean Meslier, the author of the famous *Testament*. This quiet village priest, who all his life faithfully observed everything he was obliged to do as an official servant of Christ and in his lifetime did not manifest the slightest heresy, left a written testament in which he pours out his bitter heart and discloses to the world his profound life's drama. With intense hatred, with contempt and scorn, he attacks the Church and Christianity. The simple village priest, who all his days was humbly subservient to the secular and spiritual powers, speaks here in such a sharp tone and expresses such heretical and "blasphemous" ideas as not a single one of the most militant enlighteners and freethinkers of the eighteenth century permitted himself. For the fact that in life he had not the courage to fight and, as a priest, was obliged publicly to sing prayers and praises to the God in whom he did not believe, he takes vengeance in his testament by spitting on the founder of the Christian faith and pelting him with such abusive words as are not to be found either in *Toledot Yeshu* or in any other anti-Christian tract. "I did not have the courage," writes Meslier, "to speak openly in life; let men therefore read the truth after my death." And with his own hand he wrote his *Testament* in three copies and hid one of them under the very chair of the village church where every Sunday he used to conduct services.

Leo de Modena was also not a fighter by nature. But he did not wish to reveal, even after death, his true face and openly express for future generations the truth he had attained. When he lists in his autobiography the compositions that he wrote,[90] he adds: "This at least is my great consolation—that despite death and my bitter fate, my name will never be erased among the Jewish people."[91] But he wished to remain in the memory of later generations as a scholar in Israel, not with the hated name of "heretic" and "troubler of Israel," like Hiwi Ha-Balchi or Elisha ben Abuyah. He therefore resolved to carry on his battle against rabbinic Judaism not openly, on his own account, but from a hiding place, disguised, with a mask on his face.

De Modena relates that in 1622 a friend supposedly came to him and informed him that there had come into his hands a manuscript which a bitter opponent of the Talmud had written in Alcalá one hundred and twenty years before. Since de Modena had acquired fame as an extraordinary polemicist with his *Magen Ve-*

90. *Ḥayyei Yehudah*, 42–52.
91. *Ibid.*, 42.

Tzinnah, his friend gave him the manuscript with the request that he write a reply to all the attacks of this heretic.

"After I became familiar with this manuscript," further relates de Modena, "I was convinced that these attacks were made with great skill, and one must therefore reflect on them for a long time in order to be able to answer and dispose of all the contradictions cited by such a powerful and experienced opponent." He then turns with an earnest face to the reader and writes: "You, too, acquaint yourself with all the arguments and reflect well upon them. He who can hear, let him hear; he who is deserving will understand."[92]

There can be no doubt that the whole story of the discovered manuscript is nothing more than pretense. Even the name of the heretic testifies that all this is merely a story. The author, relates de Modena, is called Amittai ben Yedaiah Ibn Raz. This name means "the true one, the son of the God-knower, the scion of the secret." The work is supposed to have been written in the year *heres* (1500), but the word *heres* has a definite meaning—"destruction." De Modena does not indicate the title of the work but he himself gives it the name *Kol Sachal* (The Voice of a Fool) and calls his reply *Shaagat Aryeh* (The Roar of a Lion). But de Modena's answer is also nothing but pretense; the whole of it consists of two rather small and colorless chapters. Ostensibly this is to be merely the beginning of a large work, but in the course of twenty-five years[93] de Modena did not manage to write the sequel and complete the work that had been begun. He devised this entire masquerade in order to blind the eyes of men, so that they should not be able to complain of him and so that others might think that he does not in fact agree with the theses of the heretic of Alcalá and even intends to write a sharp response and refute the latter's attacks. In these two chapters of *Shaagat Aryeh* de Modena puts on a pious mien, as if he were responsible to God for his soul, represents himself as a simple, godfearing man of faith who believes blindly in everything the sacred tradition demands and the rabbis ordain. But it is not difficult to see under this pious mask the crafty, scornful smile of the mystifier and freethinker.[94]

Kol Sachal is not only de Modena's most remarkable book but also occupies a special place in the entire old Hebrew literature. Just as the *Testament* of the Catholic priest Meslier, with its viru-

92. *Kol Sachal*, 5.
93. De Modena died on the twenty-sixth of Adar (March 21), 1648.
94. For a more detailed discussion, see Reggio in *Beḥinat Ha-Dat*, pp. 253–68.

lent hatred for the Church and its dogmas, does not have its analogue in all of Christian literature, so the work of the Italian rabbi of the seventeenth century is truly exceptional in all of Hebrew literature. Even the fiercest opponents of the rabbis, the Karaites, rarely allowed themselves to speak with such fierce anger and hatred of the bearers of the tradition and of the Oral Law as does Leo de Modena in the name of Amittai ben Yedaiah.[95]

See, angrily calls out Amittai, what our "sages" made of the Mosaic Torah, of the divine Law! In the Torah it is explicitly written, "All the things which I, the Lord, command you, you shall observe to do; you shall not add to them or diminish from them." But these, our teachers, our sages, have done precisely the opposite. They have surrounded the commandments of the Torah with new rules and all kinds of restrictions to such an extent that the divine law is literally no longer recognizable. And they even have the impudence to appeal to the authority of the tradition; they speak of *halachah le-Mosheh mi-Sinai* (laws of Moses from Sinai) and demand that the people blindly observe everything they command, even when they say of left that it is right and of right that it is left. The legend about the millennial chain of tradition from Moses to our times is something that never was, something that they, the rabbis, have fabricated. How can one speak of an uninterrupted chain of tradition, Amittai ben Yedaiah argues, when in the Bible itself it is related that after Joshua's death, in the generation of the Judges and Kings of Judah and Israel, the Torah was so thoroughly forgotten that when, in the days of Hezekiah, a Torah scroll was found in the sanctuary, this was great news both for the king and for the priests? The same thing happened again in the Babylonian exile, and at the time of the building of the Second Temple Ezra the Scribe revealed the Torah of Moses anew.[96] I have, God forbid, no doubt—Amittai adds with, as it were, a hidden smile—that Ezra did not change even a single letter in the Torah and that all his explanations and ordinances are indeed correct and agree perfectly with the meaning of the Torah; nevertheless we are entitled to say that we have really received the Torah from Ezra the Scribe and not from Moses. And how can we be such fools as to believe our sages, who lived many generations after Ezra, that all the heaps upon heaps of customs and laws which they, the rabbis, introduced—even the ordinance that Jews

---

95. That Amittai ben Yedaiah is only the voice of de Modena himself was conclusively demonstrated by Reggio, Geiger, and Libowitz. Halevi's counterarguments are not convincing.
96. *Kol Sachal*, 24.

on Friday evening must eat garlic as a charm for bearing children—were transmitted from him by way of tradition?[97]

"We know very well," Amittai argues further,

that just after the times of Ezra various sects multiplied among the
Jews—Sadducees, Pharisees, Boethusians, etc. All these carried on intense controversies among themselves about the meaning of the Torah.
Each sect made its own ordinances and refused to recognize the ordinances of the others. This alone shows best that there was no solid,
universally recognized tradition. If a certain manner of putting on
the *tefillin* were really a "law of Moses from Sinai," an ordinance
resting on the sanctified chain of tradition, how would controversies
about it be possible? Who would undertake to fight against this ordinance and refuse to recognize it?

Only after the destruction of the Second Temple did our "sages"
show what they could do. In reality, with the destruction of the Temple and the loss of its land by the Jewish people, many commandments
and precepts became null and void. The teachers of the people should
have adapted the Torah to the new circumstances prevailing in the
exile. They should have lightened the yoke of the punctilious commandments for the miserable exiles, with their difficult situation in
the land of their enemies and oppressors, so that it would not hinder
them in their struggle to live nor arouse any hatred in the surrounding
populace. But our leaders did just the opposite. All the strict regulations
which the Pharisees ordained particularly for the pietists who wished
to separate themselves from the world they enlarged even more fear-
fully and cast upon all the people. They endlessly multiplied their
prohibitions and commands, which press like a heavy burden on every
individual, embitter and grieve his life, and make the whole people
a mockery and a scorn. All this they did with a definite purpose:
to rule over the people, so that the people might be completely dependent upon them, so that they might not be able to take a single
step without them, the scholars and lawgivers.[98]

This idea—that the sages of the Talmud and the rabbis of later
generations did not intend any "heavenly" purposes with their
ordinances and regulations but simply exploited them as a means
of increasing their power over the masses of the people—dominates
the entire *Kol Sachal*. Over and over again we encounter in it
such expressions as "to play the ruler over the congregation," "they
seize dominion over the multitude," "to increase the minutiae of
the laws in order to rule," "to consume the wealth of Israel and
to grieve their lives," etc., etc.

With his strictly rationalist outlook, which measured everything

97. *Ibid.*
98. *Ibid.*, 25–26.

with the commonplace yardstick of sober sense, de Modena was not able properly to appreciate the significance of the role of the Oral Law and its historical development. Blinded by hatred and anger, he saw in the history of the unfolding of rabbinic Judaism merely the malevolence of narrow-minded and small-hearted people who avidly pursued power and whose entire thought was only to embitter the lives of others as much as possible. Hatred blinds, and de Modena's historical perspective became so vague that he frequently charged the sages of the Talmud with responsibility for ordinances that originated only in much later generations.

Even after the close of the Mishnah, when the Oral Law also became a written law, Amittai ben Yedaiah complains, the sages were still not content and continued to create new hedges and ordinances. In order to rule over the people, the leaders endeavored to show that the laws of the Mishnah also require commentaries and explanations. They created new mountains of laws and prohibitions, they surrounded all of life with their cobwebs, so that the people should be totally dependent on them, with their verdicts and decisions. In this way the great tower called the Babylonian Talmud was constructed. But the creators of the Talmud lived in a very ignorant country with a very narrow outlook, and so they measured the breadth of the world, the heavenly distances, indeed everything, with their petty yardstick and narrow-gauged view. Is it surprising, then, that the tower they built is so strangely crude, so truly chaotic? They themselves, the creators, had to admit that with regard to the Babylonian Talmud, the Biblical expression "He hath made me to dwell in dark places" is most appropriate.[99]

The author of *Kol Sachal* speaks with particular anger and contempt of the narrative, non-legal part of the Talmud. This unique world of imaginative legends and wondrous tales is, after all, exceedingly inconsistent with practical common sense. And so de Modena fights against this world mercilessly and pelts it with arrows of mockery and scorn. Instead of clear precepts, cries Amittai, they gave us whole mountains of overly pointed hairsplitting and thick nets of cobwebs. Instead of true wisdom, science and philosophy, they gave us Aggadah and Midrash which swarm with ignorance and foolishness and are full of wild exaggerations, lascivious talk, and foolish notions about God and the world. Only here and there does one encounter useful ethical maxims which teach good qualities and proper conduct. And all this they call the "sacred tradition"!

99. *Ibid.*, 31.

These sages of the Talmud served as the pattern for the later scholars—for the Geonim, the Tosafists, the codifiers and the legal decisors. Just as the Amoraim obscured the Mishnah, these did likewise in regard to the Talmud. In vain, laments Amittai ben Yedaiah, did the great genius, the light of Israel, Rabbi Moses ben Maimon, endeavor to spread light in the pitch-darkness and with his *Mishneh Torah* to bring order into the fearful chaos and change the *Talmud Bilbuli* (Talmud of confusion) into the *Talmud Aruch* (Talmud of order). After him in later generations came all kinds of decisors and codifiers and "uprooters of mountains" by the thousands. They began to "improve" Maimonides, to add new precepts, and to declare the most insignificant custom "law from Sinai." Only so could they display their sharpness, for all other wisdoms are alien to them, philosophy and the natural sciences are beyond their understanding.

"What harm do all these customs and hedges really do?" stubborn fools will ask.[100] "The harm is tremendously great," Amittai exclaims.

It is a question here not only of the fact that our sages distorted the content of the Torah and obscured with their innumerable laws the consciousness of the people, so that no one of the multitude can now distinguish the important from the secondary, and when he violates some of the most foolish customs thinks that his sin against God is just as great as if he had denied the root principle and cast away the major precepts of the Torah. These sages of ours, with their hedges, ordinances, and laws, are the ones who have brought it about that the Jewish nation is so degraded in the lands of exile. They should have simplified the commandments and laws of the Torah in exile; they should have remembered the golden words of the Torah, "For this word is very nigh unto thee, in thy mouth and in thy heart, that thou mayest do it." Light is the yoke and easy it is to observe it, for the chief thing is the heart, not the minutiae of the commandments, but knowing God, loving Him, and following His ways. If our sages had understood this, they would have known that in exile the yoke of the Torah must be made lighter, not heavier, and we should long ago have lived to see the glorious hope of "the end of days," and the time of the advent of the Messiah and the redemption of Israel would have come. For the most powerful peoples of that time[101] were then seeking the true faith, and they would have found among us the Torah of Moses in its pure form and not have had to accept it in its falsified and distorted form.[102] They would have united with it, and all would have become one people—the *Jewish* people.

100. *Ibid.*, 32.
101. The time of the destruction of the Temple.
102. I.e., the form of Christianity.

David's throne in Jerusalem would have been firmly established, the sanctuary would have glistened in all its splendor, and God's grace and radiance would have shone over all of us. But our sages with their restrictions and ordinances made us a mockery and a scorn. They made our faith despicable in the eyes of all peoples, who treat us like slaves, and every day our shame and degradation grow greater.[103]

The author of *Kol Sachal* cannot forgive the sages of the Talmud for having ordained that the commandment of circumcision is obligatory on a prospective proselyte and that without it he cannot become a Jew. This is of the "commandments of Sodom," he declares with great indignation. If they had instituted the rule that only the newborn children of proselytes must be circumcised and the proselytes themselves need only go through ritual immersion in water, then many peoples and kingdoms would have joined themselves to us. They would have accepted our faith, and our redemption would long since have come. "Ah, woe to us," he cries out with feeling, "how many troubles, how many afflictions did our people have to endure throughout the generations—all because our sages, out of great foolishness and ignorance, always devised new laws which the Torah did not command!"[104]

"Certainly these sages of ours are justified," the author of *Kol Sachal* remarks with bitter irony, "in always calling themselves the 'pillars of the exile.' They are, indeed, the foundation and keystone of the exile, and it is because of them that we languish in it and still see no end."[105]

After battling in the first two parts of *Kol Sachal* against the Oral Law in general and the Talmud in particular, Amittai ben Yedaiah moves in the third and last part to particular laws and commandments and attempts to show how many of these are completely inconsistent with the plain meaning of the Torah and are nothing more than stupidity and foolish notions of "old women and children." But, he adds, they were ordained so that their creators might, with their aid, rule over the people. Our author finds numerous ordinances in regard to Sabbath-keeping,[106] the prohibition against leaven on Passover,[107] the laws of ritual slaughter and examination of animals,[108] of marriage,[109] and of milk and

103. *Kol Sachal*, 33.
104. *Ibid.*, 56.
105. *Ibid.*, 59.
106. *Ibid.*, 44–46.
107. *Ibid.*, 47.
108. *Ibid.*, 52–53.
109. *Ibid.*, 63–64.

meat,[110] barbaric and foolish. Amittai also complains strongly of the fast days, and concludes that even on Yom Kippur one should fast only according to his powers, and that if one feels weak he is not obliged to fast at all.

This sharp critique is conducted by Amittai ben Yedaiah in an extremely enraged tone. In every word and outcry the breath of poisonous hatred and cold contempt is discernible. When the author mentions, for example, the prohibition against the wine of idolaters, he cries out angrily: "As far as possible they have always devised such things as are never referred to in God's Torah—and all this in order to make us more hated and contemptible in the eyes of the surrounding peoples!"[111] Even such an innocent ordinance on the part of the sages of the Talmud as that on Purim "joy is to be increased" is not allowed by the author of *Kol Sachal* to pass without caustic and ironic remarks. He even considers it possible to employ in his battle against the Talmud the poisoned arrows that he borrowed from such an intense Jew-hater and bitter opponent of Judaism as the apostate Abner of Burgos.[112]

Typical also is Amittai's attitude to the Jewish prayers. As a great lover of music, Leo de Modena was very desirous that worship in the synagogue be conducted with great solemnity and with the most beautiful musical instruments.[113] But convinced rationalist and battler for sober common sense that he was, he found alien the feeling of the moving prayers, the enthusiasm of the religious sentiment, the mystical tremor of the believing soul when it prays in its longing for God. De Modena's mouthpiece, Amittai ben Yedaiah, declares that the weekday prayers are too long. He proposes his own rather short ones to be said every day in the place of the established prayers of the *Siddur*. These new prayers, as well as those that were printed under de Modena's name in *Tefillot Yesharim* (published in Venice in 1622), are written in a clear and even in places rather lovely style, but they lack one thing, and that the most important—true fervor, the pathos of the believing soul.

In *Kol Sachal*, written in the first quarter of the seventeenth century, all the arguments and attacks on Talmudic and "*Shulhan Aruch*" Judaism that we find so widely much later among the

110. *Ibid.*, 54.
111. *Ibid.*, 55.
112. *Ibid.*, 51.
113. See de Modena's introduction to Salomone de Rossi's compositions (1615). De Modena wrote a special *responsum* on the question of music during the public synagogue service (see Libowitz, *Leo Modena*, pp. 96, 117).

reformers and enlighteners of the first half of the nineteenth century are already assembled. It is therefore no surprise that Samuel David Luzzatto, when he became familiar in 1846 with the manuscript of *Kol Sachal*, wrote to Z. Stern: "Have you seen *Shaagat Aryeh* with *Kol Sachal?* There is no doubt that *Kol Sachal* is also Leo de Modena's work. This rabbi hated the sages of the Mishnah and the Talmud much more than the Karaites, and was a significantly more radical reformer than Geiger—and this 220 years ago, and in Italy!"[114] When Isaac Samuel Reggio several years later, in 1852, published *Kol Sachal* with *Shaagat Aryeh*, he created a great sensation.[115] There were even some who expressed the conjecture that not de Modena but Reggio was the mystifier. It cannot be imagined, they argued, that a famous rabbi of the seventeenth century should have written such a heretical work, but this was done by the *maskil* Reggio, the author of *Ha-Torah Veha-Pilosofiah*, and, to blind people's eyes, he pretended that he found this work among de Modena's writings.[116]

At the end of *Kol Sachal*, the author addresses the following words to the reader:

You must not think that I succeeded in revealing completely the folly of these men who are called by us "sages." Everything that I have disclosed is merely a very small part, one in a thousand. This is no more than the first hammer blow to awaken man from the intellectual slumber in which our oppressors have placed him. Let man open his eyes and see how very backward our people are and who is responsible for this. Let him see and understand how greatly they have obscured and darkened the brilliance and radiant light of our divine Torah. I could not be silent at such a fearful crime, and I wrote this work even though I know very well that as soon as the rabbis and heads of the Talmudic academies learn of it they will make a great outcry. They will declare the author a heretic and apostate, cover him with curses and bans, and deafen the world with their cries. But—who knows?—perhaps my book will fall in the hands of a very unique person, of a man with a clear, proper understanding who is not infected with the universal disease of foolish ignorance and wild, barbarous pride. And if I succeed in helping this understanding person, this

114. *Iggerot Shadal* (Przemysl, 1882), p. 980.
115. *Kol Sachal* was twice translated into German, by D. Einhorn in 1856 and S. Stern in 1902 (*Der Kampf des Rabbiners gegen den Talmud im 17-Jahrhundert*). There is also an English translation (1871).
116. Reggio wrote in 1854: "I have learned that some German scholars accuse me of having invented the entire book *Kol Sachal*" (*Otzar Nehmad*, I, 127). For a discussion of the views expressed after the publication of *Kol Sachal* see Libowitz, *op. cit.*, Chapter 11.

one among thousands, I will not be disturbed by the tumult of the multitude of fools and ignoramuses.

In point of fact *Kol Sachal* could not fall into the hands of this very unique individual, of this "one among thousands," simply because de Modena did not have the courage to publish the work, even under a pseudonym. Lacking character and with a flabby will, de Modena was extremely fearful of the anger of the "multitude of fools and ignoramuses," and he did not have the moral courage to fight for the truth he had attained. De Modena himself relates frankly in his autobiography what a fright he had merely at the notion that he would have to give account for his freely expressed views. In 1616, at the suggestion of an English nobleman, he composed for the English king James I a special work in Italian in which are described in systematic form the Jewish customs connected with the cult and the religious way of life, *Historia dei riti hebraici, vita e osservanze degli Hebrei di questi tempi.* Because the work was designated for a Protestant and without any intention of printing it, de Modena did not consider it necessary to take account of the strict principles of the *Canon purificationis* and of the inquisitorial eye of the Catholic censor. Many years later, in 1635, de Modena's friend the French scholar Giacomo Gafarelli became interested in his *Riti.* He took the manuscript from him and promised that he would have it published in France. Gafarelli fulfilled his promise, and two years later de Modena's work appeared in print.[117] When de Modena became aware of this, he was beside himself with fear. When he leafed through the copy of his work that he had kept, he noticed that some passages might call forth displeasure on the part of the censor. "I sobbed and groaned," he relates,

I tore my beard and barely kept myself alive. I thought: As soon as they learn of my work in Rome, it may become a stumbling block

117. *Historia dei riti* went through numerous editions. It was also translated into various languages—English (1650, 1707, and 1753), French (by the well-known scholar Richard Simon, 1671, 1681, and 1710), Dutch (1683), and Latin (1693). In 1863 Solomon Rubin translated Modena's work into Hebrew under the title *Shulḥan Aruch* with Jellinek's comments. On other works of de Modena in Italian see Steinschneider, *Die italienische Literatur der Juden* (*MGWJ*, 1899, pp. 311–16). De Modena's projected translation of the Bible into Italian could not be executed because it was forbidden by the Catholic censorship. De Modena only published (1612) a Hebrew-Italian dictionary (*Galut Yehudah: Novo Dittionario Hebraico e Italiano*) in which the difficult words of the Bible are explained.

for all Israel . . . and especially for myself. I did not know where to turn, for it was impossible for me to flee either to Ferrara or to another Italian city. I imagined the danger much greater than it was . . . I nearly lost my mind out of fear and grief.[118]

De Modena promptly went to the Inquisition and declared that this work had appeared without his knowledge and not under his redaction. But it became apparent that all his fears were in vain. Gafarelli himself had been sufficiently cautious and eliminated all the passages which might arouse suspicion among the censors. But de Modena was not satisfied with this, and when he reprinted his work two years later (Venice, 1639), he threw out many other passages which, in his view, might be offensive to the Christian reader.

In this remarkable man "two souls" struggled with each other. He did not have the courage to publish Kol Sachal, but he also could not be silent. He could not allow his hated opponent rest and craftily thought of a new attack from a hidden corner, so that the enemy might not notice. Soon after Kol Sachal was completed, de Modena undertook a new work with which he acquired a great reputation and obtained many admirers. This work is called Bet Yehudah.[119]

At the end of the fifteenth century, one of the exiles of Spain, Jacob Ibn Ḥabib, after settling in Salonika, had assembled all the stories and legends of the Talmud and published them in a separate volume entitled Ein Yaakov. This quickly became one of the most beloved of popular books.[120] The work incidentally also became the most essential handbook for all preachers, who would utilize the aggadot gathered in it to ornament their sermons. Ein Yaakov was therefore much loved by Leo de Modena as well. We have observed that de Modena was a brilliant preacher. Already in his youth he was extremely successful with his sermons, not only among Jews but among Christians as well. He had a reputation as one of the most gifted preachers of his time, and it happened not infrequently that on the same day he had to give talks in several synagogues, one after the other.[121] The most eminent representatives of the Venetian republic came to hear the talented preacher.

118. Hayyei Yehudah, 56–57.
119. Bet Yehudah was completed in 1625 and was to have been published the same year. However, because of various obstacles, the work was first printed in 1635 (see the introduction to Bet Yehudah and Bet Leḥem Yehudah; see also Hayyei Yehudah, 52).
120. For more about this matter, see infra.
121. While de Modena wrote hundreds of sermons, he published only twenty-two in his Midbar Yehudah, 1602.

One of his sermons was even attended by the French king's brother.[122] Following the custom of that time, de Modena would quite frequently adorn his sermons with Talmudic legends and parables, and in this connection Jacob Ibn Ḥabib's collection was very useful to him.[123] In 1625, de Modena published a special "key" to *Ein Yaakov* under the title *Bet Leḥem Yehudah*. This was a kind of index in which all the sources for each individual *aggadah* or story are noted. It then occurred to de Modena to write a second work, *Bet Yehudah*, in which he would be able to sneak in his critical attacks on the Talmud and the Oral Law in general under a disguise. In his *Ein Yaakov* Ibn Ḥabib had not included those legends and parables which, because of their exaggerated forms or overly sharp expressions, could be falsely understood by the simple reader. All these passages omitted by Ibn Ḥabib were gathered by de Modena with the definite intention of presenting the sages of the Talmud in an unfavorable light. In order to make the impression even stronger, de Modena deliberately went beyond the bounds that Ibn Ḥabib had set himself and brought into *Bet Yehudah*, besides *aggadot*, certain laws and rules as well. "Even though they do not fit the place and do not belong to the subject matter," de Modena defends himself, "they may be useful to the reader."[124]

De Modena in *Shaagat Aryeh* gives the ostensible author of *Kol Sachal* the name *ha-hores*, "the destroyer," but in his *Bet Yehudah* he calls himself *ha-boneh*, "the builder."[125] But he was a very peculiar kind of "builder," and precisely in the most important questions is very frequently in agreement with the "destroyer."

When de Modena quotes the well-known statement of Rabbi Johanan that "a prophet is not permitted to add anything new to the Torah of Moses," the "builder" immediately explains: " 'The Law of the Lord is perfect'—this means that God's Torah is harmoniously complete, and that which is perfect must neither be diminished nor increased. . . . And if this is forbidden even to a prophet, then certainly a common mortal may not make any change in the Torah."[126] But all this, de Modena adds with caustic

---

122. *Ḥayyei Yehudah*, 46, 47, 58.
123. It must be borne in mind that because of the intense persecutions of the Talmud on the part of the Inquisition not a single printed copy of the Talmud was obtainable in de Modena's times in all of Italy (see his *Riti*, I, 14; II, 2, 5).
124. The introduction to *Bet Yehudah*.
125. All the explanations of the legends of *Bet Yehudah* are begun by de Modena with the words: "The builder says."
126. *Bet Yehudah*, I, 28a (we quote according to the first Venice edition of 1635).

irony, was in vain. Of what avail was it that the author of the Torah or the lawgiver took pains to speak, in regard to their commandments, in a clear and understandable language so that their precepts should be precisely fulfilled, if there are men who do not wish to understand and fulfill? They will always find ways of perverting the plain meaning and doing the exact opposite. So it was with the Karaites and with all the others "who interpret the Torah in an improper way."[127]

The "builder" of *Bet Yehudah* is also in agreement with the "destroyer" of *Kol Sachal* in regard to the statutory daily prayers. "Because the Jewish people lives in exile under extremely difficult circumstances," we read in *Bet Yehudah*, "we ought to be content with very short prayers."[128] The author of *Bet Yehudah* also holds the same view as the author of *Kol Sachal* in regard to the fast days[129] and the commandment of circumcision for proselytes.[130] De Modena deliberately interjects a quotation from the Gemara to show that in Palestine, when there was occasion to conclude a bill of sale, it did not matter if one signed it at the time of the act, even if this happened to be on the Sabbath day.[131] He endeavors to show that numerous ordinances that the sages introduced were suited to a certain moment and to definite circumstances and will therefore, in time, become null and void.[132] It would certainly be well, de Modena adds, if contemporary scholars would listen to these words. "Pay close attention," he insists in another passage. "Some of our sages," he further notes, "often had occasion to speak only with hints and allusions, so that it would not be easy for the ordinary people to understand the true meaning."[133] And de Modena himself also frequently speaks in *Bet Yehudah* only with hints and allusions. In all these one and the same basic motif is heard: indignation and hatred for the sages of the Talmud. He relates with a foolish mien and a hidden smile that only those were admitted as members of the Sanhedrin who, with their keenness and overly pointed hairsplitting, could show that day is night and that unclean is clean. Further on he remarks incidentally that "the disciples of the wise" very frequently permit themselves such things as they strictly forbid the common multi-

---

127. *Ibid.*, II, 6a. For passages quite congruent, see *Kol Sachal*, 21, 22, 28, 29, 52, 53, 54, 55, and 64.
128. *Ibid.*, I, 5a.
129. *Ibid.*, 15b.
130. *Ibid.*, 17a.
131. *Ibid.*, II, 17.
132. *Ibid.*, I, 10a; cf. *ibid.*, 19a (*Eruvin*, 56).
133. *Ibid.*, 19a.

tude.[134] He utilizes every suitable and unsuitable occasion to point out that the Talmudic sages were stirrers up of conflict and pursuers of wealth, and that the honored position of High Priest used to be sold for money.[135] Even the thought expressed by the author of *Kol Sachal* that the country in which the Babylonian Talmud was created was an ignorant and foolish corner of the world, or his anger at the Talmudic sages for their ordinance that on Purim "one should increase joy," are met again in the comments of the "builder." In *Bet Yehudah* appears very clearly the definite tendency to represent the Talmudic sages on the ridiculous side and to show how "unwise" and superstitious they were. The "builder" deliberately emphasizes all the passeges in the Talmud in which old wives' tales, superstitions, incantations, spirits and demons—in short, everything that is inconsistent with "sound common sense"—are discussed.[136] The naive Talmudic legend to the effect that when the prophetess Miriam was leprous, God Himself served her as priest is also not passed by the rationalist de Modena without his sarcastic smile.[137] He deliberately quotes a Talmudic legend which Jacob Ibn Ḥabib had not omitted and which is found in *Ein Yaakov,* only so that the "builder" might be able to make the following ironic remark:

Now see how great is the reward for observing the commandment of *mezuzah* [affixing a small box containing Biblical passages to the door-post of a house]. . . . It can save a whole city and turn aside from it the decree of ruin and destruction which has been determined for its grievous sin of idolatry. Even such a sinful city and all its environs are forgiven everything for the merit of observing the commandment of *mezuzah.*[138]

In the year *Bet Yehudah* appeared, de Modena was requested by one of his pupils, David Finzi, to express his view on the belief in transmigration of souls which plays such a significant role among the Kabbalists. De Modena soon gave an answer in his work, *Ben David.*[139] "Know," he says to his pupil,

that if someone else had applied to me with this question, I would have tried to reply to him in generalities. I would have explained to him that in this matter I rely on the view of our scholars, our recognized authorities. You know that the world develops unquestion-

134. *Ibid.,* 26.
135. *Ibid.,* II, 1.
136. *Ibid.,* I, 35a; II, 3a and b, etc.
137. *Ibid.,* II, 38, at the end of the tractate *Zevaḥim.*
138. *Ibid.,* 32a.
139. Published in 1855 in *Taam Zekenim,* 61–64.

ing faith in what has long been accepted, and whoever has the presumption to express his own view and not blindly drag himself along the old way trodden by all is at once attacked by everyone and declared either crazy or heretical. But I will not fool you, my pupil, who are as precious to me as my own son; to you I will reveal my thoughts.

Then he proceeds sharply to criticize the idea of transmigration of souls and to show that it derives from alien sources, from the nations of the world.

But *Ben David* was only a prelude to the struggle which the rationalist de Modena undertook against his despised enemy, the Kabbalah. Already in *Kol Sachal*, Amittai ben Yedaiah remarks that the Kabbalah calls itself "the true wisdom" in a euphemistic sense, for it is the complete antithesis of truth. To this he immediately adds, "and elsewhere I have already spoken at length about this Kabbalah."[140] De Modena did in fact write a special work on the Kabbalah, but he wrote it many years later, at the end of 1638. We have noted earlier how successfully, at the end of the sixteenth century, the new mystical tendencies which had blossomed on the banks of the Jordan and the Sea of Galilee spread in Italy. De Modena's relative and good friend, the previously mentioned Azariah da Fano, was the "chief of the Kabbalists in the lands of the west." With Israel Saruk, Rabbi Isaac Luria's disciple and faithful emissary, de Modena frequently carried on debates.[141] The Kabbalist books, which, thanks to the printing press, were then accessible to all, confused the minds of the common reading public, which was ill prepared for them. One of the contemporary scholars, Rabbi Moses Isserles, who was himself favorably disposed to the Kabbalah, strongly complains of this. "Many also of the multitude," he laments,

have taken to the Kabbalah. The newest Kabbalist books, which explain and popularize the ideas of the men of the secret wisdom, are read with special diligence, especially at the present time when such works as the *Zohar*, the writings of Recanati, *Shaarei Orah*, etc., are printed and available to everyone. All read these works and everyone thinks that everything in them is clear and understandable, but in truth the correct meaning is hidden from them. Even plain householders, ignoramuses who understand nothing, read these books. They are not able to understand a chapter of the Pentateuch with Rashi, and they undertake to study the Kabbalah![142]

140. *Kol Sachal*, 31–32.
141. *Ari Nohem* (1840), 35, 70.
142. *Torat Ha-Olah*, III, Chapter 4.

As in earlier generations the rationalist ideas of Aristotle and
Maimonides had become a thing of fashion, so the Kabbalah became in the period in question. From the isolated chamber of the
thinker, it passed into the open marketplace. There were fervent
adherents of the Kabbalah who looked with contempt on those
who did not penetrate into the secret wisdom. Arrogantly they declared that he who does not enter into the mysteries of the Kabbalah will have to grope in the darkness forever, and that he who
does not believe in the *sefirot* is a heretic and a denier.[143]

All this of necessity strongly offended such a thoroughgoing
rationalist as Leo de Modena. But he did not dare publicly attack
a doctrine which enlisted so many convinced followers and admirers. Only in his old age, as a man of sixty-eight, did he write
his famous work against the Kabbalah, *Ari Nohem*, in which his
polemic talent is manifested in all its brilliance.[144] Since a number
of respected authorities had already issued forth against the Kabbalah in earlier generations, de Modena now did not consider it
necessary to make any pretense and wrote *Ari Nohem* under his
own name.[145]

"People always speak," says de Modena,

about the "wisdom of the Kabbalah." How can one pair two words
of which one is the complete antithesis of the other? This can only
cause the greatest confusion. Every wisdom and science, after all, rests
on its own investigations. It controls its assumptions, and obtains its
truths through searching and investigation. The Kabbalah, however,
rests not on scientific arguments but on the authority of the tradition.[146]

In the so-called wisdom of the Kabbalah there is in fact neither
wisdom nor tradition. It is not wisdom because its assumptions
do not rest on any scientific foundations and know of no logical
rules. But it is also not true tradition because it does not rely on
the heritage of the fathers, on ideas and conclusions that have
passed over as a legacy from generation to generation. The whole
doctrine of the "hidden wisdom" is, after all, relatively recent.
Its proponents themselves cannot deny this. Indeed, for this reason,

143. *Ari Nohem*, 1–2.
144. De Modena did not have the courage to publish his sharply polemical
work in his lifetime. It remained in manuscript and was first published
in modern times by J. Fürst (1840). Many copies of the edition
were burned by pious adherents of the "true wisdom," and *Ari Nohem*
became a bibliographical rarity. Only in recent times (1930) did de
Modena's work appear in a new edition.
145. *Ari Nohem* was also written by de Modena for a pupil of his, Joseph
Ḥalif, an ardent adherent of the Kabbalah.
146. *Ari Nohem*, 10.

they are not in agreement with each other and diverge in the most important questions. This, naturally, would be absolutely impossible if they really based themselves on the tradition hallowed by the chain of generations. To be sure, they always rely on works which were presumably written in ancient times. The *Sefer Yetzirah* is supposed to derive from the patriarch Abraham, the *Sefer Ha-Bahir* from Rabbi Neḥunya ben Ha-Kanah, and the holy *Zohar* is supposed to have been written by Rabbi Simeon ben Yoḥai. All this, cries de Modena, is vanity and falsehood, fabricated old wives' tales! To be sure, de Modena has too fine a literary taste not to admit that in the *Zohar* there are some brilliant passages[147] but, with the aid of a historical-critical analysis, he attempts to show that the *Zohar* was written not in the time of the Tannaim but much later, no earlier than the thirteenth century.[148] "The followers of the 'wisdom of the Kabbalah,'" de Modena further says,

see in combinations of letters and in all kinds of *notarikon* tremendous mysteries, and believe that a wondrous power is hidden in amulets and incantations. But this means simply to mock man's understanding, his common sense. To fancy that by combinations of letters and twisting various names one can perform miracles that are beyond nature is either madness or the greatest folly.[149]

And such persons still have the presumption to speak of "the true wisdom." They dare to declare men of eminence, great Jewish scholars, heretics and ignoramuses merely because these do not wish to believe in their "true wisdom."

The "wisdom of the Kabbalah," de Modena further says, is not only void of both wisdom and tradition; it is actually a stumbling block for the whole people of Israel, because its doctrine of the ten *sefirot* undermines the foundation of their faith—the unity of God. The "true wisdom" plants anthropomorphic concepts of God in the people's minds, and it is not without reason that all the apostates and Christian mystics are so intensely interested in the Kabbalah.[150]

147. *Ibid.,* 48.
148. *Ibid.,* Chapters 17–18.
149. *Ibid.,* 62.
150. *Ibid.,* 7, 79. Several years before his death (in 1645) de Modena also composed a special polemic work against Christianity entitled *Magen Va-Ḥerev* (a few fragments of the work were published by A. Geiger together with *Magen Ve-Tzinnah*). While the heretical priest Malia regards the founder of Christianity with contempt and hatred, the Jewish freethinker, de Modena, speaks of Jesus as a person with great respect. See also the memoirs of de Modena's pupil, the apostate Giulio Morosinis, in the Berliner *Festschrift,* 340.

To be sure, de Modena points out, the Kabbalists themselves admit that there is a definite relationship between the basic ideas of their books and Plato's ideas. But they explain this through the old legend that Plato was for a time a pupil of the prophet Jeremiah, and Aristotle a pupil of Simon the Just. But how can one believe in such ridiculous foolishness? They themselves glory in the claim that the Kabbalah is a "hidden wisdom" and that even many Jewish scholars were not privileged to have its marvelous secrets revealed to them; and here all the secrets have been disclosed to strangers who even denied the unity of God. They were considered worthy to be the bearers and preachers of the holy wisdom.[151] The point, however, de Modena concludes, is that it is not they who benefited from us but we from them—and this not in the times of Jeremiah but much later, only subsequent to the generation of Maimonides. Only after the mystical doctrine of the Kabbalah had developed under the influence of Plato's ideas and those of other thinkers, de Modena asserts, was the *Zohar* produced and the tale that it derives from Rabbi Simeon ben Yoḥai fabricated.

In his "testament" de Modena insists that he was not a hypocrite or two-faced.[152] But his true form and real face were seen neither by his own generation nor by later generations, for de Modena himself did not exhibit them. A man without character, without moral power or the will to fight, he deliberately hid his real countenance. He either concealed his free thoughts and critical explanations in allusions or locked them up in manuscripts which were not published for centuries. Apparently de Modena understood this very well and himself expressed it in the epitaph he composed for his own tombstone:

> Here on the field, a plot of four cubits,
> Which were determined by God Himself,
> For Jehudah Aryeh, born in Modena.
> Here he lies buried, hidden and lost.

151. *Ari Noḥem,* 44.
152. *Ḥayyei Yehudah,* 69.

CHAPTER SIX

Joseph Solomon Delmedigo

OSEPH Solomon Delmedigo,[1] Leo de Modena's younger contemporary, who is better known as Yashar (Yosef Shelomoh Rofe) of Candia (or Crete), also sought to remain "hidden and lost" to his generation. His father Elijah, who was a great-grandson of the author of *Behinat Ha-Dat* and served as chief rabbi of the island of Crete, gave his son a well-rounded education. As a child Joseph Solomon learned Italian and Spanish, as well as Latin and Greek, and at the age of fifteen was accepted at the University of Padua. His rich natural endowments, immense diligence, and strong thirst for knowledge helped make him, by the time he was twenty, a student of all of the many-sided knowledge of his time. A respected physician, Delmedigo was also a significant mathematician and astronomer. He studied these sciences under the famous Galileo,[2] who also familiarized him with the new system of the great Copernicus.

When Joseph Delmedigo was studying in Padua, he used to travel frequently to Venice and there visit Leo de Modena, who had a large influence on the world outlook of the young, knowledge-hungry student.[3] In 1613 Delmedigo returned to his home, where he very diligently continued his studies, spending day and night in scientific labors. The son of a wealthy family, he did not

---

1. The genealogy of Delmedigo's family is given in the letter of Moses Metz in *Elim*, 29. Here it is also noted that Delmedigo was born on June 16, 1591.
2. See *Mayan Gannim*, 148, where Delmedigo speaks of Galileo as of his teacher.
3. See Modena's *haskamah* (approbation) to *Elim*.

have to worry about earning a livelihood and was even in a position to spend a great deal of money on books and manuscripts. He proudly declares that there is no worthwhile book required for his work that is not in his library.[4] Sitting under the roof of his father's house, Delmedigo conceived a scientific work of encyclopedic compass to be entitled *Yaar Ha-Levanon*, but he was not destined to complete it, for he soon had to leave his home. The young man would often give utterance to his liberal ideas in regard to religious matters,[5] and this brought him into controversies with the orthodox environment in which he lived. The upshot of the matter was that in 1616 he had to take the wanderer's staff in hand and leave his native city. From then on he led a wandering life all his days. First he went to the major Moslem centers of culture, Cairo and Constantinople, to which he was attracted by the treasures of their libraries.[6] In Cairo he soon acquired fame with the triumph he scored in a public debate with the famous Moslem professor of mathematics Ali Ibn Rahmadan.[7] This made a name for him in Arabic circles. He also entered into close relationships with the local Karaites, since among them he could, as a stranger, express his thoughts more freely than in the rabbinic circles. He became especially friendly with the *hacham* of the community, the learned mathematician Jacob the Alexandrian, at whose request he composed a work on mechanics, *Niflaot Adonai*.[8] Coming to Constantinople, he became acquainted with the cultured Karaite Moses Mezordi.[9] But Delmedigo could not long remain in one place. New countries always attracted him. Through Wallachia and Moldavia he went to Poland and Lithuania, where he engaged in the practice of medicine. For a short time he was court physician to Prince Radziwill.

The very inferior cultural condition of the populace made a great impression on the encyclopedically learned foreigner. Interesting in this respect is Delmedigo's letter to his pupil Samuel Ashkenazi, in which he describes how he spent his time in Lithuania and Poland:

4. See the introduction to *Novelot Hochmah* and also *Melo Chofnajim*, where Delmedigo indicates that his library consisted of seven thousand volumes.
5. See *Elim*, 30, 62 (we quote according to the first edition).
6. In his letter to the Karaite Zerah (*Melo Chofnajim*, 18, 23) Delmedigo notes: "He who wishes to see precious manuscripts should go to Constantinople, a father and mother in scholarship."
7. For a discussion of this incident, so interesting from a cultural-historical point of view, see *Mayan Gannim*, 41; *Elim*, 16, 42–50.
8. See *Mayan Gannim*, 4 ,165; *Mayan Hatum*, 23.
9. *Melo Chofnajim*, 18.

I have here not a single minute of rest. Day and night I constantly travel around outside the city to visit my patients, for the local princes and nobles do not live in the city but in their castles and palaces. I spend all my time in a carriage travelling over forests and fields, alone with the servants of the nobility, and there is no one with whom to speak a word, for the common folk here are terribly ignorant and benighted. They are literally like dumb beasts, truly a people like unto an ass.[10]

An even greater impression was made on Joseph Delmedigo by the cultural situation of the Polish-Lithuanian Jews. Everything seemed to him strange and crude. "Pitch blackness," he laments,

covers the earth, and the ignorance is fearful. Despite the fact that the whole land is filled with Talmudic academies and houses of study, even the study of Talmud is extremely backward, for all the thousands of people who hasten to the academies and beat on the doors of the Torah and *halachah* have in mind only physical matters, purely material purposes: livelihood, honor, pride, and other extraneous motives. Men are interested only in careers—to become rabbi, judge, rector of an academy, or head of a community. This plague has infested everything. The highest and most important has become secondary, merely a means for petty goals and little desires. . . . They waste the best times riding around to the fairs.[11] Of secular wisdoms, they have no concept whatsoever. Every science is hateful to them. God, they say, needs no grammar, no rhetoric, no mathematics or astronomy, no logic, and certainly no philosophy. All these secular sciences were devised by the peoples of the world. One must flee from them, for they may—God forbid—lead one away from the right path.[12]

For this reason Delmedigo preferred, in Lithuania, as he had earlier in the lands of the east, to make acquaintance with the local Karaites rather than with the rabbinic scholars. "There," he relates,

I occupied myself much with secular sciences, especially when I would study with the Karaites who, as soon as they came to know me, became my best friends. They are greatly interested in external wisdoms and, indeed, it was at their request that I wrote my scientific works—not for our rabbis and Talmudic scholars, for I know very well that the latter are interested only in the Talmud and its commentaries.[13]

10. Introduction to *Novelot Ḥochmah.*
11. Here there is certainly a reference to the assemblies of the *Vaad Arba Ha-Aratzot.* The role and significance of the *Vaad* for the autonomous government of the Jewish community in Poland and Lithuania apparently remained completely unfamiliar to Delmedigo who came from a distant country.
12. *Mayan Gannim,* 3.
13. Introduction to *Novelot Ḥochmah.*

"And this they do very reasonably," he adds ironically;

this is, after all, their bread. They live only from the fact that they attain to the rabbinate or become rabbinic judges. Their learning, their scholarship in the Talmud and codes, consists of those things "the interest of which a man enjoys in this world and the principal of which remains for the world to come." The secular sciences can in no way be compared to these. They, after all, bring so little to the body, and for the soul they are certainly harmful; as is known, they lead one off the right path. Hence, whoever holds his soul dear must remove himself from these secular sciences, for they are contrary to the true Jewish nature. Let a Jew have even a hundred sons and he will certainly desire that all of them be great Torah scholars, for God does not need all the philosophical academies with their dialectical methods following the laws of logic. Beloved to Him is only the *pilpul* [dialectic] of the Talmud. His greatest pleasure is in subtle distinctions, and the whole world is sustained only by the breath[14] of the pilpulists. God does not need rhetoricians, ingenious preachers or orators. He is pleased only by the Biblical expositors who were raised on *aggadot* and *midrashim*. And all the people come into God's house to hear their instruction, to learn how one must be pious and serve God and praise His beloved name.[15]

This quotation is very characteristic of Delmedigo's style and manner of writing. The historian Heinrich Graetz portrays Delmedigo as a man "in whom opposing ideological currents were paired." And S. Dubnow writes, "His many-sided encyclopedic education did not give him any clear world outlook and firm convictions. On the contrary, his great knowledge only mixed up his mind. All his life he confused science and tradition, philosophy and the Kabbalah, and would contradict himself at every step."[16]

Whoever has taken the trouble carefully to study Delmedigo's work knows how inaccurate such a characterization is. This talented disciple of Galileo was the first Jewish scholar who had a clear grasp of what a tremendous revolution had been effected by the brilliant discoveries of Copernicus and Kepler, not only in the realm of astronomy but in all of man's understanding of

14. "For the world exists only through their breath (*be-hevleihem*)." This is an untranslatable play on words. *Be-hevleihem* may mean the breath of the scholars when they carry on their pilpulistic discussions but it may also mean "follies" (from the Hebrew word *hevel*).
15. Introduction to *Novelot Hochmah.*
16. *Weltgeschichte des jüdisches Volkes* (1908 edition), III, 63. A false picture, of a diametrically opposed nature, is given of Joseph Solomon Delmedigo by S. Bernstein in his *Hazon Ha-Dorot*, 1928. For a discussion of this, see our article in *Yevreyskaya Starina*, XII, 172–75.

the world. All of a sudden the whole ingenious structure of Aristotle's system with its teaching about the spheres and intelligences, at first blush so harmoniously constructed, fell apart like a house of cards. Suddenly all the attempts of the Jewish Aristotelians to make peace between the narratives of the Bible and Aristotelian conceptions, between the problem of the immortality of the soul and the "active intellect," and the belief in angels and seraphim associated with the doctrine of the conscious spheres, turned out to be absolutely unnecessary and childishly naive. Also childish and naive appeared the separation of heaven and earth, the stories about "heavenly" gates and foundations, when "heaven" and "earth" are in fact both equally small dots in the infinite space of the universe. An excellent mathematician and competent astronomer, Delmedigo was extremely skeptical of metaphysical theories and philosophical-speculative systems. He believed only in the positive natural sciences, in the strict demonstrations of experiment and proven facts. "All of these metaphysical, so-called divine sciences," declares Delmedigo's disciple Moses ben Meir of Metz in his name, "rest on very weak foundations. The doctrine of the spheres, of the matter which exists only in potentiality—all this is something that never was, a fabricated web. And yet what tremendous arguments were carried on about all this! How much energy was expended, how many pens broken and ink spilled!"[17]

The old question about the relationship between faith and knowledge is illuminated by Delmedigo from an entirely new perspective. He is firmly convinced that two separate and distinct truths are inconceivable. "If the faith is correct, it must not contradict truth," he declares.[18] But the attempt to make peace between faith and the philosophical systems and theories, which change so frequently, he points out, is an altogether superfluous thing.[19] "See," he adds, "how great was the error of the Jewish scholars who held so firmly to the doctrine of the 'spheres' and blindly believed in the conclusions and theories of a certain philosophical system. Most present-day scholars have rejected precisely what these men believed in so strongly and have acknowledged what they denied."[20]

Hence Delmedigo emphasizes with special sharpness "how great the distinction is between knowledge which relies on solid argu-

---

17. *Elim*, 41 (we quote according to the first edition of 1639).
18. *Ibid.*, 38: "If the faith is correct, it will not be in opposition to the truth." See also *Novelot Ḥochmah*, 6b: "If the religion is right, it will reject miracles."
19. *Elim*, 41.
20. *Ibid.*, 60.

ments and ideas which rely merely on faith or on logical consisten-
cies."[21] Only the first is real truth that is beyond every doubt.
The other two, however, show themselves to be incorrect and false.
Hence faith must take account only of positive knowledge, not
of philosophical theories which may prove ungrounded and false.
And whoever relies too much on speculative dialectic and
purely logical assumptions actually follows the same way as the
naive, ignorant men who trust hearsay and all kinds of stories transmitted from mouth to mouth and think that they are pure truth.
"I have in my life heard so much in which there was so little truth,"
Delmedigo says, "that I firmly decided to believe only what I have
myself many times proved and about which I have persuaded myself that it is really true. But what I have not investigated and
my own eyes have not seen—of that I will not speak, for I cannot
decide whether I must acknowledge it or deny it."[22]

In these words of Galileo's disciple the skeptical, critical spirit
of the new era is clearly heard. Joseph Solomon Delmedigo was
the first to acquaint the Jewish reader with the rich treasures of
the new world of ideas the brilliant Copernicus disclosed to mankind. He was the first in Jewish literature to proclaim that the
old Ptolemaic conception of the universe had crumbled and that
our earth is not the immovable center around which the whole
universe revolves, but one of the insignificant planets which move
in a tremendous cycle around the enormously huge sun.[23] But
Delmedigo goes even further. He insists that Copernicus' discovery
brilliantly confirms the bold conjecture expressed by Ḥasdai Crescas in his day: If the creation of the world is the result of God's
infinite goodness, how can one assert that the divine power of creation is limited to our world? Is it not easier to believe that count-
less other worlds exist along with our world in the infinite space
of the universe?[24] Delmedigo frequently repeats Crescas' idea about
constant and everlasting creation, i.e., that the creative process is
an eternal and uninterrupted one.[25] The world, which is an
emanation of divine light, says Delmedigo, is as eternal as the light
itself.[26] The created world is as eternal as its Creator; both of
them together have been from eternity.[27] And he who does not

---

21. *Ibid.*: "And from this you will understand the difference between
knowledge demonstrable by argument and speculation and faith."
22. *Ibid.*, 83.
23. *Ibid.*, 7, 17–18; *Mayan Gannim*, 141–48 ff.
24. See Volume Three of our work.
25. The influence of Crescas on Delmedigo is admitted by Delmedigo
himself (see *Novelot Ḥochmah*, 106–7).
26. *Novelot Ḥochmah*, 38a.
27. *Ibid.*, 106, 107.

believe in the temporal creation of the world is not at all a denier
of one of the "root principles" of the Torah. He merely denies
one of the many stories which are related in the Torah but which
in fact have no essential relationship to the faith.[28]

This Spinozist idea, that God and the world are closely connected and that one is unthinkable without the other, is often reiterated by Delmedigo. "Not without reason," he insists precisely,
"have some thinkers expressed the idea that the world [i.e., nature]
is God Himself." Proceeding from this pantheistic idea, Delmedigo
denies the existence of angels and independent spiritual intelligences and endeavors to show that wherever an "angel" is spoken
of, what is meant is not a separate spiritual creature but one of
the powers in man or in nature through which the divine creative
will is revealed.[29] "But how great and harmful is blind foolishness,"
he exclaims.

Try to tell one of those who think they are the sages of Israel that
God sends an angel to penetrate the womb of a woman and there
produce the structure and form of a child, and he will accept this
as truth and consider it altogether natural. Indeed, he will see in it
a new proof of God's power and great wisdom, despite the fact that
the same "sage" believes that the angel is a flaming fire and occupies,
with his stupendous size, perhaps a third of the whole world. All
this he will find quite natural. But try to explain to him that God
has endowed man's seed with a wondrous power bearing in itself the
germ of the child to which the mother will later give birth and that
this power is called "an angel," and he will reject this completely
and not be able to understand it at all.[30]

Delmedigo attempts to explain to the reader that whenever the
Bible speaks of an angel, this is simply a metaphorical expression,
as, for example, in the narrative relating how Sennacherib's army
perished from the plague in one night. In another place—for example, in the story of Manoah's wife—it is really nothing more than
the imagination of an ignorant woman with a diseased fantasy.
Regarding other stories, such as the long description in the Book
of Chronicles how at the time of the plague in Judea in the time
of King David the angel stood with his drawn sword, we cannot

28. *Ibid.*, 92.
29. *Ibid.*, 96–97, 139; *Matzref Le-Ḥochmah*, 29; *Elim*, 41.
30. *Novelot Ḥochmah*, 96b.

rely on these at all, for "we know very well from modern historians how many exaggerations they report about former times and how one historian contradicts and denies what the other says."[31]

Concerning the belief in demons and witches, Delmedigo remarks ironically that he believes only in what he sees with his own eyes, and that in his long wanderings over various lands he has never had occasion to meet anything that could confirm belief in demons. Furthermore, in Egypt they say that the demons dwell in the northern lands, and in the north they say that they are common in Egypt.[32]

A man with such a positivist-rationalist outlook was destined to live in a period when mystical currents were completely dominant and the Kabbalists filled the world with all kinds of destroying angels, whisperings, and incantations. Fate brought it about that he spent many years in Lithuania, where Jews had an attitude of extreme suspicion toward secular knowledge, toward every spark of free speculative thought, and that he later occupied the post of rabbi and preacher of the orthodox community in Hamburg and later in Amsterdam, where just then the last act of the tragic struggle in which the unfortunate "denier" and "heretic," Uriel Acosta, perished took place. But Delmedigo, like Leo de Modena, was not a fighter by nature. He did not have the courage to go the martyr's way of his teacher, Galileo, and Acosta. He attempted to conceal his thoughts under the mask of ostensible piety. This masquerade, this constant pretense, did not, however, come easy to Delmedigo. He paid for it dearly with his nerves and heart's blood. It was his life's drama, the deep tragedy of his soul. And the drama of this richly endowed man has a great psychological and cultural-historical interest.

Already in his youth he dreamt of literary and scientific activity. "Life is, after all, so brief," Delmedigo writes, "and every man is therefore obliged to leave some memorial in the world, so that he may not be like a swiftly disappearing shadow and his name not be forgotten as soon as he completes his life's way."[33]

So Delmedigo, with great diligence, composed one work after another in various fields. He wrote on chemistry, mathematics, astronomy, and also on religious questions. He composed a special work, *Taalumot Hochmah*, on the Kabbalah, incantations, magic, and the belief in destroying angels, and a large treatise entitled

---

31. *Matzref Le-Hochmah*, 29b (we quote according to the first edition of 1629).
32. *Elim*, 83.
33. *Mayan Gannim*, 183.

Gan Naul on the basic foundations of the faith.[34] But Delmedigo realized quite well that his scientific activity, the spirit discernible in his work, harmonized very little with the currents dominating the environment in which he lived. "I was afraid," he laments in a letter to his disciple Samuel Ashkenazi, "to put my finger between the teeth of my enemies. They would immediately make a great to-do about the fact that I employ foreign sources and be quite prepared to destroy me with their mouths, with the blazing torches of their foxish tails."[35] Indeed, his disciple Samuel Ashkenazi declares that Delmedigo himself burned many of his manuscripts. "It is bitter to relate," he laments, "how he cast into the fire many of his valuable works which cost him so much effort. This was his manner: he used to write and then burn what he had written." Delmedigo himself wrote to Ashkenazi when the latter wished to publish his teacher's *Novelot Hochmah:* "If you had not taken the manuscript without my knowledge, I would long ago have thrown it into the fire."[36]

While Delmedigo had to place a bridle on his mouth and found it more proper to burn his own works than to hand them over into the public domain, he witnessed with indignation how the Jewish book market was flooded with all kinds of Kabbalist books, full of incantations, *notarikon,* and combinations of letters, which in his view confused and barbarized men's minds. Then Gutenberg's splendid invention became hateful to him, and he saw in the printing press not the major instrument of culture but the bearer of obscurantism and barbarism. "In former times," complains Delmedigo,

when handwritten books were very expensive, people would buy only useful and valuable books. These alone would find purchasers, while useless and empty books had to perish. But now along comes any ignoramus, any fool who wishes the world to know of him, and he takes to printing books. He thinks that thereby he will become a bright star and his name shine for future generations.[37]

Delmedigo disclosed his true form only in personal conversation or in friendly correspondence. In this respect the long letter that he sent to his friend and admirer the Karaite Zerah ben Nathan

34. For a list of all of Delmedigo's works see *Elim*, 30–31, 82; *Melo Chofnajim*, 25–27.
35. A reference to the story of how Samson avenged himself on the Philistines (Judges 15:4–5).
36. *Novelot Hochmah*, 148.
37. The introductions to *Novelot Hochmah*, 7b.

of Troki in 1623 is especially interesting.[38] In a friendly letter which, furthermore, was addressed not to a Rabbanite but to a Karaite, Delmedigo did not deem it necessary to write in a disguised way. He expresses his views on religious questions, especially mysticism and the Kabbalah, openly and freely and gives a critical evaluation of Jewish literature. Only the introduction to this letter was published in Delmedigo's lifetime in the form of the introduction to *Mayan Gannim* (1629). The letter itself was first published (following the copy in the possession of the Karaite *hacham* in Halicz) by Abraham Geiger in *Melo Chofnajim* (Berlin, 1840).[39] Michael suspected without reason that the Karaites gave Geiger a falsified text. In Abraham Firkovich's first collection, under Number 523, is an old (seventeenth-century) copy which Firkovich brought from Troki together with Zerah ben Nathan's writings. It is highly probable that this copy was made directly from the original. At the beginning of the manuscript is the superscription of the copyist: "This is the text of the letter that the godly scholar, the honorable master Joseph Solomon the physician of Crete, sent to the honorable master Zerah the Karaite the son of Nathan." The expression "Zerah the Karaite" shows clearly that the copyist was not a Karaite but a Rabbanite. After the general introduction to the letter come some other remarks of the copyist:

The text up to this passage has appeared in print [i.e., in *Mayan Gannim*]. The rest was not included by the printer, possibly because he was not pleased at how the author openly expresses his view of the Kabbalists who exult in their true wisdom. In the manuscript, however, is everything which is here further given.

The text of this manuscript[40] is similar in all details (aside from some insignificant stylistic differences) to that which Geiger published.

"By nature," writes Delmedigo, "I am a social man. I am drawn to the broad strata, to the ways on which the masses walk. I wish

---

38. Zerah ben Nathan was born in 1555. His unpublished manuscripts—a commentary to the Song of Songs, poems, and a letter to the renowned Menasseh ben Israel—are in the Leningrad National Library and in the library of the Society for the Dissemination of Enlightenment Among Jews.

39. In the same year Firkovich also published the letter in Gözlöw (Yevpatoriya) under the title *Iggeret Ha-Yashar*.

40. In the manuscript the last page with the closing lines of Delmedigo's letter is missing (the manuscript is broken off at the words *lo aarich be-inyanam*).

to enlighten them, to give them essential information, aside from the profound and difficult ideas which must be held secret and which I shall reveal only to the chosen few, to my close associates and friends." He writes further,

You ask me to aid you in your strong desire to become better acquainted with the world outlook of your opponents [the followers of the Talmud]. You must know that these men have great contempt for the investigation of nature and for philosophical speculation. Everyone who thirsts after knowledge is hateful to them. "Away with you, unclean one!" they cry to him. These blind men, filled with hatred and wickedness, pursue wind and smoke, gather straw and dust. They spend their days in foolishness. Some have to do with *sefirot*, others concern themselves with *kelipot* and pore over the *Sefer Yetzirah*, *Ginnat Egoz* and *Shaarei Orah*. Like old women who chatter sitting under the moon, so these tell bizarre stories about all kinds of mysteries that inhere in the *shofar*, in the patriarch Jacob's lamed thigh, and other such matters. They speak obscenities of God and the patriarchs. Like the Philistines, they believe in magic and magical names, trust in amulets and nostrums, in exorcisms and incantations. It is simply shameful to listen to their old wives' tales about the young and old Lilith, Ashmodai, and Mahalat the mother of all the demons, about the twenty-two letters of the alphabet and their part in the creation of the world. And it is this that is called tradition, the heritage of the fathers! I have settled accounts with these idolaters in a special work,[41] annihilated their teaching about emanation and *sefirot*, and demonstrated to all with clear arguments that *Pardes Rimmonim*[42] is full of thorns and wild growths, that *Sefer Ha-Bahir* was written not by Rabbi Nehunya ben Ha-Kanah but by some unknown author, that *Maarachot Elohim* is distorted and confused, and that the well-known Moses de Leon is deficient in knowledge and ideas. They always carry God's name on their lips, but He is far from their hearts. They glory in their incantations, amulets, and whisperings. They persuade themselves that they can perform great wonders with their formulas, but all this is pure fraud and hocus-pocus. They cannot drive away even the smallest flea. They are petty, vain, obscure little men. Remove yourself from them, my friend. Let them not cross your threshold. Do not let yourself be seduced by their ostensible piety. . . . Do not think that you will find light in their books. Better to warm yourself with these when destroying them in fire. Burn to coal and ash the works of Ḥayyat and Recanati. Only fools and madmen can seek God's words in such books as *Raziel*, *Midrash Ha-Ne'elam*, *Avodat Ha-Kodesh*, or *Tikkunei Zohar*, which smolder and fume like the smoke of chimneys.

41. Delmedigo here no doubt means his *Taalumot Ḥochmah*.
42. For a discussion of *Pardes Rimmonim*, see Volume Five.

"You must not think," Delmedigo further writes,

that I speak of the Kabbalists merely on the basis of what others have told me. God is my witness that I have taken pains to study the stories and speculations of the Kabbalah with the greatest authorities, and I can swear to you that I even endeavored always to judge them favorably. But this was of no avail, and all attempts to cover their shame could only have the same result as the desire to cover the bright sun in the middle of the day. If, at least, they were silent, as is proper for fools, one could somehow endure them. But they attack us like the worst enemies, arouse the mad dogs against us, and spoil our vineyards. They cry that we serve false gods and lie around in the rubbish of philosophy. They have the arrogance to say that whoever denies the *sefirot* denies both Torahs, and they themselves do nothing but look for secrets in the Torah and forget the Torah itself! They exult in the *Zohar,* but they cannot even hide their swindlery so that it should not be obvious to everyone. They assure us that the Tanna Rabbi Simeon ben Yoḥai is its author, and yet in it opinions of Amoraim who lived hundreds of years later are given.

But it is not only with the Kabbalists that Delmedigo is displeased. "Not they alone," he cries out,

but all of my people Israel are lost and grope on false paths, pursue mirages and fantastic dreams, and gather only thorns and wild growths. There was a time, in the generations of the great prophets, the faithful guardians of the people, when many scholars and sages lived among the Jews. How beautifully the sciences and arts then bloomed among the Jewish people. But now the spirit is broken, the wells of knowledge are dried up, the leaders of the people are ignorant and obscurantist. They have hidden themselves in narrow little rooms. They look with suspicion on every ray of knowledge. All sciences have become for them "external" wisdoms, brought from the "outside," and it has become dark in the tents of the Jews. The present-day rabbis, the guardians of the people, know no more of natural science than the ox and the ass. What good is knowledge to them? What need have they of the laws of nature? They do not grasp God's work, they refuse to understand His marvelous creation. They are deaf to the prophet's word: Lift up your eyes to the heavens, and see Who has created these.[43]

After Delmedigo indicates to the Karaite Zeraḥ of Troki what studies he should engage in and in what order, he considers it necessary to warn him that only he who pursues honor or wishes to be recognized as a scholar and great man in Israel, or who hopes

43. *Taalumot Ḥochmah,* 9–13.

to earn a living thereby, should concern himself with the "books of the Gemara"; the Karaites, however, have no need of these things, especially the Midrashim, with their stories and parables which are as much needed as ants' wings.[44]

Also closely associated with the name of Zerah ben Nathan are the few works of Delmedigo which he himself published. This Karaite of Troki who was so eager for knowledge addressed a letter to Delmedigo requesting that the latter explain to him in detail twelve questions that he regarded as of crucial importance in various fields of knowledge—theology, philosophy, and natural science. He also begged him to explain seventy paradoxical mathematical problems. Delmedigo promptly acceded. He answered each of the twelve questions posed to him in a separate work, and in a special work entitled *Mayan Hatum* explained the seventy mathematical paradoxes. However, he found it possible to publish only the first three of the twelve works. These deal with astronomical matters and the explanation of Copernicus' new system; they appeared in 1629 under the title *Mayan Gannim* in Amsterdam from the press of Menasseh ben Israel, at which Delmedigo's *Mayan Hatum* was also published in the same year.

It is not merely a figure of speech when Delmedigo writes in his letter to Zerah ben Nathan: "I am drawn to the wide road, on which the general public, the common multitude, walk, so that I may enlighten them and give them useful information." The temperament of the enlightener and propagandist was too strong in him for him to stifle his desire to teach the masses of the people and to carry on a struggle against the old-fashioned conceptions and tendencies which he considered reactionary and pernicious. But he was also not a fighter by nature. Like Leo de Modena, Delmedigo, as we have observed, did not belong to those proud and firm spirits that have the courage and moral power openly and decisively to wage a stubborn battle for their ideals and for the truth they carry in their hearts. But Delmedigo was ashamed to admit his moral weakness and, to defend himself, endeavored to show that not he alone but all the great scholars of all times used to hide their convictions and ideas from the world at large. The sages of the Talmud were wont to conceal their convictions,[45] and so was as courageous a battler as Maimonides.[46] The great Plato also feared openly to express the truth and therefore used to speak in allusions and parables.[47] Present-day thinkers, too, Del-

---

44. *Ibid.*, 14.
45. *Novelot Hochmah*, 34–37.
46. *Matzref Le-Hochmah*, 20.
47. *Novelot Hochmah*, 111.

medigo adds, do not speak the truth but flatter the clergy and pretend that they are in agreement with their false views.[48] To defend himself, Delmedigo quotes a lovely old legend in which it is related that when King Saul summoned the shade of the prophet Samuel at Endor, Samuel explained to him: "When I was in the terrestrial world, in the world of falsehood, I did not utter the whole truth, because I was afraid you would kill me. Now that I am in the world of truth, you will hear from me only pure truth."[49]

An ancient proverb says: Socrates is dear to me, Plato is dear to me, but dearer than all else is truth. But, as Delmedigo interprets it, this precious truth is to be given only to the elect few, and not without reason do the proverb-sayers urge that among all the creatures in Noah's ark falsehood was also to be found, for without falsehood the world can have no endurance. "You may take it as a general principle," Delmedigo explains to the reader, "that you should never think you will succeed in clearly knowing the real outlook of an author from his works; to God alone are the hidden depths of the human heart revealed."[50]

Delmedigo, who did not have the courage publicly to express his liberal ideas, was also unwilling to be completely silent. But in this connection he utilized means other than those of Leo de Modena. The latter, as we have seen, would frequently play in disguise, hide behind fabricated names of persons who never existed, or follow the ancient path of Abraham Ibn Ezra and Moses Narboni, speaking in sign language with allusions, hints, and half-words. Delmedigo, however, employed a unique disguised style and would hit upon such inventions as smacked of truly Jesuitical hypocrisy. Typical of Delmedigo's style are his *Elim* and *Matzref Le-Hochmah*. In *Elim*, which deals not only with astronomical and mathematical questions but also with problems of a philosophical-theological character, Delmedigo makes the pretense of being orthodox while he is heterodox, and hides under the umbrella of his two admirers, the Karaite Zerah ben Nathan and Moses of Metz. He reprints the letters they wrote to each other and to him. Geiger, however, has clearly demonstrated[51] that in these letters Delmedigo secretly inserted much that was his own. In this way, hiding under the names of two Karaites, he smuggled in, as contraband, his own ideas, extremely liberal for that time. He does not express his views

48. *Ibid.*
49. *Matzref Le-Hochmah*, 20b.
50. *Ibid.*, 20.
51. *Melo Chofnajim*, Introduction, 1. In the German text see 50, 89, 90, 92 ff.

under his own name, but they are given in Moses' letter to Zerah ben Nathan (*Elim*, 27–51) in which Moses presents biographical details about his teacher and also describes Delmedigo's views on the discoveries of Copernicus and on several important theological problems.

Especially characteristic is the story of the *Wunderkind*. At the time Delmedigo lived as a physician at the court of Prince Radziwill, all the Jewish communities throughout Poland resounded with reports of a four-year-old boy of Greiding who uttered prophecies and performed the greatest miracles before the eyes of all. Despite the fact that the child hardly knew Hebrew, he would recite whole passages from the Talmud and *Zohar* by heart. People would come from all the cities to witness the great miracle with their own eyes and, along with this, present beautiful gifts to the happy father of the *Wunderkind*. The foremost rabbis confirmed with their own signed testimonials the great miracles which they themselves saw and also expressed the hope that perhaps this miraculous child, chosen by God and graced with the holy spirit, would merit disclosing the "end." Delmedigo went to Greiding to see for himself all the miracles reported about this child. On the spot he managed to show that it was all nothing more than a swindle on the part of the little boy's father, who, in this way, defrauded people of large sums of money and gifts. Delmedigo decided to use the swindle as an occasion for propaganda against the superstition of the ignorant multitude and the pernicious activity of various wonderworkers. But here also he did not appear under his own name. He employed in this connection one of Zerah ben Nathan's letters to him which were published in *Elim*. Delmedigo "reworked" this letter considerably before printing it. Zerah ben Nathan asks Delmedigo what his attitude is toward the belief in demons and the miracles that may be performed with the aid of amulets, incantations, whisperings, and magical formulas. Zerah also incidentally asks a simple question: how can one explain the prophecies which the little boy of the Podolia region speaks? Does an angel speak through him, or is this a deed of magic? Of the miracles which the little boy performs there can be no doubt, and here is the proof thereof: before me lies a letter of one of the greatest rabbis, Rabbi Hayyim of Satanov, who testifies that he and many other great scholars have seen all this with their own eyes. "And I am sending this letter to you in order that you may yourself become acquainted with it."[52] Zerah ben Nathan, however, does not receive an answer to this question directly from Delmedigo, but again

52. *Elim*, 15.

through an emissary, Moses of Metz. In his letter to Zeraḥ, Moses
pretends to be completely innocent and simple and relates incidentally how the foremost Polish rabbis and many thousands of
people went to see the miracles which the child of Greiding would
perform, but his teacher, Delmedigo, showed that all this was plain
fraud on the part of the child's father.[53]

Delmedigo himself does not react to this with a single word.
He does only one thing—prints verbatim the letter of the rabbi
of Satanov that Zeraḥ presumably sent to him.[54] In this letter which
the rabbi of Satanov dispatched to Lemberg the miracles and marvelous things which the *Wunderkind* performed before his own
eyes are related with great enthusiasm. "All the things I relate
here," concludes Rabbi Ḥayyim, "are only a drop in the sea in
comparison with what I saw of this child." At the end of the letter,
the rabbi exclaims, "Happy is the eye that has witnessed all these
things!"

This document showing how a charlatan and swindler deceived
the pious and credulous rabbi was published by Delmedigo without
comment. He understood quite well that this friendly letter sent
by one rabbi to another was much more effective than the sharpest
lampoon. "We must not rely on our guardians, on our rabbis. See
how naive, how credulous they are. The pettiest swindler, any
good-for-nothing easily leads them by the nose": so speaks Delmedigo, but he says this without words, merely reprinting the enthusiastic letter of the pious rabbi of Satanov.

The story of the wonder-working little boy was, however, nothing more than an accidental episode. It was much more important
for Delmedigo to besiege and undermine the major fortress of
obscurantist superstition, the chief source from which stemmed,
in his view, all the legends concerning the supernatural and the
miraculous, and thanks to which all the magical formulas and whisperings, the blind belief in incantations and amulets and all kinds
of destroyers and demons, increased and multiplied so greatly—the
practical Kabbalah and the compendium of mysticism, the *Zohar*.
Like Leo de Modena, Delmedigo was a fierce opponent of mysticism and the Kabbalah, and considerably before de Modena wrote
his *Ari Nohem*, Delmedigo determined to "unmask" the practical
Kabbalah and discredit the *Zohar*. But in this struggle Delmedigo
issued forth with very unique weapons. His great-grandfather
Elijah Delmedigo's anti-Kabbalist *Beḥinat Ha-Dat*, in which critical, scientific arguments are presented against the view that the
Zohar is an ancient book, was still in manuscript, and in Joseph

53. *Ibid.*, 50.
54. *Ibid.*, 65.

Delmedigo's day, when mystical tendencies blossomed so richly, it was quite forgotten and only a few rare persons knew anything at all of it. Joseph Delmedigo now decided to revive in the memory of his generation the forgotten work of his great-grandfather, together with the summary of such a bitter opponent of the Kabbalah as Saul Ashkenazi. But Delmedigo did not have the courage openly to show that he was in agreement with the author of *Behinat Ha-Dat*. He therefore pretends to be its decided opponent. Presumably he is greatly distressed that this pernicious book "is spread throughout the whole world" and has therefore decided to overthrow all its arguments But, incidentally, together with his refutation, he also prints *Behinat Ha-Dat* itself with Saul Ashkenazi's summary. Indeed in Delmedigo's counterargument[55] his style and unique polemical manner are revealed most clearly. Like the unknown authors of the famous *Epistolae obscurorum virorum*, so Delmedigo appears under the mask of a foolish pietist. He declares himself to be a fervent Kabbalist. He is greatly enamored of mysticism, and to all the attacks of the author of *Behinat Ha-Dat* and his disciple (Saul Ashkenazi), he will reply not with philosophical arguments but as a simple believer.[56] This "friend" of the Kabbalah, however, is more dangerous than an open enemy. He repeats in his *Matzref Le-Hochmah* all the attacks which the author of *Behinat Ha-Dat* makes on the Kabbalah and also quotes the opinions of other opponents of the Kabbalah—all this ostensibly in order to answer all of them and to demonstrate how ungrounded their arguments are. But the reply is extremely colorless and unconvincing. Then suddenly the author removes the mask from his face, and the reader unexpectedly sees before himself the skeptical critic with an ironic smile on his lips. The author even makes fun of the naive reader. "It happens quite frequently," calmly relates Delmedigo,

that for the purpose of gaining the favor of a patron or a prince, things are written in a book which the authors themselves do not believe. . . . Here, for example, I now write against the philosophizers and uphold the wisdom of the Kabbalah. But I do this only because I was so requested by one of the most prominent Jewish lords who is now greatly taken with the Kabbalists. Because I am very friendly with him, I do it for his sake. But if tomorrow he should change his mind and become enamored of philosophy and then beg me to glorify philosophy, I would promptly gird up my loins and with great enthusiasm battle for philosophic thought.[57]

55. Published under the title *Matzref Le-Hochmah* in Basel in 1629.
56. *Matzref Le-Hochmah*, 28.
57. *Ibid.*, 20.

Immediately after this cynical, arrogant explanation the mask is again put on, and before us stands once more the ardent mystic who, with starry eyes and a pious mien, relates marvelous legends about the ancient Kabbalists and tells about the miracles and wonders which the saintly Rabbi Isaac Luria not long ago performed. "Has there ever been even a single philosopher about whom such marvelous things were related?" asks the author of *Matzref Le-Hochmah*.[58] And immediately thereafter, quite unexpectedly, comes the following remark: "But the story of the Polish boy of Greiding is pure deception, as I showed on the very day I came there."[59]

Not without justification does Delmedigo's older contemporary, Leo de Modena, include in his *Ari Nohem* the passages just quoted from *Matzref Le-Hochmah* to confirm his view that Delmedigo "represents himself supposedly as a defender of the wisdom of the Kabbalah but in fact is its definite opponent."[60] Such passages may be found in considerable numbers in *Matzref Le-Hochmah*. For example, Delmedigo introduces all the arguments which the author of *Behinat Ha-Dat* set forth to show that the *Zohar* is not an ancient book. He pretends that these arguments do not satisfy him and that he does not agree with them. His criticism, however, is such that he concludes with the following triumphant statement:

We thus see from the arguments of the author of *Behinat Ha-Dat* himself that the author of the *Zohar* was in any case a significant person, not such an ignoramus as most of the Kabbalists, who have no knowledge of the Talmud and its commentaries and know nothing besides the Kabbalah. . . . Even the opponents, those who do not believe that Rabbi Simeon ben Yohai wrote the *Zohar*, admit that its author, let us say Moses de Leon, was a great man and a great scholar in the wisdom of the Kabbalah.[61]

The author of *Behinat Ha-Dat* emphasizes that passages so strange that they are impossible to digest and to grasp with the human mind are very frequently encountered in the *Zohar*. "This is indeed true," answers Delmedigo the "defender of righteousness," introducing many quotations from the *Zohar* which brilliantly confirm the complaint of the author of *Behinat Ha-Dat*. "But we know,"

58. *Ibid.*, 15b.
59. *Ibid.*
60. *Ari Nohem*, 64. See also *ibid.*, 50, 65–66. See especially p. 41, where he says of Delmedigo: "Rabbi Joseph Solomon Rofe wounds as a way of healing."
61. *Matzref Le-Hochmah*, 21–22.

Delmedigo adds with a naive mien, "that in the Talmud also there are such difficult passages; we are certain, however, that a secret meaning is probably concealed in them."[62] From this unique "friend of the Kabbalah" and "defender of righteousness" we also learn that to occupy oneself with the Kabbalah is merely a pastime and that it is certainly not worthwhile to devote much attention to it. He also tells us that amulets and incantations are unmitigated foolishness, and that *notarikon, gematriot,* and combinations of letters are nothing but child's play.[63] Delmedigo also informs us that he does not at all intend to follow the way of "the present-day Kabbalists" and preachers who pervert and corrupt the true meaning of the Torah, while naive persons think that this is "not corrupting the text but revealing mysteries."

Matzref Le-Hochmah was written by Joseph Solomon Delmedigo in Hamburg, where he was rabbi and preacher. He completed his work in the little town of Glückstadt, to which he went from Hamburg at the time of the cholera epidemic. It was published, however, not by the author but by his Amsterdam pupil Samuel Ashkenazi in Basel in 1629. This pupil has a close relationship to another work of Delmedigo's which appeared in 1631 under the title *Novelot Hochmah.* Thanks to Samuel Ashkenazi, Delmedigo's allusive manner of writing obtains in *Novelot Hochmah* an altogether unique style. From Delmedigo's numerous manuscripts in his possession Ashkenazi selected various essays and notices which deal with philosophic-religious questions and with problems closely associated with the theoretical Kabbalah. These works he deliberately mixed together without any order. The most contradictory ideas and views follow one another. The doctrine of Rabbi Isaac Luria and his disciples is lauded with the greatest enthusiasm, but their thoughts and views are rendered in such form that they obtain a strange, bizarre, crude appearance—and all this is done with a pious mien, with the starry eyes of an ardent devotee. And indeed, along with this, Delmedigo's own extremely radical views on the creation of the world, the nature of angels, divine providence, etc., are incidentally woven. At the beginning of the work Delmedigo's letter to the editor, also written in a euphemistic style with feigned indignation and hidden, caustic laughter, is printed. He is ostensibly very angry at his pupil for publishing, without his consent, fragments and sketches that are not at all ready for publication. How can one publish such a strange mixture of compositions, of which one contradicts the other—and all this under Delmedigo's name? He, Delmedigo, is

62. *Ibid.,* 27–28.
63. *Ibid.,* 13a.

simply ashamed to appear before the public with such a monster that wishes to know nothing of the laws of elegant style and structured rhetoric.

Apparently, Delmedigo was in fact unhappy that he could express his ideas only in allusions and under various masks. In *Matzref Le-Ḥochmah*, noting how frequently scholars must conceal their thoughts, he immediately adds: "But I swear that in my work *Bosmat bat Shelomoh* I will take account of no one and will openly utter my convictions." *Bosmat bat Shelomoh* was, indeed, especially dear to him, and his great desire was to see this work published.[64] His wish, however, was not fulfilled. Under the circumstances of that time it was not possible to publish a work which wishes "to take account of no one." For many generations the manuscript of *Bosmat bat Shelomoh* was transmitted from hand to hand and diligently studied by a chosen few in whom the thirst for knowledge was not yet destroyed. In the second half of the eighteenth century, the only manuscript of Delmedigo's encyclopedic work was in the hands of the intellectually curious Rabbi Samson of Slonim, to whom the young Solomon Maimon used to come from Nieszwicz on foot to borrow scientific books. The rabbi of Slonim guarded Delmedigo's legacy with great reverence. Nevertheless, this work had the same sad fate as the rest of Delmedigo's unpublished works. A fire broke out in which Rabbi Samson's entire library, including the manuscript of *Bosmat bat Shelomoh*, was destroyed.[65]

Thus, after the appearance of his *Novelot Ḥochmah*, Joseph Solomon Delmedigo became completely silent, despite the fact that he lived a full twenty-five years longer.[66] Already in his lifetime, in his full powers, he was a forgotten man, alien and unknown to his orphaned generation which lived through the Thirty Years' War and the Chmielnitzki massacres and in which a heavy melancholy and dark twilight veiled the Jewish quarter.

Even in the magnificent city of Delmedigo's native country, in life-loving Venice, the foremost position in Jewish society was occupied by pietists and orthodox men who took pains to see to it that the commandments and customs should be observed as strictly as possible and whose whole education and program consisted of a single motto: study of Torah. In complete contrast to Leo de Modena and Joseph Delmedigo, these men knew nothing

64. *Elim*, 31–32.
65. See *Literaturblatt des Orients*, 1848, p. 124.
66. Delmedigo died in 1655 in Prague, where he came in 1648 from Frankfort. The inscription on his tombstone is published in *Literaturblatt des Orients*, 1840, p. 332.

of a rent in the heart, of conflict and inner doubts. They were of one mold, monotonously and obdurately consistent. Strict and merciless toward themselves, they were the same also in communal life, in their whole world outlook. From the very pulpit in which in earlier times the young Leo de Modena used to appear with his lovely and ingenious sermons, the preacher Azariah Figo (died 1647), the well-known author of the popular homiletical work *Binah La-Ittim*,[67] now threatened the people with the most fearful punishments and summoned them with great ardor to repentance, prayer, and pious deeds.

Not too many years separate Azariah Figo from his brilliant predecessor, Jehudah Moscato, but what a tremendous difference is discernible in the whole mood and spiritual atmosphere that dominates the sermonic collections of these two preachers. In Moscato's parables and similes, in the feeling with which he speaks of art and music, in the respect he has for the "divine Plato," in the whole style of his preaching—in all this the life-loving spirit of the Renaissance, with its affection for bright, lively colors, for the elegant artistic gesture, is felt. An altogether different picture is to be seen in Figo's *Binah La-Ittim*. Before us here stands a typical preacher of the old Franco-German type, a great pietist, a fanatical teacher of morality and a strict supervisor of piety, who wishes to know of no theories where it is a question of commandments and religious laws and customs. "Do not believe those," the author of *Binah La-Ittim* exclaims,

who assert that man's highest bliss consists in speculation and philosophical investigation. The wisdom that man attains with his mind is altogether false. There is nothing in it that must be admitted to be pure truth. Only the wisdom of the sacred Torah, which draws nourishment from the source of knowledge, from God Himself, is the firm foundation of truth.[68]

"My sons, occupy yourselves with Torah and commandments"—this is the basic motif of Figo's sermons. Do not, he admonishes, believe those who say that the chief thing is understanding, not observing, the commandments. To fulfill God's will one must not be content with the thought but also incorporate it in the deed. Understanding the reason of the commandments is not the major thing. The highest level is attained through the act, the

67. First published in Venice in 1647.
68. *Binah Le-Ittim*, I, 122 (Lublin edition, 1875).

will, through *doing* the commandments.[69] Figo addresses the young people with the following heartfelt request:

My dear children, I beg each of you, lift your eyes and consider well the way of life that stands before you. If you serve God in youth, your old age will be blessed and your name will be inscribed forever among the people of Israel.[70]

Therefore repent, do as many good deeds as possible, and pray to God from early in the morning till late at night, for great is the power of prayer spoken with devotion; it is healing for all pains and the best salve for all the wounds of the heart.[71]

"Great is our distress," laments Figo,

and terrible the sufferings that we endure from our enemies. We have become a mockery and a scorn, a shame and a reproach; we are insulted and shamed by every wretch. Our enemies are ruthless. There is no limit to our pain. But we must not despair. For happy are those who ever hope and are certain that God's judgment will come speedily.[72] Do we not even now see God's great wonders? Is it not a miracle that we still exist among our enemies in exile? Our hope that the glorious day of the greatest miracle will come must be firm and secure, and then even the blind will see and understand the wonders that God does for those who fulfill His sacred Torah.[73]

"Is there any greater consolation," Figo feelingly exclaims,

than the fact that, despite all our sufferings and afflictions, we, our children, and our children's children remain to the end of all generations God's faithful servants, His chosen people? We recognize Him alone, and no people or tongue can have the upper hand over us. He is our Father, He is our King, He is our God, and we are His faithful children. Unbreakable is the bond between us. As a king dresses his beloved son in royal garments and adorns his head with crowns so that all may know that he is a prince, so God says to us, his people Israel: "Do you wish that all should know that you are My beloved children? Then, study My Torah, fulfill My precepts."[74]

"Occupy yourselves with Torah and commandments"—this is Figo's slogan. He wishes to know nothing of secular matters. Love for art objects, for plays and masquerades, which were so dear

69. *Ibid.,* II, 34–35.
70. *Ibid.,* I, end of the fourth sermon.
71. *Ibid.,* II, 175, etc.
72. *Ibid.,* I, 12.
73. *Ibid.,* I, 156.
74. *Ibid.,* II, 120 (Sermon 55).

to the Venetians in the seventeenth century—all this was "sinful" in the eyes of the pious preacher, and he poured fire and brimstone on them in his sermons. In one of his addresses, for example, Figo complains sharply that at Jewish weddings, when the bride goes with her friends to the synagogue or to the house of her groom's parents, on both sides of the street curious people stand in rows and look with enchantment at the lovely young women with their costly attire and ornaments.[75] "Woe to the eyes that look on this," Figo cries out; "remove yourselves from such temptation, avoid the society of women so that your eyes may not sin."

The following case is very interesting. The inhabitants of the Venetian Ghetto had no smaller fondness than their Christian fellow citizens for public ceremonies and colorful parades and processions. We have observed how Leo de Modena, who was a member of the Venetian rabbinate, and his family participated extensively in the theater. (Venice is, in fact, the city about which we have the oldest information concerning a special Jewish theater.)[76] During the years that Azariah Figo was a preacher in Venice, a prominent and wealthy member of the Venetian community constructed a lovely building for dramatic presentations. This new Jewish theater was extremely popular. All, young and old, ran to its performances, and the theater was always filled to overflowing. The pious Figo was beside himself. He saw in this new theater a true "agency of sin" and addressed a question about it to the great scholar of that time, the rabbi of Verona, Samuel Aboab (1610–94).[77] Aboab was a typical representative of strictest orthodoxy. An ascetic and Kabbalist who used constantly to afflict himself with fasts and study Torah day and night, he regarded the pleasures and joys of the sinful world with hatred. He complained vehemently that such a great scholar as Jehudah Minz had ruled that on Purim Jews might hold masquerades in order to fulfill the commandment of "increasing joy."[78] It is therefore not surprising that Figo's report greatly irritated the deeply pious Aboab. "I became sick with grief," Aboab writes in his reply,

as soon as I learned that this man [the one who had built the theatre] brings all into temptation and makes modesty and proper conduct forgotten. . . . Great is his sin. He has degraded the crown and pride of the Torah to the earth. Within the holy camp [i.e., in the Ghetto]

75. *Ibid.*, II, Sermon 64.
76. See our work in the forth volume of *Yevreyskaya Lyetopis.*
77. For biographical details about Aboab, see his son's introduction to *Devar Shemuel.*
78. *Sefer Ha-Zichronot, Zikkaron* Two, Chapter Two, 14b.

he has built theatres and circuses,[79] where men and women and children come together. Modest and chaste Jewish daughters sit together with profligate women of the streets, and all, great and small, violate the law of Moses.

The pious rabbi further complains: "If at least only adults went there. But what do they want of the little lambs? A great punishment awaits those who bring little children there. They lead them into temptation by having them sit with actors and listen to their obscene talk which poisons their young souls."[80]

It is very characteristic of the new tendencies that shortly after de Modena's death, the ascetic and strict Samuel Aboab was invited (in 1650) to become communal rabbi of Venice and occupied this post until 1694, when he died at the age of eighty-four.

No less typical in this respect is the literary activity of the only talented poet of that time, Moses ben Mordecai Zacuto. Zacuto was not a native Italian. He came from Amsterdam (born around 1625) but spent his entire life in two major Italian centers of culture, first in Venice and afterwards, from 1673 until his death in 1697, in Mantua, where he was invited to occupy the rabbinic office.

Zacuto was educated together with Spinoza in the academy of Amsterdam, the Bet Midrash Etz Ḥayyim. Even in his youth he manifested a special love for poetry and the Kabbalah, which he always calls *ḥochmat ha-nistar* (the secret wisdom).[81] In order to become better acquainted with this "wisdom," Zacuto went to Poznan.[82] From there he proceeded to Venice, intending to emigrate thence to Palestine.[83] But nothing came of his intended journey to Palestine, and he remained in Italy all his life. Coming to Venice as a young man of twenty,[84] Zacuto brought with him his initial poetic work, *Yesod Olam*, the first dramatic work in Hebrew literature. In this work of the young poet can be discerned the influence of the Marranos fleeing from Portugal who found protection in the hospitable republic of the Netherlands. From the

79. Aboab speaks in the plural simply because he employs the well-known Talmudic expression.
80. Aboab's *Responsa, Devar Shemuel*, No. 4.
81. For interesting details about the young Zacuto's attitude toward the Kabbalah, see Ghirondi's *Toledot Gedolei Yisrael*, p. 225.
82. *Iggerot Remez*, 35.
83. Azulai, *Shem Ha-Gedolim*.
84. In the poem that Zacuto placed before Figo's *Binah La-Ittim* (1647), he indicates that he came to Venice two years earlier. The elegy Zacuto wrote after Figo's death is published in Paperna's *Kol Ugav*, 15–16.

beginning of the seventeenth century on, Holland was a place of refuge for the Spanish-Portuguese Marranos who managed to escape from the claws of the Inquisition. The refugees felt great love and gratitude for their new home, but could not forget the beautiful land beyond the Pyrenees, their cruel stepmother, and its culture. The seventeenth century, when the names of Calderón and Lope de Vega flared up brilliantly, was the golden era of Spanish national drama. This had a definite influence on the literary creativity of the refugee Marranos. Zacuto's older contemporary, the talented poet and learned Marrano Antonio Enriquez Gomez, who fled to Amsterdam and there publicly returned to the Jewish faith, composed twenty-two dramas, among them several on Biblical themes. Zacuto's *Yesod Olam* is also a Biblical drama, and its central figure is the patriarch Abraham, who courageously destroys his father's idols. The young poet sets forth as a symbol of the Marranos who fled from the Spanish Inquisition the heroic figure of Abraham, the courageous battler prepared to sacrifice his life for the faith he carried in his heart. Indomitable is only one who is unshakable in his belief and knows of no doubts and conflicts. The great miracle occurs: the integrally whole Abraham, with firm faith in his heart, emerges from the fiery furnace without even a hair of his head touched, but the conflict-ridden and doubt-filled Haran perishes.

The young poet manifests extraordinary skill in the construction of verse. The whole work is written in rhymed verses which flow easily and smoothly. Zacuto is not particularly fond of the old, cumbersome Arabic meter and therefore eagerly employs the sparkling, swift, four-footed choriambus and particularly the sonnet, which Immanuel of Rome had introduced into Hebrew poetry. Unfortunately the learned editor of *Yesod Olam*,[85] Abraham Berliner, had rather slight knowledge of meter and verse construction. He therefore printed Zacuto's verses in such a way that it cannot even occur to the reader that all the personages in Zacuto have a special fondness for sonnets. The editor himself apparently did not realize this. For example, on pages 35–36 he makes a mixture of six whole sonnets, and soon thereafter leaves, in a further sonnet, a strange line which does not at all belong to the subject and distorts the entire content. It is literally astounding that Berliner did not notice that the line in question wandered into this place through the oversight of an ignorant copyist, for he also had before him the Mantua manuscript of Zacuto's drama in which the sonnet is written correctly, without the alien addition.[86]

85. Printed with a long introduction in 1874.
86. See *Yesod Olam*, p. xxvi.

Living in Italy under the influence of Dante's immortal *Divine Comedy*, Zacuto wrote his poem *Tofteh Aruch* (*L'Inferno figurato in rima*).[87] Italian influence is discernible not only in the subject but in the form of Zacuto's poem. *Tofteh Aruch* consists of 185 five-line stanzas and the rhymes of all of the stanzas follow the strict order: *a, bb, aa*. On the other hand, the poet gave the subject a highly nationalist dress. Zacuto utilizes the old popular belief about *ḥibbut ha-kever* (torment of the grave), to the effect that as soon as a deceased person is buried and his grave covered with earth, he comes to himself, his consciousness is aroused to a certain level, the angel Dumah knocks on the grave, and his judgment begins. In his poem Zacuto portrays the *ḥibbut ha-kever* of a very sinful man, describing how his senses awaken in him and he feels how he lies forsaken by all in a fresh grave. Then the angel Dumah with his attendants, the destroying angels, appears, and the man is dragged into the abysses of hell. The sinner inquires in terror where he is being led, and one of Dumah's attendants explains to him with mockery and cold laughter the fearful tortures that are prepared for him on account of his sinful life. The destroying spirit shows him one after the other all seven departments of hell, with all their inhabitants, who are burned, cooked, threshed, and tortured with the most terrible chastisements. The destroying angels surround the sinner on all sides with wild laughter. He perceives and feels that there is no escape. Now the terrible judgment, the severe punishment for his great sins, begins. On this note the poem ends.[88]

In *Tofteh Aruch* also Zacuto exhibits his great mastery of versification. With no less artistry than Moses Ibn Ezra and Alḥarizi, Zacuto employs the full-toned *Tajnis* rhymes, in which the lines end with the same word but each time with a different meaning. In addition, the poet utilizes all possible assonances, onomatopoeia, and unexpected plays on syllables. To be sure, these overly rich pyrotechnics of sound effects weary the reader and at times weaken the distressing impression of the portrayal of the abysses of hell.

As great as Zacuto's love for poetic art was, it could not compete

87. First published in Venice in 1715.
88. Five years after Zacuto's poem appeared in print a member of the religious society "Ḥadashim La-Bekarim," Jacob Daniel Olmo, composed, precisely after the pattern of *Tofteh Aruch*, a poem entitled *Eden Aruch*. In 277 five-line stanzas, constructed according to the same meter as Zacuto's poem, Olmo portrays the beautiful reward which the righteous person receives after death. Olmo's *Eden Aruch* was published in Venice in 1744 along with Zacuto's *Tofteh Aruch*, and they are also printed together in the later editions.

with his other love, that for mysticism and the Kabbalah. The mystic in Zacuto finally overcame the poet. Benjamin Halevi of Safed familiarized Zacuto with the Kabbalah of Rabbi Isaac Luria, and the poet himself enthusiastically relates how he found in the books of Luria's disciple, Ḥayyim Vital, the most precious treasures of true wisdom.[89] Zacuto soon established a Kabbalist school in Venice, wrote a large commentary on the *Zohar* called *Mikdash Adonai*,[90] composed a dictionary especially for the Kabbalah entitled *Shorashei Ha-Shemot*, occupied himself at times with the practical Kabbalah,[91] and carried on a very extensive correspondence with his pupils on the ten *sefirot*, combinations of letters, and other mystical problems.[92] Particularly interesting is his exchange of letters with his beloved disciple, the Kabbalist Benjamin Kohen. Their correspondence during the year of Benjamin Kohen's wedding lead us into the intimate world and experiences of exalted mystical natures. We see in a very clear way how religious enthusiasm is permeated with erotic elements. Earthly desire is transformed in the mystic into ecstatic prayer and celestial cleaving to God. Love for woman is closely associated with the drive for the intoxicating pleasure of harmonious wholeness.

Zacuto on occasion also wrote hymns and liturgical poems,[93] but there is very little genuine poetry in these. We see in them, above all, the Kabbalist with his combinations of names and *gematriot*. He sings of the "four worlds" of the Kabbalah in a poem called *Elef Alpin*[94] because it consists of a thousand words, each one of which begins with the letter *alef*. Only the tragic condition of the Jewish people, the exile that becomes ever more bitter and grievous, awakens the poet in Zacuto, and at the end of *Elef Alpin* he hurls his stormy protest at the heavens:

Where are Thy wonders, my proud hope and consolation? . . . God Almighty, I can no longer be silent, I cannot look on and see how

89. See *Iggerot Remez*, 42b.
90. A magnificent manuscript copy of Zacuto's commentary to the *Zohar* is located in the museum of the Jewish Historical-Ethnographic Society in Leningrad.
91. Zacuto provides, for example, prescriptions on how to drive out a *dybbuk* from a woman (*Iggerot Remez*, 2, 24, and 28).
92. Part of the correspondence was published in Leghorn in 1780 under the title *Iggerot Remez*.
93. Part of them were published by Moses Ottolenghi in Amsterdam (1712) under the title *Hen Kol Ḥadash*. Several of Zacuto's prayers entered the *Maḥzor Minhag Kaffa* as well as Hannover's *Shaarei Tziyyon*. Manuscripts of all of Zacuto"s hymns are to be found in Baron Günzburg's manuscript collection (Nos. 687, 720).
94. Printed at the end of *Iggerot Remez*.

those who are afflicted and tortured to death are compelled to bend the knee before *asherot,* to fall in the dust before dumb idols. I can no longer listen to the heartbreaking cries of those who languish in chains. . . . The bitter wailing of children who have been orphaned, of widows robbed of their husbands . . . I have no more strength to wait, to hope for light, and all the while languish in the dark. . . .

It is no wonder that as soon as the joyous tidings of the messianic pretender Shabbetai Tzevi came to Italy, Zacuto at once became his ardent follower and welcomed him with hymns and songs of praise. His disciple Benjamin Kohen also promptly joined the movement and wrote enthusiastic letters about the redemption.

Thus the Renaissance spirit in Italian Jewry gradually declined towards its setting and was completely extinguished. Ever stronger and more widespread in the Italian Jewish community became the influence of two spiritual and intellectual centers which then placed their stamp on the entire Jewish people: on one side, the home of mysticism and Kabbalah, the Turkish-Palestinian community, and on the other the fortress of rabbinism, German-Polish Jewry.

Of these centers we shall speak in the volumes that follow.

BIBLIOGRAPHICAL NOTES

Italian Jewry in the Renaissance Era

CHAPTER ONE

ITALIAN JEWRY IN THE RENAISSANCE ERA; JEHUDAH ABRAVANEL

For a bibliography of older works on the Jews and Jewish history and culture in Italy, see G. Gabrieli, *Italia Judaica* (1924). A more recent and complete classified bibliography is found in A. Milano, *Bibliotheca historica italo-judaica* (1954), with supplements in 1964 and in *Rassegna mensile di Israel* (November, 1966). Among the most valuable historical accounts are P. Orano, *Gli ebrei in Italia* (1938); G. Bedarida, *Ebrei d'Italia* (1950); C. Roth, *A History of the Jews in Italy* (1946); *idem, The Jews in the Renaissance* (1959); *idem, A History of the Jews in Venice* (1930); H. Vogelstein, *A History of the Jews in Rome* (1940; based on H. Vogelstein and P. Rieger, *Die Geschichte der Juden in Rom*, two volumes, 1895–96); M. Shulvass, *Ḥayyei Ha-Yehudim Be-Italyah Be-Tekufat Ha-Renaissance* (1955); A. Milano, *Storia degli ebrei in Italia* (1963); G. Volli, *Breve storia degli ebrei in Italia* (1961); and Gregorovius, *The Ghetto and the Jews of Rome* (1948).

Still of immense value as a comprehensive portrait of the Italian Renaissance is Jacob Burckhardt's classic *The Civilization of the Renaissance in Italy* (translated by S. G. C. Middlemore, 1928).

On Menaḥem Recanati and the introduction of the *Zohar* into Italy, see G. Scholem, *Major Trends in Jewish Mysticism* (revised edition, 1946); *idem, Ursprung und Anfänge der Kabbalah* (1962); *idem, Von der mystischen Gestalt der Gottheit* (1962); *idem, On the Kabbalah and its Symbolism* (1965). See also E. Gottlieb, *Ha-Kabbalah Be-Chitvei Rabbenu Baḥya ben Asher* (1970), pp. 259–63, and Y. Nadav in *Tarbitz*, XXVI (1956–57), 440–58.

Moses ben Isaac da Rieti's *Mikdash Meat* was published in its entirety in 1851 by J. Goldenthal, with an introduction in Italian and in Hebrew. On Rieti and his work, see M. Steinschneider, *Hebräischen Übersetzungen* (1893), pp. 28–29, 76–77, 462, 600; H. Vogelstein and P. Rieger, *Geschichte der Juden in Rom*, II (1895), 68–74 ff.; A. Milano, *Storia degli ebrei in Italia* (1963), pp. 657–58; and G. Karpeles, *Geschichte der jüdischen Literatur*, third edition, 1921, II, 745 ff.

Jehudah Abravanel's *Dialoghi di amore* appeared in a new edition, with introduction and bibliography, by C. Gebhardt (1929). The work was translated into English by F. Friedeberg-Seely and J. H. Barnes under the title *The Philosophy of Love* (1937). On Jehudah Abravanel and his work, see B. Zimmels, *Leo Hebraeus* (1880); *idem, Leo Hebraeus: Neue Studien* (1892); H. A. Wolfson, *The Philosophy of Spinoza* (1934), index s.v. "Leo Hebraeus"; J. Guttmann, *Philosophies of Judaism* (1964), pp. 259–63; J. B. Agus, *The Evolution of Jewish Thought* (1959), pp. 291–99; H. Pflaum, *Die Idee der Liebe: Leone Ebreo, zwei Abhandlungen zur Philosophie der Renaissance* (1926); idem, "Leone Ebreo und Pico della Mirandola," *MGWJ*, LXXII (1928), 344–50; I. Sonne, in *Tarbitz*, III (1931–32), 287–313; J. Klausner, in *Tarbitz*, III (1931–32), 67–98; N. Slouschz, in *Revista de estudios hebráicos*, I (1928), 192 ff.; and Dinizotti, in *Italia medioevale e umanistica*, II (1959), 409–28.

CHAPTER TWO

JEWISH MYSTICISM AND THE ITALIAN HUMANISTS; GRAMMARIANS AND SCHOLARS

On Christian appropriations and interpretations of the Kabbalah, see D. Saurat, *Literature and Occult Tradition: Studies in Philosophical Poetry* (1930); E. Anagnine, *Pico della Mirandola: sincretismo religioso-filosofico* (1937), pp. *1463–1494*; I. Abrahams, "Pico Della Mirandola," in *Hebrew Union College Jubilee Volume* (1925); J. L. Blau, *The Christian Interpretation of the Cabala in the Renaissance* (1944); F. Secret, *Le Zohar chez les Kabbalistes chrétiens de la Renaissance* (1958); idem, *Les Kabbalistes chrétiens de la Renaissance* (1964); E. Benz, *Die christliche Kabbala: Ein Stiefkind der Theologie* (1958); M. Brod, *Johannes Reuchlin und sein Kampf* (1965); and G. Scholem, "Zur Geschichte der Anfänge der christlichen Kabbala," in *Essays in Honor of Leo Baeck* (1954).

Elijah ben Moses Abba Delmedigo's *Beḥinat Ha-Dat* was published with notes and commentary by Isaac Samuel Reggio in Vienna (1833). On Delmedigo and his work, see J. Guttmann, *Philosophies of Judaism* (1964); *idem*, "Elia del Medigos Verhältnis zu Averroes in seinem *Bechinat Ha-Dat*," *Jewish Studies in Memory of Israel Abrahams* (1927); U. Cassuto, *Ha-Yehudim Be-Firenzi Be-Tekufat Ha-Renaissance* (1967), index, s.v. "Elia del Medigo"; I. H. Weiss, *Dor Dor Ve-Doreshav*, V (1904), 275–78; J. Dukas, *Recherches sur l'historie littéraire du XVe siècle* (1876), pp. 25–77; A. Huebsch, in *MGWJ*, XXXI (1882), 555–63; and M. Steinschneider, in *MGWJ*, XXXVII (1893), 185–88.

On Yoḥanan ben Isaac Alemanno and his work, see I. S. Reggio, in *Kerem Ḥemed*, II (1836), 48–53; F. Perles, in *REJ*, XII (1886), 244–57; H. Vogelstein and P. Rieger, *Geschichte der Juden in Rom* (1896), pp. 75–77; U. Cassuto, *Ha-Yehudim Be-Firenzi Be-Tekufat Ha-Renaissance* (1967), index, s.v. "Yohanan Alemanno"; G. Scholem, in *Kiryat Sefer*, V (1928–29), 273–77; and H. Pflaum, *Die Idee der Liebe* (1926), pp. 67–70.

On Jacob Mantino and his work, see D. Kaufmann, in *REJ*, XXVII (1893), 30–60, 207–38; A. Milano, *Storia degli ebrei in Italia* (1963), pp. 242, 625, 631; *idem*, *Ghetto di Roma* (1964), pp. 60, 68 f.; C. Roth, *The Jews in the Renaissance* (1959), index; Muenster, in *Rassegna mensile di Israel*, XX (1954), 310–21; M. Steinschneider, *Hebräischen Übersetzungen* (1893), pp. 145, 438, 673, 685, 976; and H. Vogelstein and P. Rieger, *Geschichte der Juden in Rom*, II (1896), 94 ff.

On Moses ben Shemtov Ibn Ḥabib and his work, see W. Bacher, *Die hebräische Sprachwissenschaft vom X. bis zum XVI. Jahrhundert* (1892), pp. 110, 113; E. Renan-A. Neubauer, *Les Écrivains juifs français du XIVe siècle* (1893), pp. 39–42; M. B. Amzalak, *Portuguese Hebrew Grammars and Grammarians* (1928), pp. 10–12; and J. Schirmann, in *Sefarad*, II (1956), 663 f., 700.

Nofet Tzufim, by Messer Leon (Jehudah ben Yeḥiel), was reprinted by A. Jellinek (1863). On Messer Leon and his work, see M. Shulvass, in *Tziyyon*, XII (1946–47), 17–23; L. Loew, in *Ben Chananja*, VI (1863), 817–19; N. Brüll, in *Ben Chananja*, VI (1863), 509–14, 527 f.; A. Neubauer, in *Israelitische Letterbode*, X (1884–85), 106–11; M. Steinschneider, *Catalogus Librorum Hebraeorum in Bibliotheca Bodleiana* (1852–60), cols. 1331–32; *idem*, *Gesammelte Schriften*, I (1925), 218–28; I. Husik, *Judah Messer Leon's Commentary on the "Vetus Logica"* (1906); and J. Schechter, in *REJ*, XXIV (1892), 118–38.

On Abraham ben Meir de Balmes and his work, see D. Amram, *Makers of Hebrew Books in Italy* (1909, reprinted 1963), pp.

169–72; M. Steinschneider, *Hebräischen Übersetzungen* (1893), pp. 972–73, and index, s.v. "Abraham de Balmes"; and N. Ferorelli, "Abramo de Balmes ebreo di Lecce e i suoi parenti" (offprint from *Archivio Storico per le Province Napoletane*, XXXI [1906], pp. 632–54).

Elijah Levita's major work, *Massoret Ha-Massoret*, on the Masoretic text of the Bible, was translated into English, with notes, by Christian David Ginsburg (1867, reprinted 1968). On Levita and his numerous writings, see H. F. W. Gesenius, *Geschichte der hebräischen Sprache und Schrift* (1815); S. Buber, *Leben und Schriften des Elias Bachur, genannt Levita* (1856); W. Bacher, "Elija Levitas wissenschaftliche Leistungen," in *Zeitschrift der deutschen morgenländischen Gesellschaft*, XLIII (1889), 206–72; *idem*, in *MGWJ*, XXXVII (1893), 398–404; D. Kahana, in *Ha-Shaḥar*, XII (1883–84), 498–505, 539–48; J. Levy, *Elia Levita und seine Leistungen als Grammatiker* (1888); M. Erik, *Die Geshichte fun der Yiddisher Literatur* (1928), pp. 179–202; J. Shatzky, *Elia Bochur* (Yiddish, 1949; includes bibliography); J. A. Joffe, *Elia Bochur* (Yiddish, 1949); M. Weinreich, *Shtaplen far Etuden tsu der Yiddisher Shprachivsenshaft un Literaturgeshichte* (1923), pp. 72–86; *idem, Bilder fun der Yiddisher Literaturgeshichte* (1928), pp. 124, 142, 149–91; G. E. Weil, *Elie Levita humaniste et massoréte, 1469–1549* (1963); and N. Snaith, *Prolegomenon to "Jacob ben Chajim ben Isaac ibn Adonijah's Introduction to the Rabbinic Bible" and "The Massoreth Ha-Massoreth of Elias Levita"* (1968).

On the origins and development of Hebrew printing and on its significance in the history of Jewish literature, see article, "Typography," *Jewish Encyclopedia*, XII (1906), 295–335; article, "Printing, Hebrew," *Encyclopedia Judaica*, XIII (1971), cols. 1095–1115; A. Berliner, *Über den Einfluss des ersten hebräischen Buchdrucks auf den Cultus und die Cultur der Juden* (1896); D. W. Amram, *Makers of Hebrew Books in Italy* (1909, reprinted 1963); E. N. Adler, *Gazetteer of Hebrew Printing* (1917); H. D. (Bernard) Friedberg, *Toledot Ha-Defus Ha-Ivri Ba-Medinot Italyah, Aspamyah-Portugalyah, Togarmah, Ve-Artzot Ha-Kedem* (1934, second edition 1956); J. Bloch, *Venetian Printers of Hebrew Books* (1932); A. Yaari, *Ha-Defus Ha-Ivri Be-Artzot Ha-Mizraḥ* (two volumes, 1936–40); *idem, Meḥkerei Sefer* (1958); Y. Z. Cahana, in *Sinai*, XVI (1945), 49–61, 139–51; A. Freimann, *Gazetteer of Hebrew Printing* (1946); A. M. Habermann, *Ha-Sefer Ha-Ivri Be-Hitpatteḥuto* (1968); and G. Zilberg, *Ha-Ot Ha-Mudpeset Be-Yisrael* (1961). On the pioneering Soncino family of printers, see A. M. Habermann, *Ha-Madpisim Benei Soncino* (1933); M. Marx (Hieronymus), in *Hebrew Union College An-*

nual, VII (1930), 427–50; and A. Yaari, in *Kiryat Sefer*, XIII
(1936–37), 121–30.

On Bonet de Lattes, see A. Milano, *Ghetto di Roma* (1964),
pp. 67–68, 419; H. Vogelstein and P. Rieger, *Geschichte der Juden
in Rom*, II, 35, 83; and C. Roth, *The Jews in the Renaissance*
(1959), 162, 210, 232–34.

CHAPTER THREE

HISTORICAL LITERATURE IN THE FIFTEENTH AND SIXTEENTH CENTURIES

On Abraham ben Mordecai Farissol, see M. Steinschneider,
Catalogus Librorum Hebraeorum in Bibliotheca Bodleiana (1852–
60), cols 689–90; *idem*, *Hebräischen Übersetzungen* (1893), p. 81;
H. Graetz, *History of the Jews*, IV (1894), 411–13; and A. Pesaro,
in *Vessillo Israelitico* (1879), p. 170.

Part three of Joseph Ha-Kohen's *Divrei Ha-Yamim Le-Malchei
Tzarefat U-Malchei Bet Ottoman Ha-Togar* was edited, with an
introduction, by D. A. Gross (1955). His *Emek Ha-Bacha*, with
notes by S. D. Luzzatto and M. Letteris, was published in 1852
and reprinted in 1895. It was translated into German, with an introduction, by M. Wiener in 1858. On Joseph Ha-Kohen and his
work, see A. Kahana, *Sifrut Ha-Historiah Ha-Yisre'elit*, II (1923),
91–108; M. A. Shulvass, *Ḥayyei Ha-Yehudim Be-Italyah Be-
Tekufat Ha-Renaissance* (1955), index; I. Loeb, "Josef Haccohen
et les Chroniqueurs juifs," in *REJ*, XVI (1888), 28–56, 212–23;
M. Steinschneider, *Die Geschichtsliteratur der Juden* (1905), pp.
101–3; and G. Musso, in *Scritti in Memoria di Leone Carpi* (1967).

The first modern edition of Abraham ben Samuel Zacuto's *Sefer
Ha-Yuḥasin* was published by H. Filipowski from an Oxford manuscript (1857). This edition was reprinted, with a biographical and
critical introduction and with corrections and notes, by A. H.
Friemann (1925; second edition 1963). On Zacuto and his work,
see M. Steinschneider, *Die Geschichtsliteratur der Juden* (1905),
pp. 88–93; J. de Carvalho, in *Revista de estudios hebráicos*, I (1928),
9–56; A. Marx, in *Studies in Jewish Bibliography and Related Subjects in Memory of Abraham Solomon Freidus* (1929), pp. 247 f.;
idem, in *Essays and Studies in Memory of Linda R. Miller*
(1938), pp. 167–70; F. Cantera Burgos, *El judío Salmantino Abraham Zacut* (1931); *idem*, *Abraham Zacut* (1935); *idem*, in *Revista
de la Academia de Ciencias de Madrid*, XXVII (1931), 63–398;

R. Levy, in *JQR n.s.*, XXVI (1935–36), 385–88; and C. Roth, in *Sefarad*, IX (1949), 1–9, and XIV (1954), 122–25.

Solomon Ibn Verga's *Shevet Yehudah* was edited by F. (Yitzḥak) Baer, with notes and commentary by A. Shochat (1947). It was also edited and translated into German in two volumes by M. Wiener (1855; second impression, 1924). On Ibn Verga and his work, see Baer, *Untersuchungen über die Quellen und Komposition des Schebet Jehuda* (1923); *idem*, "He'arot Ḥadashot La-Sefer Shevet Yehudah," *Tarbitz*, VI (1935), 152–79; *idem*, *Galut* (1947), pp. 77–82; and A. Neuman, in *Louis Ginzberg Jubilee Volume* (1945), pp. 253–73.

Samuel Usque's *Consolaçam as tribulaçoens de Israel* was edited by J. Mendes dos Remedios (1906–8). It was also edited and translated into English by M. A. Cohen (1965). A Yiddish version appears in E. Lipiner, *Bie die Teichen fun Portugal: Rabbi Shmuel Uski, zein Tekufoh und zein "Treist tzu die Leiden fun Yisroel"* (1949).

Some selections from Elijah Capsali's *Seder Eliahu Zuta* (commonly referred to as *Sefer De-Vei Eliahu*) were published by M. Lattes under the title *Likkutim Shonim Mi-Sefer De-Vei Eliahu* (1869). On Capsali and his work, see G. Margoliouth, *Catalogue of the Hebrew and Samaritan Manuscripts in the British Museum*, III (1909–15), 429–34; D. S. Sassoon, *Ohel David*, I (1932), 349–57; and N. Porges, in *REJ*, LXXVII (1923), 20–40, LXXVIII (1924), 15–34, and LXXIX (1924), 28–60.

On Gedaliah Ibn Yaḥya and his work, see E. Carmoly, *Divrei Ha-Yamim Le-Venei Yaḥya* (1850); M. A. Shulvass, *Ḥayyei Ha-Yehudim Be-Italyah Be-Tekufat Ha-Renaissance* (1955), *passim*; A. Marx, in *Hebrew Union College Annual*, I (1926), 605–9; I. E. Benjacob, *Otzar Ha-Sefarim* (1880), p. 590; H. H. Michael, *Or Ha-Ḥayyim: Ḥachmei Yisrael Ve-Sifreihem* (second edition, 1965), No. 303; and A. Neubauer, in *Israelitische Letterbode*, X (1886), 139.

On Abraham ben David Portaleone II and his work, see C. Roth, *The Jews in the Renaissance* (1959), pp. 315–19; D. Kaufmann, in *JQR, o.s.*, IV (1892), 333–41, and X (1898), 455; and N. Shapiro, in *Ha-Rofe Ha-Ivri*, XXXIII (1960), 137 ff.

CHAPTER FOUR

THE BELATED BATTLE AGAINST PHILOSOPHY; AZARIAH DEI ROSSI

On Messer David ben Jehudah Leon and his writings, see H. H. Michael, *Or Ha-Ḥayyim: Ḥachmei Yisrael Ve-Sifreihem* (second edition, 1965), No. 727; J. Schechter, in REJ, XXIV (1892), 118–38; M. Steinschneider, *Gesammelte Schriften*, I (1925), pp. 219 f.; S. A. Rosanes, *Divrei Yemei Yisrael Be-Togarmah*, I (second edition, 1930), 79, 85–88, 110–13; S. Asaf, *Mekorot Le-Toledot Ha-Ḥinnuch Be-Yisrael*, II (1931), 99–101; and D. Tamar, in *Kiryat Sefer*, XXVI (1949–50), 96–100.

On Obadiah ben Jacob Sforno and his work, see E. Finkel, *Obadja Sforno als Exeget* (1896); H. Vogelstein and P. Rieger, *Geschichte der Juden in Rom*, I (1895), 77 ff.; L. A. Wohlgemuth, in *Scritti in memoria di Sally Mayer* (1956), pp. 120–25 (Hebrew section); J. Volk, in *Sefer Niger* (1959), pp. 277–302 (contains bibliography); C. Roth, *The Jews in the Renaissance Era* (1959), index; and Colorni, in *Rassegna Mensile di Israel*, XXVIII (1962), 78–88.

Jehudah Leone ben Isaac Sommo's *Dialoghi in materia di rappresantanzioni scheniche* were edited by F. Marotti (1969). They were translated into English by A. Nicoll under the title *Dialogues on the Art of the Stage*. Marotti also edited Sommo's comedy *Le Tre sorelle* (1970). Sommo's *Tzaḥut Bediḥuta De-Kiddushin*, the oldest Hebrew drama extant, was edited by J. Schirmann (second edition, 1965; contains bibliography on Sommo, pp. 173–76). On Sommo and his work, see A. Nicoll, *The Development of the Theatre* (fifth edition, 1966), p. 253 (bibliography); I. Gour, in *Bamah*, XXXI (1967), 14–25; and A. Holtz, in *Tarbitz*, XXXVI (1967).

On the important Jewish cultural center in Mantua during the Renaissance era, see S. Simonsohn, *Toledot Ha-Yehudim Be-Dukkasut Mantova*, two volumes (1962–64); A. Milano, *Bibliotheca historica italo-judaico* (1954), index, s.v. "Mantova"; *idem*, *Storia degli ebrei in Italia* (1963), index, s.v. "Mantova"; C. Roth, *A History of the Jews in Italy* (1946), index; *idem*, *The Jews in the Renaissance* (1959), index; D. W. Amram, *Makers of Hebrew Books in Italy* (1909, reprinted 1963); and H. D. (Bernard) Friedberg, *Toledot Ha-Defus Ha-Ivri Be-Italyah* (second edition, 1956), pp. 15 ff.

On Jehudah ben Joseph Moscato and his work, see A. Apfelbaum, *Toledot Ha-Gaon Rabbi Yehudah Moscato* (1900); I. Bettan, *Studies in Jewish Preaching* (1939), pp. 192–225; *idem*, "The Sermons of Juda Muscato," in *Hebrew Union College Annual*, VI (1929), 297–326; S. Simonsohn, *Toledot Ha-Yehudim Be-Dukkasut Mantovah*, II (1964), index; and C. Roth, *The Jews in the Renaissance* (1959), index.

Azariah dei Rossi's *Meor Enayim* and *Matzref Le-Kesef* were edited by D. Cassel, who also supplied an introduction (1864–66).

On dei Rossi and his work, see C. Roth, *The Jews in the Renaissance* (1959), index; D. Kaufmann, "Contribut a l'histoire des luttes d'Asarja de Rossi," *REJ*, XXXIII (1896), 77–87; S. W. Baron, "La Methode historique d'Azaria de Rossi," *REJ*, LXXXVI (1928), 151–75, and LXXXVII (1929), 43–78; *idem*, "Azariah de Rossi's Attitude to Life," in *Israel Abrahams Memorial Volume* (1927), pp. 12–52; and S. Simonsohn, *Toledot Ha-Yehudim Be-Dukkasut Mantovah*, II (1964), 462 ff.

CHAPTER FIVE

THE DECLINE OF THE RENAISSANCE ERA; LEO DE MODENA

On the effect of the Catholic Counter-Reformation on the Jews of Italy, see C. Roth, *A History of the Jews in Italy* (1946); I. Sonne, *Mi-Paulus Ha-Revii Ad Pius Ha-Hamishi* (1954); P. Orano, *Gli ebrei in Italia* (1938); G. Bedarida, *Ebrei d'Italia* (1950); H. Vogelstein and P. Rieger, *Geschichte der Juden in Rom*, two volumes (1895–96); and A. Milano, *Storia degli ebrei in Italia* (1963).

On the censorship and destruction of Hebrew books in the period of the Reformation, see I. Sonne, "Expurgation of Hebrew Books: The Work of Jewish Scholars," *Bulletin of the New York Public Library*, XLVI (1942), 975–1013; A. Berliner, *Censur und Confiscation hebraischer Bücher im Kirchenstaate*, Rabbiner-Seminar zu Berlin, *Jahresbericht* (1889–90) and Supplement (1891); J. Hilgers, *Die Bücherverbote in Papstbriefen* (1907); W. Popper, *Censorship of Hebrew Books* (1899, reprinted 1968); and M. Carmilly-Weinberger, *Sefer Ve-Sayif* (1966).

On Israel Saruk (Sarug), the disseminator of the Lurianic Kabbalah in Italy, see G. Scholem, in *Tziyyon*, V (1940), 214–43; S. A. Horodetzky, *Torat Ha-Kabbalah Shel Rabbi Yitzhak Ashkenazi-Ari Ve-Rabbi Hayyim Vital Rahu* (1947), pp. 79–82; G. Scholem, in *Revue d'histoire des religions*, CXLIII (1953), 33; and D. Tamar, in *Tziyyon*, XIX (1954), 173.

On Menahem Azariah da Fano, see L. Woidslawski, *Toledot Rabbenu Menahem Azariah Mi-Fano* (1903); S. Simonsohn, *Toledot Ha-Yehudim Be-Dukkasut Mantovah* (1964), index; and M. A. Shulvass, *Hayyei Ha-Yehudim Be-Italyah Be-Tekufat Ha-Renaissance* (1955), pp. 196, 220.

On Jehudah Minz, see I. H. Weiss, *Dor Dor Ve-Doreshav*, V (1924), 280–82; I. E. Benjacob, *Otzar Ha-Sefarim* (1880, reprinted

1956), p. 557; H. H. Michael, *Or Ha-Ḥayyim: Ḥachmei Yisrael Ve-Sifreihem* (second edition, 1965), No. 1020; L. Finkelstein, *Jewish Self-Government in the Middle Ages* (1924), pp. 27, 306, 308; M. Güdemann, *Geschichte des Erziehungswesens und der Cultur der abendländischen Juden*, Vol. III (1888), *passim*; M. A. Shulwass, *Hayyei Ha-Yehudim Be-Italyah Be-Tekufat Ha-Renaissance* (1955), index; D. Cassuto, *Ha-Yehudim Be-Firenze Be-Tekufat Ha-Renaissance* (1967), p. 229.

Some newly discovered responsa of Joseph Colon were edited and published by E. D. Pines under the title *She'elot U-Teshuvot U-Fiskei Ha-Maharik Ha-Ḥadashim* (1970). On Joseph Colon and his work, see V. Colorni, in *Annuario de studi ebraici*, I (1934), 169–82; H. Rabinowicz, in *Journal of Jewish Studies*, VI (1955), 166–70; *idem*, in *JQR*, XLVII (1956–57), 336–44; *idem*, in *Historia Judaica*, XXII (1960), 61–70 and D. Tamar, in *Tziyyon*, XVIII (1952–53), 127–35.

A complete, emended, and collated edition of Jacob Landau's two works, *Hazon* and *Ha-Agur*, was published, with an introduction, by M. Herschler, under the title *Ha-Agur Ha-Shalem* (1960).

On Meir ben Isaac Katzenellenbogen (Maharam of Padua), see M. Ghirondi, in *Kerem Hemed*, III (1838), 91–96; I. Eisenstadt and S. Wiener, *Daat Kedoshim* (1897–98), pp. 82–84; S. Assaf, *Mekorot U-Meḥkarim* (1946), pp. 240–46; M. Straschun, *Mivḥar Ketavim* (1969), pp. 168–86; Schwarzfuchs, in *Scritti in Memoria di Leone Carpi* (1967), pp. 112–32 (Italian part); Siev, in *Hadorom*, XXVIII (1968), 160–95; I. Tishby, in *Perakim*, I (1967–68), 131–82; and I. S. Lange, in *Misscellanea di Studi in Memoria di D. Disigni* (1969), pp. 49–76 (Hebrew part).

On Samuel Archevolti, see S. Bernstein, in *Tarbitz*, VIII (1936–37), 55–68, 237; C. Roth, *The Jews in the Renaissance* (1959), index; *idem*, *A History of the Jews in Italy* (1946), pp. 234–35; D. Kaufmann, in *JQR*, IX (1896–97), 263–69; *idem*, *Schriften*, I (1908), 93–96.

Leo de Modena's Hebrew poems were edited by S. Bernstein under the title *The Divan of Leo of Modena* (1932). His Hebrew correspondence was edited by L. Blau under the title *Leo Modenas Briefe und Schriftstücke* (1905–6), and his letters in Italian to Christian Hebraists were published by C. Roth in *Jewish Studies in Memory of Israel Abrahams* (1927). De Modena's autobiography, *Hayyei Yehudah*, was edited by A. Kahana (1911). His anti-Christian polemic, *Magen Va-Ḥerev* was edited by S. Simonsohn (1960). Simonsohn also edited a collection of de Modena's responsa, *Ziknei Yehudah* (1956), in the introduction to which he provides a complete bibliography of de Modena's writings, published and unpublished. The best study of de Modena's work is E. Rivkin, *Leon da Modena and the Kol Sakhal* (1952). See also U. Cassuto, "Leon Modena e l'opera sua," *Rassegna Mensile di Israel*, VIII (1933–34), 132–42; I. Sonne, in *Hebrew Union College Annual*, XXI (1948), 1–28; N. Samaja, in *Rassegna Mensile di Israel*, XXI (1955), 73–84; C. Roth, in *Transactions of the Jewish Historical Society of England*, XI (1924–27), 206–26, and XVII (1951–52), 39–43; I. Rivkind, in *Tarbitz*, IV (1933), 366–76; *idem*, in *Sefer Ha-Yovel . . . L. Ginzberg* (1946), pp. 401–23; and B. Klar, *Meḥkarim Ve-Iyyunim* (1954), pp. 357–78.

CHAPTER SIX

On Joseph Solomon Delmedigo, see A. Geiger, *Melo Chofnajim* (1840), Introduction, pp. 1–95 (German part), and pp. 1–29 (Hebrew part); *idem, Nachgelassene Schriften*, III (1876), 1–33; L. Roth, in *Chronicon Spinozanum*, II (1922), 54–66; C. Roth, *A Life of Menasseh ben Israel* (1934), pp. 132–34; and F. Kobler, ed., *A Treasury of Jewish Letters*, II (1952), 486–96.

On Azariah Figo, see A. Apfelbaum, *Azariah Figo* (1907; in Hebrew); I. Bettan, "The Sermons of Azariah Figo," in *Hebrew Union College Annual*, VII (1930), 457–95; M. Shulvass, *Ḥayyei Ha-Yehudim Be-Italyah Be-Tekufat Ha-Renaissance* (1955), index; and H. R. Rabinowitz, *Deyokenaot Shel Darshanim* (1967), pp. 150–58.

On Samuel Aboab, see Loewenstein, in *MGWJ*, XLVIII (1904), 674–82; C. Roth, *A History of the Jews in Venice* (1930), pp. 231–36; I. Sonne, in *Tziyyon*, III (1938), 145–52; A. Yaari, *Sheluḥei Eretz Yisrael* (1951), pp. 65, 277; M. Benyahu, in *Eretz Yisrael*, III (1954), 244–46; *idem*, in *Sinai*, XXXIV (1953–54), 156–202; *idem*, in *Yerushalayim*, V (1955), 136–86; *idem*, in *Scritti in memoria di Sally Mayer*, (1956), pp. 17–47 (Hebrew section); and G. Scholem, *Shabbetai Tzevi Veha-Tenuah Ha-Shabbetait Be-Yemei Ḥayyov*, II (1967), 408–12; 418 ff., 648–51.

Moses ben Mordecai Zacuto's *Yesod Olam*, the first Biblical drama in Hebrew literature, was published in 1874 in two editions, one by A. Berliner and one by D. J. Maroni. His *Tofteh Aruch* was edited by D. A. Friedman (1922). The latter work, which was inspired by Dante's *Divine Comedy*, was twice translated into Italian, in verse by S. I. Luzzati (1819) and in prose by C. Foa (1901).

On Zacuto and his work, see A. Apfelbaum, *Rabbi Mosheh Zakut: Hayyav, Sefarav, Shitato Be-Kabbalah, Talmidav, Piyyutav, U-Peulotav Ha-Tzibburiot* (1926); L. Landshuth, *Ammudei Ha-Avodah*, Vol. II (1862), pp. 214–21; G. Scholem, *Kitvei Yad Be-Kabbalah* (1930), pp. 150–55; *idem*, in *Tziyyon*, XIII–XIV (1949), pp. 49–59; A. Yaari, *Taalumot Sefer* (1954), pp. 54–56, 67–75; M. Benayahu, in *Yerushalayim*, V (1955), pp. 136–186; *idem*, in *Sefunot*, V (1961), pp. 323–26, 335; and I. Tishby, *Netivei Emunah U-Minut* (1964), Index.

Glossary of Hebrew and Other Terms

Acquired Intellect: Among the Jewish and Arabic Aristotelians, the new intellect produced in man when he has acquired abstract concepts through the operation of the Active Intellect (see below).

Active Intellect: Among the Jewish and Arabic Aristotelians, the universal "Intelligence" which serves to control the motions of the sublunar world and especially to develop the human faculty of reason, which, in the infant, is merely a capacity or potentiality—a "material" intellect.

Aggadah (or Haggadah): The non-legal part of the post-Biblical Oral Torah, consisting of narratives, legends, parables, allegories, poems, prayers, theological and philosophical reflections, etc. Much of the Talmud is aggadic, and the Midrash literature (see below), developed over a period of more than a millennium, consists almost entirely of Aggadah. The term *aggadah*, in a singular and restricted sense, refers to a Talmudic story or legend.

Amora (pl. Amoraim): The title given to the Jewish scholars of Palestine and especially of Babylonia in the third to the sixth centuries whose work and thought is recorded in the Gemara of the Talmud.

atzilut: Literally, "emanation." The term used in Kabbalist literature to designate the emanation or radiation of the divine through the *sefirot* (see **sefirah**).

blood libel: The charge frequently made in the Middle Ages, and even later, to the effect that Jews murder Christians in order to obtain blood for the Passover *seder* and other rituals. The first recorded case of such an accusation was in 1144, in connection with a Christian child named William at Norwich in England. Despite the fact that the charge was declared absurd by many Christian scholars and numerous papal edicts, it continued to be made sporadically as late as the twentieth century.

Boethusians: A religious-political party among the Jews during the century before the destruction of the second Temple in 70 C.E. The Boethusians were closely associated with the high priesthood, and their principles were, in many cases, similar to those of the Sadducees (see below).

Exilarch: From the Aramaic *Resh Galuta*, i.e., "head of the exile." The title given to the political head of Babylonian Jewry. The office was hereditary and its occupant, according to legend, was a descendant of the House of David. From the eleventh century on the office was imitated, often under the same name, in Egypt and elsewhere.

Gaon (pl. **Geonim**): The spiritual and intellectual leaders of Babylonian Jewry in the post-Talmudic period, from the sixth through the eleventh centuries C.E. The head of each of the two major academies of Babylonia, at Sura and Pumbeditha, held the title Gaon. The Geonim had considerable secular power as well as religious authority, and their influence extended over virtually all of world Jewry during the larger part of the Geonic age. The title Gaon is occasionally applied in a general honorific sense to a very eminent Judaic scholar.

Gemara: The second basic strand of the Talmud (see below), consisting of a commentary on, and supplement to, the Mishnah (see below).

gematria: A system of exegesis based on the interpretation of a word or words according to the numerical value of the constituent letters in the Hebrew alphabet.

ḥacham: Hebrew for "wise man". Originally, an officer of the rabbinic courts in Palestine and Babylonia. Later the term was applied to an officiating rabbi in Sephardic communities.

Halachah: In Hebrew, "law"; derived from the verb *halach*, "to go" or "to follow." The legal part of Talmudic and later Jewish literature, in contrast to Aggadah or Haggadah (see above), the non-legal elements. In the singular, *halachah* means "law" in an abstract sense or, alternatively, a specific rule or regulation; the plural, *halachot*, refers to collections of laws.

Haskalah: The movement for disseminating modern European culture among Jews from about 1750 to 1880. It advocated the modernization of Judaism, the westernization of traditional Jewish education, and the revival of the Hebrew language.

Hasmoneans: The name of the priestly family and dynasty founded by Mattathias of Modin. Mattathias and his five sons, including Judah the Maccabee, led the popular revolt against the Syrian king Antiochus Epiphanes in the second century B.C.E. which led to the re-dedication of the Temple and later to the gaining of about a century of independence for the Jewish state.

Ineffable Name: YHWH, the Tetragrammaton or *Shem Ha-Meforash*. The particular name of the God of Israel in the Bible. Its original pronunciation is no longer known, though it is generally conjectured to have been Yahweh. By the second century B.C.E. it was no longer pronounced, except by the High Priest on Yom Kippur (see below), but read as *Adonai*.

Kabbalah: The mystical religious movement in Judaism and/or its literature. The term Kabbalah, which means "tradition," came to be used by the mystics beginning in the twelfth century to signify the alleged continuity of their doctrine from ancient times.

Karaites: A Jewish sect, originating in the eighth century C.E. in and around Persia, which rejected the Oral Torah or Oral Law (see below) and wished to interpret the Bible literally and to deduce from it a code of law without reliance on Talmudic tradition. Major factors in the evolution of the Karaites were their ardent messianic hopes and their ascetic tendencies.

maaseh bereshit: Literally, "work of creation." The term refers to the first chapter of Genesis, the exposition of which was one of the primary concerns of early Jewish mysticism.

Marrano: A Spanish term meaning "swine"; the equivalent term in Hebrew is *Anusim*, i.e., those "forced" or "coerced." A term applied in Spain and Portugal to those descendants of baptised Jews who were suspected of continued covert loyalty to Judaism. The class became particularly numerous in Spain after the massacres of 1391 and in Portugal after the forced conversions of 1497. The Marranos achieved high standing socially, economically, and politically, but were frequently persecuted by the Inquisition.

Maskil (pl. **Maskilim**): An adherent of Haskalah (see above).

Masorites: A group of scholars who preserved the body of traditions regarding the correct spelling, writing, and reading of the Hebrew Bible. A major school of Palestinian Masorites was located at Tiberias.

matzah (pl. *matzot*): The unleavened bread prescribed by Jewish tradition for consumption during the Passover season as a memorial of the bread baked in haste by the Israelites departing from Egypt.

midrash (pl. **midrashim**): The discovery of new meanings besides literal ones in the Bible. The term is also used, capitalized, to designate collections of such Scriptural exposition; the best-known of these Midrashim are the *Midrash Rabbah, Tanhuma, Pesikta De-Rav Kahana, Pesikta Rabbati,* and *Yalkut Shimeoni.* In a singular and restricted sense, "midrash" refers to an item of rabbinic exegesis.

Mishnah: The legal codification containing the core of the post-Biblical Oral Torah (see below), compiled and edited by Rabbi Judah Ha-Nasi at the beginning of the third century C.E.

Notarikon: A method of abbreviating Hebrew words and phrases by writing only single letters, usually the initials.

Oral Torah (or **Oral Law**): The body of interpretation and analysis of the written law of the Pentateuch created in post-exilic Judaism and handed down orally from generation to generation. The Oral Law consists of the Mishnah (see above) and the Gemara (see above), both of which were combined to form the Talmud (see below). Even after the redaction of the Talmud, the body of tradition contained in it continued to be known as the Oral Law because its roots were in an oral tradition.

parashah: The weekly portion of the Pentateuch read in the synagogue during the Sabbath service, or, more restrictedly, the shorter passages read to or by each person called up to the reading of the Torah. Synonomous with *parashah* in the first sense is the term *sidra.*

Pharisees: A Jewish religious and political sect during the period of the Second Temple. The Pharisees, who were committed to the idea of evolution in the law of the Torah, began the process of developing the Oral Torah (see above), which they regarded as equally authoritative with the Written Law or Pentateuch. In contrast to the Sadducees (see below) they believed in life after death, the resurrection of the dead, the advent of the Messiah, and the Day of Judgment. The rabbis of the Talmudic Age are the successors of the Pharisees.

pilpul: In Talmudic and rabbinic literature a clarification of a difficult point. Later the term came to denote a sharp dialectical distinction or, more generally, a certain type of Talmudic study emphasizing dialectical distinctions and introduced into the Talmudic academies of Poland by Jacob Pollak in the sixteenth century. Pejoratively, the term means hairsplitting.

Purim: Hebrew, "lots." A festival commemorating the saving of Persian Jewry through the efforts of Esther from the threat of destruction on the part of Haman, as recorded in the Biblical Book of Esther. Purim is observed on the fourteenth day of the Hebrew month of Adar.

Rosh Ha-Shanah: Hebrew, literally "head of the year." The Jewish New Year, a holiday which inaugurates the Ten Days of Penitence culminating in the Day of Atonement or Yom Kippur (see below). It is regarded as a day of judgment for the entire world and for individuals when the fate of each man for the coming year is inscribed in the Book of Life.

Sadducees: A Jewish sect of the period of the Second Temple whose membership was drawn primarily from the priestly and aristocratic circles. Their religion centered around the temple cult. In contrast to the Pharisees (see above), the Sadducees attempted to adhere strictly to the Written Law and had no faith in a future life, resurrection, or immortality of the soul.

They also rejected the existence of angels and spirits. Since the Sadducees were so closely connected to the Temple cult, they disappeared after the destruction of the Temple.

Sanhedrin: A Hebrew word of Greek origin designating, in rabbinic literature, the assembly of seventy-one ordained scholars which served both as the supreme court and the legislature of Judaism in the Talmudic age. The Sanhedrin disappeared before the end of the fourth century c.e.

sefirah (pl. *sefirot*): A technical term in Kabbalah, employed from the twelfth century on to denote the ten potencies or emanations through which the Divine manifests itself.

Shechinah: A term used to imply the presence of God in the world, in the midst of Israel, or with individuals. In contrast to the principle of divine transcendence, Shechinah represents the principle of divine immanence.

Sheol: In the Bible, the dwelling place of the dead, situated below the earth, where the shades of the dead continue a kind of existence in which they can no longer praise or give thanks to God.

Shofar: A horn of a ram, the sounding of which is prescribed by Biblical law for the New Year as well as to proclaim the year of release. At various times the *shofar* was also sounded on fast days, on the occasion of proclaiming a rabbinic edict, at times of famine or plague, and as a part of the ceremony of excommunication.

Siddur: Hebrew, "order." Among Ashkenazic Jews, the volume that contains the statutory daily prayers.

Talmud: The title applied to the two great compilations, distinguished as the Babylonian Talmud and the Palestinian Talmud, in which the records of academic discussion and of judicial administration of post-Biblical Jewish law are assembled. Both Talmuds also contain Aggadah or non-legal material.

Tanna (pl. **Tannaim**): A teacher mentioned in the Mishnah, or in literature contemporaneous with the Mishnah, and living during the first two centuries c.e.

Tosafists: The authors of the Tosafot (see below).

Tosafot: Hebrew, "addenda." Critical and explanatory notes on the Talmud by Jewish scholars in France and Germany during the twelfth to fourteenth centuries. Among the most famous of the Tosafists are Rabbenu Tam, Rabbi Samuel ben Meir, and Rabbi Isaac of Dampiere.

Tosefta: A supplement to the Mishnah (see above). The one version that has survived has six Orders with the same names as those of the Mishnah and its treatises correspond to all but four of the treatises of the Mishnah.

yeshivah (pl. *yeshivot*): A traditional Jewish school devoted primarily to the study of the Talmud and rabbinic literature.

Yom Kippur: Hebrew, "Day of Atonement." A solemn fast day observed on the tenth day of the Hebrew month Tishri and serving as the culmination of the Ten Days of Penitence. It is a day on which the individual is to cleanse himself from sin and to beg for the forgiveness of God through confession, prayer, and atonement.

Zohar: The chief work of the Spanish Kabbalah, traditionally ascribed to the Tanna Simeon ben Yoḥai (second century) but probably written by the Spanish Kabbalist Moses de Leon at the end of the thirteenth century.

Index

Index

Index

Index